W9-DIF-499

UNIVERSITY OF WINNIPEG
LIBRARY
DISCARDED
515 Portage Avenue
Winnipeg, Manitoba R3B 2E9

STUDIES IN IRISH HISTORY, SECOND SERIES
edited by

T. W. MOODY
Professor of Modern History
University of Dublin

J. C. BECKETT
Professor of Irish History
Queen's University, Belfast

T. D. WILLIAMS
Professor of Modern History
National University of Ireland

VOLUME VI
THE IRISH CONVENTION, 1917-18

STUDIES IN IRISH HISTORY, SECOND SERIES

DA
962
.M26

THE
IRISH CONVENTION
1917–18

by

R. B. McDOWELL

LONDON: Routledge & Kegan Paul
TORONTO: University of Toronto Press
1970

First published in 1970
by Routledge and Kegan Paul Ltd
and in Canada and the United States of America
by University of Toronto Press
Printed in Great Britain
by Cox and Wyman Ltd,
London, Fakenham and Reading

© *R. B. McDowell 1970*
No part of this book may be reproduced
in any form without permission from
the publisher, except for the quotation
of brief passages in criticism

SBN 7100 6511 6

UTP SBN 8020 1670 7

CONTENTS

~~~~~~

INTRODUCTION

THE CONVENTION which met in 1917 was one of the most striking failures in Irish history. Indeed, if the intellectual calibre of many of its members is taken into account, it may reasonably be called a brilliant failure. Its convening could be considered a declaration of faith in the principles of nineteenth-century liberalism. Liberals believed that the free exchange of opinion should lead to the triumph of truth; that if men of good-will got down together and discussed rationally their political differences, by conversion and compromise they could reach agreement. This method of tackling political problems had worked very successfully in the very sphere, constitution-making, in which the Irish convention attempted to apply it, when it had been employed in the creation of the United States, the Dominion of Canada, the Commonwealth of Australia and the Union of South Africa. But the convention failed to find an answer to the Irish question. The gaps were too wide, or, to put it another way, the main groups clung too tightly to their prepared positions. Moreover, the majority of the convention's members were constitutional nationalists who were rapidly losing the confidence of the sections they were supposed to represent. For the most part, responsible, established, middle-aged men, they were plainly and pathetically out of touch with the new nationalism. The war had encouraged the feeling that direct action was the most efficient solvent for political problems. In Ireland the rising of 1916 had kindled widespread admiration for bold action and the spirit that put it

> . . . unto the touch
> To win or lose it all

With Europe on the move, home rule as a policy was far too limited and far too slow. But although soon after it finished its labours the convention's approach to the Irish problem already seemed archaic and the plans it mulled over antiquated, it deserves attention. It made a serious, if futile, effort to achieve agreement by conference. Its members' views, expressed frankly in debate and in correspondence, provide an anthology of Irish political opinion. And the plans the convention discussed have acquired a new interest. In the era when the doctrine of self-determination was enunciated, home rule schemes for Irish self-government which, practically speaking, fell short of complete independence, seemed inadequate and over-complex. Now, when Europe is striving to combine a degree of national diversity with a large measure of unified control, such schemes and the anxiety of many members of the convention to find a compromise may be regarded more sympathetically.

R. B. MCDOWELL

ACKNOWLEDGEMENTS

I AM MOST grateful to my friend and colleague Professor T. W. Moody for the invaluable advice and help he has afforded me at every stage of this work. I am also very grateful to Miss K. Digby for first drawing my attention to the mass of material relating to the convention in the Plunkett papers, to Professor J. C. Beckett for reading and commenting on the work, to Mr Patrick Buckland for helpful comments, to Professor J. W. Boyle for very useful information concerning the labour members of the convention, and to Dr Edward MacLysaght (a member of the convention) and Lord Southborough (a member of its secretariat) for discussing the convention with me.

For access to material I am indebted to the trustees of the Beaverbrook foundation and for permission to use material to the Plunkett Foundation for Co-operative Studies, the Beaverbrook newspapers, Mr Mark Bonham Carter, Dr Oliver Chance, His Eminence Cardinal Conway, the earl of Granard, Dr MacLysaght, Madeleine Lady Midleton, Mr Dennis Morris, Lord O'Neill, Mr Godfrey Samuel and Mr R. Stewart.

Finally I must express my thanks to the staffs of the libraries and record offices in which I have worked.

I

THE IRISH QUESTION

THE EIGHTEENTH CENTURY left two legacies to Ireland, the union and the republican separatist tradition. Pitt's solution for the Anglo-Irish problem was strongly opposed in Ireland and aroused relatively little enthusiasm in England. But within a generation it was being fervently supported by influential sections of opinion in Ireland and treated as axiomatic in England. Before the act of union had been on the statute book twelve years, Canning, adept at embodying a theory in a ringing phrase, declaimed: 'Abolish the union! Restore the heptarchy as soon!'[1] Twenty-three years later Macaulay, the eloquent exponent of level-headed liberalism, discussing the repeal of the union, remarked, 'I know it to be impracticable: and I know that if it were practicable, it would be pernicious to every part of the empire and utterly ruinous to Ireland'.[2] And in 1868 Gladstone referred to the union as 'an inexorable political necessity'.[3]

The roots of Irish nationalism have been discerned in the middle ages. Its later prophets were Molyneux, Swift and Grattan, and during the last few decades of the eighteenth century a strong urge in Ireland towards autonomy coincided with an upsurge of revolution in America and France. Radical revolution in many areas in Europe fused with a growing

[1] *Hansard 1*, xxi, 530.
[2] *The complete works of Lord Macaulay* (1898), xi, 522.
[3] *The Times*, 15 Oct. 1868.

I

national consciousness. The United Irishmen at the end of the eighteenth century were influenced by this tendency and assumed that a distinctive community should express itself through a sovereign state. Later the tradition was strengthened by the romanticism of the Young Irelanders and the vigorous militancy of the Fenians. And it may be added that each manifestation of the separatist tradition – eighteenth-century radicalism, Young Ireland, and Fenianism – went down in catastrophic defeat.

The union and complete independence were the poles in Irish politics, but from about 1830 attempts were being made to find a compromise which would both preserve the political unity of the British Isles and yet enable Ireland to enjoy a high degree of autonomy. In time this policy was formulated and given a short, catchy and descriptive label – home rule. Home rule meant that purely Irish matters were to be managed by an Irish legislative assembly and an Irish executive, and that matters of common concern to the two islands, defence and foreign affairs for instance, were to remain under the control of the United Kingdom Parliament. By the middle eighties home rule had won an impressive degree of support, measured in parliamentary terms. About eighty-five Irish M.P.s were home rulers and with Gladstone's conversion home rule became one of the major planks in the programme of the liberal party.

The attitude of British liberals to home rule was relatively simple. They were convinced that it provided an adequate answer to the morally disturbing and time-consuming problem of Irish discontent. It might reasonably be asked, did English liberals, who during the nineteenth century were profoundly conscious of nationalism as a potent force shaping contemporary Europe, believe that home rule would really satisfy Ireland? Three distinguished liberals early in the home rule struggle confidently asserted that in the long run it would. Spencer, who had twice held office in Ireland as viceroy, admitted that there were those who thought that home rule must lead to separation. But, he wrote, 'I cannot believe in this fear, for I know of no English statesman who looks upon the complete separation of Ireland from Great Britain as possible. The geographical position of Ireland, the social and commercial connections between the two peoples renders such a thing impossible. The

Irish know this.' Bryce, a vigorous liberal, of Ulster protestant stock, a historian and a student of constitutional forms, expressed the same view in slightly different terms. If the force of national sentiment in Ireland, he wrote, was recognized and satisfied in every way which was compatible with imperial unity, then Irishmen would accept the laws of economics and 'an island which finds its chief market in England and draws its capital from England will prefer a connection with England to the poverty and insignificance of isolation'. And Morley, a philosophic radical and Gladstone's active lieutenant in the home rule struggle, said the same thing. 'The sentiment of nationality', Morley remarked, 'is a totally different thing from a desire for separation'. The Irish were quite shrewd enough to know that a separation, if attainable, would do no good to their markets.[4] A quarter of a century later, when the liberals were for the third time attempting to carry a home rule bill, Herbert Samuel, a rising young liberal politician, having insisted that for a parliament at Westminster to try to legislate for Ireland was 'like an artist trying to paint a picture on a wall twenty feet away with brushes six yards long', went on to assert that the separation of Ireland from the British Empire 'is and always will be an impossibility'. 'The geographical propinquity of Ireland to Great Britain', he stressed, 'the strategic importance of the union between the two, the greater size, wealth and population of Great Britain – these things are facts, just as much as the facts of difference of race, and difference of history – and those facts must always maintain the United Kingdom under one undivided sovereignty'.[5]

The attitude of Irish nationalists to home rule is less easily explained. The extreme nationalists of course rejected it. Ireland, they fervently believed, should be a sovereign state; anything less than full political independence was almost worthless; and to accept home rule, even with the aim of using it as a stepping-stone to full independence, might imply a dangerous and treacherous weakening of Ireland's claims. Moderate, constitutional nationalists, when they were

[4] The views of Spencer, Bryce and Morley are given in essays they contributed to a *Handbook of Home Rule*, ed. James Bryce (1887).

[5] Printed copy of speech delivered by Samuels to the Belfast liberals, 6 Oct. 1911 (Samuel papers, A/41/1).

discussing home rule, were well aware that they were being contemptuously watched by the political rigorists who demanded complete separation from Great Britain and who were prepared to employ physical force to attain it. Moreover, constitutionalists could not but be conscious that one of the most striking and inspiring elements in the Irish national tradition was the memory of the wars which had been waged by Irishmen against English domination since medieval times. Home rule as an objective, constitutional action as a method, may both have been highly rational. They were bound to seem drab in contrast to the martial methods of the past. Years before, Dr Johnson, in conversation with Boswell, had driven home the (possibly unfair) advantage those who advocated direct action have over those who relied on debate. 'Were Socrates and Charles XII of Sweden to be present in any company, and Socrates to say, "Follow me and hear a lecture in philosophy", and Charles, laying his hand on his sword to say, "Follow me, and dethrone the Czar", a man would be ashamed to follow Socrates . . . Sir, the profession of soldiers and sailors has the dignity of danger.' So strong was historic tradition that even John Redmond, a man of peace by temperament and conviction, speaking as leader of the parliamentary party at a great gathering in Dublin in 1907, was constrained to declare that resistance in arms 'would be absolutely justifiable if it were possible'. Admittedly he quickly added that it was not possible under existing circumstances, and that 'Thank God there are other means at our hands'.[6]

The parliamentary battle begun by Butt, Biggar and Parnell, the land war and the Plan of Campaign, with the lapse of time acquired something of the romantic excitement associated with more violent contests, and during the first decade of the twentieth century the moderate nationalists could point with pride to what had been won by constitutional methods – the elimination of landlordism, the transfer of county government to democratically elected county councils and the creation of the National University. They could argue that home rule would give Irishmen complete control over their own affairs in a number of spheres and they could emphasize – and this was most important – that it was politically attainable in the imme-

[6] *Home rule speeches of John Redmond* (1910), p. 237.

diate future. There was one argument for home rule which moderate nationalists were understandably loath to employ. Great Britain and Ireland had so many common interests both cultural and economic that they were bound to be more closely connected than any other two European communities. Home rule might be a faulty constitutional device, but it at least represented an attempt to reconcile autonomy and unity.

It is not easy to find an authoritative answer to the question, to what extent did constitutional nationalists consider that home rule would provide a permanent pattern of government for the British Isles? Carson, the Ulster unionist leader, speaking early in the great debate on the home rule bill of 1912, contended that the bill gave Ireland power to obtain national independence, the guarantees it contained of imperial supremacy being of little value 'The executive', Carson declared, 'is everything'. And, he argued, the leaders of the Irish parliamentary party were determined to get rid of the restrictions on the power of the Irish parliament. Redmond in reply emphatically declared that he and his party were willing to accept, as Parnell had been willing to accept, a subordinate parliament, created by a statute of the imperial parliament, as a final settlement of Ireland's claim.[7] Redmond was a man of sensitive honour who certainly would not have wittingly misled his opponents. Nevertheless a survey of the Irish national tradition reinforces Carson's argument. Engraved in gold on Parnell's monument in Dublin was his celebrated declaration, 'Let no man presume to set bounds to the march of a nation', Redmond himself, who early in his career laid down, that 'the one great principle of any settlement of the Irish question must be the recognition of the divine right of Irishmen and Irishmen alone to rule Ireland', when the home rule bill of 1893 was being debated candidly stated that if the bill passed it would not prove 'final or immutable'.[8] And when the home rule bill of 1912 was being debated, William O'Brien, one of the most eloquent and spirited of Parnell's followers, emphasized that the bill would involve 'a certain degree of renunciation by Irish nationalists of the old school of the dreams, perhaps only dreams that came

[7] *Hansard 5*, xxxvi, 1437, 1443–5.
[8] *Home rule speeches of John Redmond* (1910), pp. 20, 44.

in the youth of some of us as the blood of our veins – dreams for which many generations of the best men of our race were proud to risk their liberties and their lives'. However, he concluded by emphasizing that Irishmen were willing to accept 'a sensible compromise in a world of compromises'.[9] In fact it would probably be fair to say that constitutional nationalists while they were prepared to accept home rule as a workable settlement of the Anglo-Irish question, expected that as time went on the significant differences between home rule and independence would steadily diminish

When Gladstone declared himself a home ruler at the beginning of 1886 and began to draft a home rule bill, home rule from being an aspiration had to be translated into a piece of detailed legislation. Two problems, which were to play a great part in the debates on successive home rule bills and which were to be the main issues in the convention of 1917 at once loomed up – minorities and finance. It might be said that these problems were very different in magnitude. The attitude of Irish unionists and protestants to home rule was a fundamental difficulty which created in 1912–14 a major political crisis, while home rule finance might be dismissed as merely a matter of dull detail. In fact, however, the financial clauses of the home rule bills are important not only because of the acute sensitivity of mankind to money matters, but because the financial provisions of a measure settling Anglo-Irish relations involved in a concrete form major issues of general principle.

Gladstone, always interested in public finance, devoted considerable attention to the fiscal sections of the 1886 bill. He saw that there were two important issues involved, the size of the Irish contribution to joint expenses (defence and the servicing of the national debt, for instance) and the taxing powers of the new Irish legislature. After a little hesitation he decided that the Irish share of the common expenses should be in the ratio of one to fourteen. He was prepared to grant the Irish parliament the power of imposing direct taxation (in the eighties direct taxation accounted for only about sixteen per cent of the revenue of the United Kingdom),[10] but over the levying of customs and excise he hesitated. There were, he pointed out, two advantages

[9] *Hansard 5*, xxxvi, 1467.
[10] Memoir, Irish finance, 20 Mar. 1886 (Add. MS 44632).

in leaving the control of customs and excise at Westminster. It would mean the minimum of change in existing fiscal arrangements and it would eliminate any possibility of interference with trade between the two islands. There were, however, he saw, several advantages in giving the control of customs and excise to Ireland. To do so would avoid 'a great abridgement of the power of the Irish legislative body'; it would remove a reason for retaining Irish representation at Westminster; and it would put the whole administration of the revenue laws in Ireland into the hands of Irish officials, whereas the retention of control by the imperial authorities might bring United Kingdom officials into conflict with the Irish taxpayer.[11] Writing to Morley towards the end of March 1886 Gladstone went so far as to say, 'Individually I am perfectly ready to give to Ireland the right to impose protective tariffs on British goods. Had I to consider Irish prejudices I should consider this to be the superior way of eventually and thoroughly getting rid of them. But the main thing is to pass our measure. In this view we have to weigh British prejudices and the 567 (566) members in a position to back them.' Therefore he thought the best course would be to provide that neither country should raise a customs duty on an article the produce or the manufacture of the other, without imposing a corresponding excise duty.[12] But already one of Gladstone's colleagues, Childers, had protested against the suggestion that the control of customs and excise should be handed over to the Irish legislature. 'I feel confident', he wrote, 'English and Scottish public opinion would never tolerate any plan which gives an Irish legislature power to impose customs duties, to make Ireland "a foreign country" and trade with Ireland "a foreign trade"'.[13] At the end of March the problem of whether the Irish legislature should be given complete control over Irish revenue matters or whether it should be prevented from levying protective duties or duties affecting the trade between the two islands was referred to a cabinet committee under Kimberley. This committee reported that the Irish legislature should be prohibited from levying

[11] Memorandum, marked 'Send a copy to Mr Morley, 29 Mar. 1886'. (Add. MS 44647).
[12] Gladstone to Morley, 22 Mar. 1886 (Add. MS 44255).
[13] Childers to Gladstone, 18 Mar. 1886 (Add. MS. 44132).

protective duties and that the bill should provide that neither Great Britain nor Ireland should be permitted to levy duties on articles which were the produce or manufacture of the other.[14] In the bill, as finally drafted, a simple approach to the question was adopted. The control of customs and excise, it was laid down, was to be retained by the imperial parliament.

The home rule bill of 1886 was prepared under great pressure. The time, as Morley said, was terribly short between the Government taking office at the very end of January and the introduction of the bill at the beginning of April. There was more time to consider the details of the 1893 bill, Gladstone taking office in August 1892 and the bill being introduced in the middle of February 1893. When the figures for Irish revenue and expenditure were compiled and studied they suggested a pattern for the fiscal clauses of the bill. The amount collected in customs duties from Ireland was approximately equal to what it was felt the Irish imperial contribution should amount to.[15] So it was laid down in the bill that customs should be controlled by the imperial parliament, the receipts from Ireland being treated as Ireland's imperial contribution. But when the bill was in committee the government had to make a painful and absurd confession. It was discovered that the treasury had made a bad mistake in its calculations, seriously over-estimating the yield from excise in Ireland. The result was the financial clauses of the bill had to be hastily remodelled, 'with a view', Gladstone explained, 'of presenting to the house for its sanction a simple plan raising few points of debate'.[16] For a provisional period of six years the management of all existing taxes in Ireland was to remain unaltered, the Irish parliament was to have power to impose new taxes, and the Irish imperial contribution was to be one-third of the Irish revenue.

The Irish nationalist M.P.s when the 1886 and 1893 bills were under consideration were greatly concerned about the size of the imperial contribution expected from Ireland. In

[14] Note on Irish government, 31 Mar. (Add. MS 33632); Irish finance committee report, 1 Apr. 1886 (Add. MS 44647).

[15] Memorandum by Welby, Hamilton and Milner, 14 Dec. 1897 (Cab. 37/32/51).

[16] *Hansard 4*, xiii, 1682.

1886 Parnell was convinced that it should not be in the suggested ratio of one to fifteen but in that of one to twenty. In meetings with Morley and Gladstone, Parnell, with quiet tenacity, fought hard for his fraction and in later years he remarked that in financial matters 'the G.O.M. was the hardest taskmaster Ireland ever had'.[17] When the 1893 bill was being drafted, McCarthy, the leader of the larger section of the Irish nationalists in the house of commons, presented Morley with a memorandum from his party suggesting that the imperial contribution should be a fixed proportion of Ireland's revenue.[18]

When discussing the financial provisions of the first two home rule bills Irish nationalist M.P.s tended both in public and private to dwell on the imperial contribution rather than on the fiscal powers of the Irish parliament. There were obvious reasons for this. *Laissez-faire* still dominated economic thinking in the British Isles. Public finance was seen as a matter of securing the necessary funds to meet the state's expenses rather than as a great instrument of economic and social policy. And in Ireland itself, one economic problem, the land, threw all others into the shade. The relations of landlord and tenant, and methods of land purchase absorbed an incredible amount of intellectual energy and ingenuity. Finally, Irish nationalists must have been aware that if they made a determined effort to increase the fiscal powers granted to the Irish parliament they would be supplying damaging debating points to their unionist opponents. But in 1885 Parnell had claimed than an Irish parliament should have the power to protect by tariffs any Irish industry which it considered required protection. Admittedly in the following year, during the home rule bill debate, he declared he would not claim this power from a liberal government, justifying this concession by pointing to the *quid pro quo* which Ireland was obtaining by the adoption of a generous (if faulty) method of estimating the revenue derived from Ireland. However, in 1893 Redmond, having referred to both Parnell's statements, argued that Ireland should ultimately have the control of its customs duties. And two other nationalist M.P.s, who were financial experts, Clancy, a Parnellite, and Sexton, an anti-Parnellite, were also anxious

[17] *Hansard 5*, xxxvii, 1928.
[18] Paper handed to Morley (Cab. 37/33/7).

that Ireland should in the near future obtain complete control over its finances.[19]

Between 1893 and 1911 tariff reform became one of the big issues of British politics, unionists stressing what an important role tariffs could play in national economic development. At the same time Irish nationalism was being invigorated by a great revival of cultural and intellectional life which was bound to influence Irishmen's approach to economic problems. Admittedly, when at the very beginning of 1911 the general council of Irish county councils (a body which represented sedate and orthodox constitutional nationalism) considered the finances of home rule, its recommendations were directed towards limiting the size of Ireland's imperial contribution, securing a fair allocation of revenue between Great Britain and Ireland, and obtaining subsidies for certain services from the British exchequer. And the council's spokesman specifically stated that it was ready to leave the fixing of customs and excise duties to the imperial parliament. But in the same year 1911 two very able constitutional nationalists, Erskine Childers and Thomas Kettle each published a work on home rule, obviously intended to anticipate and influence the shaping of the coming home rule bill. Childers's *The framework of home rule*, authoritative and academic in tone and closely packed with well-marshalled detail, was a formidable presentation of the nationalist case. In the large section devoted to finance, he argued that as finance and policy were inseparable, without financial independence it would be impossible to realize the aims of home rule. 'Great Britain', he wrote, 'has no moral right to lay down that her views about trade shall govern the course of Irish policy'.[20] Kettle, in his short and sparkling *Home rule finance: an experiment in justice*, pointed out that everywhere the budget was at last being recognized 'as the main method of influencing the social habits of the people'. And he argued that if Ireland was refused the right 'to frame her customs and excise schemes', she not only would be denied the power of protecting her industries but would be unable 'to rearrange the unjust incidence of taxation'.[21]

---

[19] *Hansard 4*, xv, 248, 500, 510.
[20] E. Childers, *The framework of home rule* (1911), pp 567–72.
[21] T. Kettle, *Home rule finance* (1911), p 76.

When drafting the home rule bill of 1912 Asquith's government was able to benefit from the work of its predecessors in 1886 and 1893. In addition, early in 1911 it appointed a strong committee under the chairmanship of Sir Henry Primrose to report on Irish finance. This committee, which had a distinctively liberal, in the party sense, bias, heard a good deal of evidence and within a few months produced a remarkably readable and definite report. It emphasized that there had recently occurred a very significant change in Ireland's fiscal position. When the 1886 and 1893 bills were being considered, there was an annual surplus between the amount of taxation raised in Ireland and the cost of local services. So it was both reasonable and feasible to provide for an imperial contribution from Ireland. But early in the twentieth century a momentous change had taken place. The increased cost of the land commission, the provision of old age pensions, and the growing tendency for the administration to acquire new functions, had wiped out the surplus. And the committee estimated that in 1910, while Ireland's true revenue was £10,300,000, expenditure on purely Irish services was £11,344,000. Considering the question what financial provisions should be inserted in a home rule bill, the committee proposed a bold and simple solution. The future Irish government should be given full control over Irish revenue and expenditure. This, the committee emphasized, would be in complete accord with the government's general policy for Ireland, freedom within its own sphere for Irish nationality. The committee thought that the Irish government might be debarred from imposing tariffs which would differentiate between one foreign country and another, and from imposing a customs duty on any article the produce or manufacture of Great Britain, without imposing a corresponding excise duty. To meet the problem of the Irish deficit, the committee suggested that the British exchequer might accept liability for old age pensions granted before the date home rule came into operation. This would assure the new Irish government of a substantial, but steadily diminishing, subsidy.[22]

One member of the cabinet, Birrell, the chief secretary, was inclined to accept the Primrose committee's report. An able and

[22] *Report by the committee on Irish finances*, [Cd. 6799], H.C. 1912–13, xxx.

adroit debater, who had played a strenuous part in public life for over twenty years, he frequently expressed his views on political problems with an urbane detachment, incongruous in a cabinet minister. But along with this went a sensitive awareness of many facets of Irish life. 'Messrs Maunsell's list of new Irish publications and the programme of the Abbey theatre', he wrote, 'became to me of far more significance than the monthly reports of the R.I.C.'[23] And at the end of 1911 he explained to his cabinet colleagues that Ireland in the previous five years had developed a public opinion of her own, neither created nor controlled by the Irish members. He thought that the plan of giving the Irish parliament the control of taxation with the exception of customs potentially dangerous, 'because whilst Great Britain may be easily worked up to say "We will not part with customs duties", Ireland on the other side of the channel can with greater ease be made to shout "No customs, no freedom"'. Birrell was inclined to accept the Primrose committee's recommendations, but if the cabinet did not agree to this, he thought the next best plan would be to give no taxing powers at all to the Irish parliament, handing over all the revenue derived from Ireland to the Irish government, 'not as taxes but as money'.[24]

The cabinet when framing the financial clauses of the home rule bill of 1912 did not adopt either of the two simple and extreme solutions suggested by Birrell. Instead it devised a complex and highly ingenious scheme which took into account a number of considerations not all of which were easily reconcilable. It was emphasized that the Irish government must be started with a revenue sufficient to meet its expenses, that it should have the benefit of any economies it might make, and that it should have to meet the cost of any increases in expenditure for which it was responsible. Again justice had to be done and seen to be done between the British and the Irish taxpayer. If it was 'impracticable, impolitic and unjust' to saddle the Irish government at the outset with a deficit, it was obviously wrong to leave this burden permanently on the shoulders of the British taxpayer. Also, though it was thought desirable to give the Irish parliament the widest powers of taxation, there had to be

[23] *Things past redress* (1937), p. 214.
[24] Birrell, Memorandum (Cab. 37/108/161.)

left to the United Kingdom parliament a sufficient 'field of imperial taxation'. Customs and excise presented a knotty problem. To give Ireland 'full and unfettered control of customs . . . would indeed be inconsistent with devolution to other parts of the United Kingdom', the general policy the government had in view. It was also argued that to give the Irish parliament control of customs and excise would lead to the imposition of differential duties on articles passing between Great Britain and Ireland and, as the cabinet was acutely aware, it would almost certainly be pointed out during the debate on the bill that 'liberal policy aims at the diminution of customs duties'. But Herbert Samuel, the postmaster-general, who was in charge of the financial clauses of the bill, argued that though the possibility of differential duties being imposed was a serious objection to the proposal to give the control of customs and excise to the Irish parliament, 'it is not so serious . . . as the objection to denying to the Irish parliament the right of lowering the only taxes that are of real importance to its people . . . or of raising the only taxes that are fruitful'. Finally it had to be provided that changes in the finances of one country could not have detrimental effects on those of the other.[25]

The result of taking all these considerations into account was that the financial clauses of the home rule bill of 1912 were lengthy and intricate. Before summarizing these clauses it is desirable to outline the bill itself. It provided that there should be an Irish parliament with two houses, a senate and a house of commons. The Irish parliament was empowered to legislate for 'the peace, order and good government of Ireland'. But the first clause of the bill asserted the supremacy of the parliament of the United Kingdom and its second clause listed under twelve heads the subjects on which the Irish parliament was not permitted to legislate, these ranging from making peace and war and defence to the granting of bounties, and lighthouses and coinage. In addition a group of important subjects – the collection of taxes, land purchase, the Royal Irish Constabulary, post office savings banks, old age pensions, and national insurance were reserved under the control of the United Kingdom government. Six years after the passing of the act the control of the

[25] *Hansard 5*, xxxvii, 62–6; papers on Irish finance, Nov. 1911 (Cab. 37/108).

R.I.C. was to be transferred to the Irish government, and the other reserved services, with the exception of the collection of taxes and land purchase, could be transferred to the Irish government by a resolution of both houses of the Irish parliament. Ireland was to be represented at Westminster by forty-two M.P.s, and questions arising over the validity of legislation passed by the Irish parliament and fiscal disputes could be ultimately referred to the king in council.

Taxation was to be collected in Ireland by imperial departments, but the Irish parliament was empowered to vary by an addition, reduction or discontinuance, any imperial tax as respected its levy in Ireland, and to impose in Ireland any independent tax, not being 'substantially the same in character as an imperial tax'. But the taxing powers granted to the Irish parliament were subject to important limitations. The Irish parliament could not impose a customs duty unless the article on which it was imposed was already liable to an imperial customs duty and it could only vary a customs duty by increasing it. Moreover, if the proceeds of an Irish addition to any customs duty came to more than one-tenth of the yield of that duty in Ireland when levied at the imperial rate, Ireland would not be credited by the United Kingdom exchequer with the excess above ten per cent. Again the Irish parliament had not the power to vary the rate of income tax (though it could vary abatements and exceptions), it could not vary death duties so as to impose a charge upon the personal property of any person domiciled in Great Britain, and it could not vary the rates of certain stamp duties.

All taxation levied in Ireland was to be paid into the United Kingdom exchequer, but there was to be an Irish exchequer and annually the United Kingdom exchequer was to pay into the Irish exchequer a sum termed 'the transferred sum'. This was to be made up of the cost of the departments transferred to the Irish government at the time of the passing of the act, together with the proceeds of any taxes imposed by the Irish government and a grant amounting in the first year to £500,000 and decreasing annually by £50,000 until it reached £200,000. If a reserved service was to be transferred to the Irish government, the transferred sum was to be increased by the equivalent of the consequent saving to the United Kingdom exchequer.

To determine problems arising from the administration of the
financial provisions of the act there was to be a joint exchequer
board, consisting of two persons nominated by the treasury, two
by the Irish treasury and a chairman appointed by the crown.
If at any time the proceeds of Irish taxation exceeded the cost of
the transferred and reserved services the financial provisions of
the act were to be revised with a view both to extending the
financial powers of the Irish government and parliament and
of securing an imperial contribution from Ireland. Obviously
until this revision took place the Irish fiscal system would have
had to conform fairly closely to the British pattern though the
Irish government would have had the power to decide how it
would spend its revenue.

The financial clauses of the third home rule bill embodied
an intricate and interesting plan. Unfortunately, they were
never exhaustively debated. The bill reached its committee
stage in the house of commons towards the close of a long
session when the members, according to an intelligent observer,
were showing signs of strain and some of those who spoke on its
financial provisions clearly failed to grasp the meaning of what
they were talking about.[26] And the Irish nationalists were remarkably silent when fiscal matters were being discussed in
committee, being obviously reluctant either to embarrass the
Government or show over-enthusiasm for the financial provisions of the bill.

The other major and more fundamental problem which had
to be faced when a home rule bill was being formulated was
the existence of the unionist minority, or – if northern and
southern unionists are considered separately – of unionist
minorities. Nationalists tended to imply that Ireland was an
almost united community unanimously demanding self-
government. For instance, Redmond, a generous-minded man,
implied in 1886 that the Irish unionists were simply a 'faction'.[27]
In fact, if the contemporary convention of equating unionism
with protestanism and nationalism with catholicism is accepted,
the unionists must have amounted to about a quarter of the
population of Ireland. Admittedly there were exceptions to
the convention which has just been mentioned. There was a

[26] *Nineteenth Century*, xxiii, 213.
[27] J. E. Redmond, *Historical and political addresses* (1898), p. 127.

succession of distinguished protestant nationalists and in Ulster there were small groups of protestant liberals who were home rulers. On the other hand there were catholic unionists, such as Lord Fingall, who presided over the great southern unionist demonstration in 1892, Lord Morris, the law lord, Denis Henry, the first chief justice of Northern Ireland, who sat as unionist member for South Londonderry, and Thomas Maguire, the first catholic fellow of T.C.D., a Platonist and a unionist pamphleteer, who helped, in all good faith, to introduce Pigott to *The Times*. And when Maguire's colleague Edward Dowden, the gentle literary critic and fervent unionist organizer, was collecting 'songs for unionist Ireland', he had to explain to Swinburne, who had responded to his appeal, that the phrase 'black as . . . creed of priest' would not do 'for our catholic unionists'. Swinburne obligingly substituted 'beast' for 'priest'.[28]

But when allowance is made for political eccentrics and sturdy individualists, it was generally agreed that political and religious lines of division coincided. Accepting this assumption there must have been at the beginning of the twentieth century about 1,000,000 Irish unionists, the protestants in Ireland amounting to 1,147,000 out of a total population of 4,390,000. Denominational demography divided the Irish unionists into two sections – the northern and the southern unionists. The population of Belfast county borough was almost 76 per cent protestant; in a zone formed of Belfast itself and the country within a radius of about 65 miles from the city, the protestants amounted to over 75 per cent of the inhabitants. In the six north-east counties of Ulster about 66 per cent of the population was protestant; in the whole province, including the three strongly catholic counties of Cavan, Monaghan and Donegal, the protestants were about 56 per cent of the population. Numerically speaking there were nearly 300,000 protestants in Belfast, over 670,000 in Belfast and the surrounding zone, over 800,000 in the six north-east counties and in the province nearly 900,000.

In the three southern provinces the position was very different. In Leinster the protestants amounted to 14 per cent of the population, in Munster they were proportionally far

[28] *Letters of Edward Dowden* (1914), p. 383.

weaker, being only 6 per cent, in Connaught they amounted to only 4 per cent. Taking the three southern provinces together they formed only 10 per cent of the population and all told numbered about 250,000. Moreover about 60 per cent of the Leinster protestants were concentrated in Dublin city and county, forming between one-fifth and a quarter of the population of the area, and 60 per cent of the protestants of Munster were in Cork city and county. Consequently outside the Dublin and Cork areas the protestants were spread thinly in the south and west.

This striking difference in densities was bound to produce differences in attitude between the northern and the southern unionists. The unionists of the north formed a powerful, comparatively concentrated, block. Over wide areas they outnumbered their nationalist opponents, they predominated in industrial, commercial and professional life, they were well entrenched in local government, they held seventeen parliamentary constituencies and in political debate they could appeal on their own behalf to liberal and democratic principles. What size of population and what degree of homogeneity is required to constitute a community with the right to determine its own political destiny is obviously likely to be settled subjectively. It is enough to say that in Ulster (or in a portion of the province) the unionists were relatively so numerous that their feelings could scarcely be ignored by British liberals. The southern unionists on the other hand were undoubtedly a small minority, even in the Dublin area being outnumbered by three to one. So, if the general principles governing British political life at the beginning of the twentieth century were accepted, it was obviously more difficult for them to make a case. They could argue that home rule would be detrimental to Ireland and the empire, they could stress that they formed a cultural and political *élite* in Ireland, but their position was dialectically indefensible if the principle that the will of the majority should ultimately prevail was accepted.

Each of the two great sections into which Irish unionism was divided was also significantly influenced by the economic history of its region. Largely as a result of the tremenduous economic changes which occurred during the nineteenth century Ireland was clearly divided into two zones – the north-east industrial area, centred on Belfast, that great urban concentration of industrial and commercial power, and the south and west, still essentially agricultural. The difference between the two zones is simply indicated by the fact that at the close of the nineteenth century nearly half the factories and over 70 per cent of the factory workers in Ireland were in the six north-east counties.[29] The economic evolution of this north-east zone was a remarkable, indeed a romantic chapter in economic history. By the end of the eighteenth century a prosperous linen industry had grown up in Ulster, but the region lacked the two indispensible elements for industrial advance in the coming era, coal and iron. However, using their reserves of trained labour, technical skill, marketing expertise, capital and self-confidence, the Ulster businessmen strenuously and successfully participated to the full in the nineteenth-century industrial revolution. Coal, iron and flax were imported. Ulster fine linen became world famous, large quantities of linen and linen thread were exported, and foreign linen came to Ulster to be bleached. What was even more remarkable was the development of the Belfast shipbuilding industry, the yards along the Lagan usually launching well over 150,000 tons of shipping a year, including many of the great liners of the White Star line. The success of linen and shipbuilding naturally stimulated other industries – engineering, rope-making, tobacco manufacture and printing – and many of the small market towns of Ulster were full of industrial activity.

The region was dominated and directed by Belfast. With its clustering slim factory chimneys and hundreds of straight streets of redbrick working-class and middle-class houses, Belfast was undoubtedly a nineteenth-century town. Its population had increased about twentyfold between the union and the diamond jubilee, and at the beginning of the twentieth century an enthusiastic Belfastman dwelt on its spacious, well-kept streets and its palatial warehouses, offices and shops, many of them, he pointed out, having 'lifts' to the upper floors. The spirit of the city was vigorously expressed by its citizens' pride, the new city hall begun in 1898. In white stone, decorated and domed without, within lavishly covered with 'Pavonazzo and

[29] *Supplement to the annual report of the inspector of factories and workshops for the year 1900*, [Cd. 841], H.C. 1902 xii.

Breccia marbles' and wood carvings in the style of Grinling
Gibbons, its florid flamboyance is both assertive and exhilarating.[30]

Northerners at the beginning of the twentieth century were
proud of their economic achievements and quick to compare
themselves to their own advantage with the rest of Ireland. For
instance during the debates on the third home rule bill the
Belfast News Letter published a big industrial map of Ireland
on which the Ulster area, packed with economic information,
contrasted effectively with the large empty spaces in the south
and west. And Ulster businessmen, conscious of what their
firms had accomplished and very sensitive to market fluctua-
tions, were deeply perturbed by the suggestion that the political
framework in which they worked should be drastically altered.
Twice, in 1893 and 1912, the Belfast chamber of commerce sent
strong deputations to the prime minister of the day to voice
their fears. 'All our progress', the chamber declared in 1893,
'has been made under the union. We were a small, insignificant
town at the end of the last century, deeply disaffected and hostile to the British empire. Since the union and under equal laws,
we have been wedded to the empire and made a progress
second to none . . . Why should we be driven by force to abandon
the conditions which have led to that success?'[31] And Vesey
Knox, a protestant home ruler who sat for nine years as M.P.
for Ulster constituencies and who, as he himself admitted,
made few converts amongst his co-religionists to his political
creed, in an able memorandum on the Ulster question which he
drafted about 1914, pointed out that the northerners' apprehensions were understandable. 'Ulster', he wrote, 'is a little
Lancashire without coal'. And its businessmen were afraid that
'even if the southerners had every desire to be perfectly fair
they will not have the experience or understanding to govern a
country so different to their own'. The industries of Ulster, he
emphasized, could easily be killed by the pressure of direct
taxation (the result of southern extravagance); by a mistaken
tariff policy, which might for instance impose duties on flax and

[30] R. M. Young, *Belfast and the province of Ulster in the 20th Century*
(1909), pp 110–2.
[31] *Report of the council of the Belfast chamber of commerce, adopted, 17 March,
1893.*

foodstuffs; or by a philanthropic government, full of the best intentions, attempting to regulate industrial wages.[32]

Northern unionists were held together not only by economic interests but also by simple, serious loyalties, compounded of evangelical protestantism, cultural traditions and historic memories. A simple political faith, based on these memories, was enunciated in 1917 by Lord Ernest Hamilton, a member of a great Ulster house, whose estates lay in the debatable land of west Tyrone. Home rule he regarded as another of the attempts which had been systematically made in the past to rid Ulster of the British element in its population. This time, he thought, open violence would not be used because the catholic Irish were essentially 'non-combative in the British sense, that is to say face to face fighting does not appeal to them'. Instead, once home rule was in operation they would employ illegitimate electoral practices, agrarian outrage and Tammany Hall tactics to overcome their unionist opponents.[33]

There were, naturally enough, fissures in Ulster protestantism. There were denominational differences going back to the seventeenth century, the presbyterians being still sensitively suspicious of the social pretensions of the adherents of the disestablished church. There had been, until the land purchase acts changed the agrarian pattern, tension between landlord and tenant – and if the northern tenants had been more law abiding than those in the south and west, they had been equally determined to get fair rents and later ownership of their holdings. In fact it could be said that the northern tenant farmer had benefited from agrarian disorder while disdaining to indulge in it. Again, though relations between employers and employees in Ulster were on the whole good, there had been industrial disputes. Finally, there was for some time a definite division in Ulster politics between conservatives and liberal unionists. When Gladstone at the beginning of 1886 announced his conversion to home rule the Ulster liberals, with their political tradition firmly rooted in eighteenth-century whiggery and radicalism, were faced with a hard choice. Unhesitatingly the great majority decided to stand by the union, and the Ulster

[32] Memorandum drawn up by Vesey Knox, *c.* 1912 (P.R.O. N.I., 89/5/19).

[33] E. W. Hamilton, *The soul of Ulster* (1917), pp. 126–39.

Reform Club in Belfast, which had been founded 'in celebration of Mr Gladstone's great triumph at the general election of 1880' and opened with great éclat at the beginning of 1885, 'proved itself a valuable factor in the maintenance of the union during the home rule agitation'.[34] Nevertheless, as MacKnight's *Ulster as it is*, a vigorously written and very readable account of Ulster politics between 1866 and 1892, reminds us, old antagonisms lingered on for a time. MacKnight, from 1866 editor of the *Northern Whig*, the leading liberal newspaper in Ulster, was a fervent unionist, prepared to discuss the issue over a cup of tea with the G.O.M. himself. But writing in the nineties MacKnight recalls the fight for disestablishment and tenant right, dwells with gusto on how Disraeli's right-hand man, Cairns, snubbed his Belfast conservative constituents once he was seated in the lords and grumbles about the selfishness displayed by conservatives when it was a question of dividing Ulster seats between themselves and the liberal unionists.[35] But the divisions in Ulster unionism, though they should not be overlooked, must not be over-emphasized. They were far less important than the common and integrating elements in the community's tradition. And in a period of emergency one element in this tradition – the refusal of the Ulster protestants when besieged to surrender – was likely to assert itself.

The unionists of the south and west of Ireland lived in counties which had been, economically speaking, less fortunate in the nineteenth century. Moreover the backbone of their party in these areas was a declining class in Irish agrarian society – the Irish landlords. From the seventies British opinion had increasingly tended to view the Irish landowners as being from the economic standpoint of little value and from the political as a social irritant. Parliament first curtailed their powers and then provided the machinery and finance to enable their tenants to buy them out. Resentfully the Irish landlords accepted the escape offered by the land-purchase acts. Naturally they did not realize that as the first large group of landlords in Europe to be expropriated on grounds of public policy they were getting out relatively well, having a far better financial fate than

[34] T. MacKnight, *Ulster as it is*, ii, 81–2, 101–2; R. M. Young, *Belfast and the province of Ulster in the 20th century*, p. 114.
[35] T. MacKnight, *Ulster as it is*, ii, 189; i, 77–8, 157.

that which awaited the landlords of central Europe and Russia. But if they made a reasonably good financial bargain they lost definitely in status. From owning and directing large agricultural units they were transformed into rentiers with perhaps a big house, a demesne and a home farm.

Simultaneously the Irish landlords were losing their commanding position in county affairs. In 1898 county government was transferred from the grand juries to democratically elected county councils. Unionists were convinced that the grand juries had managed county business, as Lecky put it 'economically, efficiently and fairly'.[36] Nevertheless Salisbury's government felt obliged to act on unionist principles by extending the new English system of county administration to Ireland. Again, until the end of the nineteenth century, the commission of the peace in rural areas was almost monpolized by the landed gentry. But after 1892 successive liberal governments began to democratize the bench, shopkeepers, farmers and auctioneers being placed beside the landowners, land agents and retired army officers who had for so long constituted the unpaid magistracy in the rural parts of Ireland.

It would be a mistake to assume that southern unionism was entirely a landlords' movement. The southern unionists included in their ranks many professional men, protestants being disproportionately numerous in the professions in the three southern provinces, providing nearly half the lawyers, a third of the medical men and over half the engineers as well as holding nearly all the academic posts in Dublin university. Many big businessmen in the south were unionists, even if Arthur Samuels' bold assertion that 'the direction of affairs in commerce and industry is vested in the hands of unionists', was an overstatement.[37] Unionists too were prominent in the commercial patriciate of the small Irish country towns, there were protestant farmers scattered through the three provinces, there were thousands of protestant working men in the Dublin area, the strength of working-class unionism in Dublin being demonstrated by the existence of the 'City and county of Dublin Conservative Working Men's Club'.

[36] *Hansard 4*, lv, 456.
[37] A. Samuels, *Home rule: Fenian home rule, home rule all round, devolution* (1911), p. 94.

Nevertheless the landlords were the traditional leaders of southern unionism, and, it may be added, even in economic decline they were influential clients and customers of the unionist lawyers, land agents, doctors and merchants. And as a class, by the beginning of the twentieth century, the Irish gentry were unlikely to be inspired by political self-confidence and optimism. Midleton, an Irish landowner and an ex-cabinet minister, who was chosen as the leader of the southern unionists in 1909, noticed that 'the general sale of landed estates, co-operating with the tendency of the southern Irish gentry for a century past to concentrate on country life and regard themselves as a British garrison had caused a certain atrophy of political development'.[38] In short, while the northern unionists could dig in on a defensible line, the southern unionists, scattered and largely led by a discouraged class, could only hope that through some unexpected political conjuncture the inevitable would not occur.

It was clear that circumstances might compel northern and southern unionists to adopt different, and to some extent divergent, strategies. And early in the fight against home rule the Ulster unionists felt it advisable to reassure their southern friends. When the unionists of the three southern provinces in June 1892 held a great demonstration in Dublin, it was attended by a delegation from the northern unionists, who a few days earlier had held their own demonstration in Belfast. Two members of this delegation, Fellenburg Montgomery and Adam Duffin, both of whom were to play an active part in Ulster politics for the next thirty years, addressed the gathering. Montgomery, an able, somewhat arrogant, hard-fighting country gentleman from the Ulster border, assured his audience that the Ulstermen's opposition to home rule did not mean sitting still while 'the yoke of a Healyite parliament was being firmly strapped on your necks, and then saving ourselves from the consequences by setting up a little home rule shop of our own'. Duffin, a linen merchant and a liberal unionist, emphasized that though the Ulster unionists thought they could muster their resources more effectually 'in our own city of Belfast, they did not think their claims and interests were distinct

[38] Lubbock, *A page from the past* (1936), pp. 242–3.

from those of the rest of Ireland. 'Tinkers of constitution,' might, he went on, try to separate the government and political life of Ulster from the rest of Ireland, but such a suggestion would be rejected by the Ulster unionists 'with indignation and with scorn', as being unfair to the unionists of the rest of Ireland, 'who had boldly upheld the flag of the union under dangers and trials of which we in Ulster have had no experience', and to the catholic minority in Ulster, who would be put under the rule of a protestant majority, 'whom they have learned unhappily to regard with jealousy and mistrust'.[39]

In 1886, Gladstone was very conscious of the minority problem in Ireland. And though he himself believed that the best guarantee of its rights a minority could have was 'free institutions with absolute publicity',[40] he tried to find other safeguards for the Irish unionists. Sections were inserted into the clause limiting the legislative powers of the Irish parliament, restraining it from passing discriminatory legislation on religious matters. And, it may be added at once, that similar sections were included in the 1893 and 1912 home-rule bills. But the Irish unionists were afraid that they might be the victims of administrative discrimination and that attacks would be made on the economic interests with which they were associated. Gladstone in 1886 tried to meet these fears by providing that for three years after the enactment of home rule the Irish legislature should consist of two orders which would sit and deliberate together, either of which could veto the decisions of the other. The first order was to be composed of 28 representative Irish peers and 75 members possessing a fairly high property qualification, elected by persons with a rateable qualification of £25 annual value. The second order was to consist of 103 M.P.s. In the home rule bill of 1893 this unusual arrangement was replaced by a bicameral scheme. There was to be a legislative assembly of 103 members elected by the existing parliamentary constituencies and a legislative council of 48 members elected by persons possessing a rateable qualification of £20 annual value. A dispute between the two houses over a bill would be settled

---

[39] *The unionist convention for the provinces of Leinster, Munster and Connaught*, (1892), pp. 107–10.
[40] *Hansard 3*, ccciv, 1052.

at a joint sitting. The legislative council, Gladstone asserted, would secure 'a fair, full and liberal consideration' for the views of the minority. An eloquent spokesman for the minority, David Plunket, who represented Dublin University, retorted that as 'a protection' to 'the unionist minority or holders of property in Ireland', the council would prove 'a sham', almost all the voters with a £20 rateable qualification being small tenant-farmers.[41]

In the 1912 home-rule bill it was provided that the Irish parliament should consist of two houses, a senate of 40 members and a house of commons of 164. Senators were to have an eight-year term. The first senators were to be nominated by the imperial government, being replaced as they retired by senators nominated by the Irish government. The senate was to have no power over money bills. Disputes between the two houses over other bills were to be settled by their voting together at a joint session. Introducing the bill, Asquith expressed the hope that the senate should include representatives of the minority. But before the bill reached the committee stage he met a deputation from the Proportional Representation Society of Ireland, led by Sir Horace Plunkett and Lord MacDonnell, which emphatically explained to him that a representative legislature could only be secured in Ireland if P.R. was introduced.[42] This deputation made a real impression on the prime minister, and when the bill was in committee the government amended their own scheme for the senate. Senators were to sit for five years. The first senate was to be nominated by the imperial government. Thereafter senators were to be elected by parliamentary electors in the four provinces as separate constituencies, proportional representation being employed. As a result, Birrell calculated, the unionist minority might have as many as 15 seats in the senate. The unionists replied that their calculations showed that at a joint sitting of the two houses of the Irish parliament they would have 54 votes out of 200.[43]

A second chamber was one device for protecting the minority in Ireland; another was giving a special status to the area where

---

[41] *Hansard 4*, viii, 1255; x, 1868.
[42] *The Times*, 26 June 1912.
[43] *Hansard 5*, xliii, 624-5, 650.

the minority was most highly concentrated. About eight months before Gladstone announced his conversion to home rule, Bryce, then a rising young liberal M.P., on being entertained in Belfast by the Ulster liberals, 'strong on suffrage extension and Ulster tenant right', told them in a short address that liberal opinion in England was inclining to home rule and that therefore they should consider how Ulster interests could be protected. His remarks were received with surprise and incredulity.[44] And within a year, most of his audience, far from carefully considering what, if any, safeguards Ulster would need under home rule, were fighting that measure tooth and nail. Gladstone himself when drafting the first home rule bill was well aware of the Ulster problem, but he decided that the question whether any part of Ireland should be exempted from the measure or given some other form of special treatment should be left open for consideration during the progress of the bill.[45] In his speech on the first reading of the bill, having emphasized that the 'wealthy, intelligent and energetic portion of the Irish community which predominates in a certain portion of Ulster' must not be allowed to baulk the wishes of the rest of Ireland, he went to indicate schemes which demanded 'careful and unprejudiced consideration'. Ulster or a portion of Ulster, he pointed out, could be excluded from the operation of the bill, or it could be given autonomy on its own, or provincial councils could be set up in a home-rule Ireland which would control certain subjects such as education.[46]

Before introducing the third home-rule bill in 1912 Asquith's cabinet considered the Ulster problem. Lloyd George and Churchill proposed that Ulster should be excluded from its scope. Their colleagues, however, decided that the bill should apply to Ireland as a whole, but the cabinet was careful to warn the Irish nationalist leaders that the government held themselves free to make changes if it became clear that special treatment must be provided for the Ulster counties and that in this case the government will be ready to recognize the necessity either by amendment of the bill or by not pressing it on under

[44] H. A. L. Fisher, *James Bryce* (1927), ii, 208–9.
[45] Draft of memorandum, 20 Mar. 1886 (Add. MS 44632).
[46] *Hansard 3*, ccciv, 1053–4.

the provisions of the parliament act.[46A] The government's policy might be characterized as reasonable but it involved a considerable element of risk. Liberals believed in home rule for Ireland and were sure that a truncated Ireland would be an unsatisfactory unit, administratively and economically. On the other hand they were instinctively opposed to forcing a political system on a community against its settled and strongly held convictions. The government's policy enabled it to gauge the extent and depth of Ulster unionist opposition to home rule. It was also a policy which might during the discussions on the bill arouse hopes and passions which would be hard to assuage.

In the event, hopes and passions were roused, and the steadily sustained and well-advertised opposition of the Ulster unionists to the bill created a serious problem of conscience for British liberals. The Ulster unionists detested home rule. It was, however, a major presupposition of British politics that after a question had been fully discussed, the will of the majority expressed constitutionally should prevail. But it was also taken for granted that there would be sufficient agreement on fundamentals to prevent any decision being intolerable to the minority. Therefore, the Ulster unionists' problem was how to convince the British public that their resistance to home rule was deep-seated and immovable. When the second home-rule bill had been in the offing, Joseph Chamberlain had advised the Ulster unionists to take energetic measures 'to show you are determined to resist. No government will ever dare to coerce you.' And about the same time, an able Ulster unionist, Thomas Sinclair, addressing the great Ulster convention of 1892, outlined the policy they, 'the children of the revolution of 1688', should adopt if a Dublin parliament was set up. 'We shall', he declared. 'ignore its existence, its acts will be but waste paper, the police will find our barracks preoccupied with our own constabulary, its judges will sit in empty court houses'.[47]

In 1911 the position, from the Ulster unionist point of view, was much more critical that it had been in 1892. In 1892 the house of lords offered an impassable barrier. But after the

[46A] J. A. Spender and C. Asquith, *Life of Henry Herbert Asquith* (1932), ii, 15; W. S. Churchill, *The world crisis, 1911–1914* (1923), p. 181. Report of cabinet meeting, 6 Feb. 1912 (Cab. 41/33).

[47] T. MacKnight, *Ulster as it is*, ii, 288; *The Times*, 16 Feb. 1914.

parliament act was passed in 1911, it was probable that if a home rule bill was introduced in the session of 1912 it would reach the statute book in the lifetime of the parliament elected in December 1910. So the Ulster unionists took a series of spectacular steps to bring home to parliament and the British public how deep was their detestation of a measure which put them under the control of an Irish parliament. They already had a central organization, the Ulster Unionist Council, founded in 1904, representing the unionist associations and Orange lodges of the province and in 1910 they had secured as their leader Edward Carson, then outstanding at the English bar. Carson had strong convictions, the status and confidence conferred by a brilliant professional career, and a superb command of the arts of advocacy. He could quickly see the essentials of a problem and drive home his approach by concentrating on what he felt were the most telling arguments. His oratory – impressive and idiosyncratic – reflected his personality. While engaged in lucid exposition in conventional parliamentary or platform style he would begin to talk with startling directness, the broken sentences and colloquial, and often clumsy, turns of phrase conveying passionate conviction and immovable resolution. Carson was in fact a man of profound and perceptible feeling. But emotion while it infused strength into his rhetoric did not blind him. A fervent unionist he was also an able political strategist. He knew when it was opportune to negotiate, he could suggest obstinacy without seeming stolid, and without committing himself to what might prove an untenable position, and he could be unexpectedly conciliatory while surrendering little that could be held. Tall, gaunt, aloof but warm-tempered, able to express with stark and inspiring simplicity the feelings of his followers he was well fitted to be the leader and spokesman of a small, proud community in what it saw to be a fight for political survival.

It was fortunate for the Ulster unionists that Carson was able to invest their cause with a high seriousness which justified extreme measures. For they soon formed the Ulster volunteer force, drilled, organized and armed on military lines; made preparations for constituting a provisional government which could take over the administration of Ulster if the home rule bill came into operation; and held a series of great disciplined, determined gatherings which culminated in the meetings at which tens of thousands of Ulster unionists signed a Solemn League and Covenant, pledging the signatories to stand by one another in defending 'our cherished position of equal citizenship within the United Kingdom'.

Their intense and defiant opposition to home rule was bound to create a problem of conscience for British liberals. Government with the consent of the governed was one of the fundamental tenets of the liberal faith and it justified the party's self-sacrificing devotion to Irish home rule, but as the debate on the third home-rule bill proceeded with growing acerbity it seemed as if the application of the principle to Ireland was not going to be a simple operation. The Ulster unionists fervently asserted that they formed a community entitled to determine its own political fate. Moreover, they were only too clearly prepared by passive and active methods to prevent their feelings being disregarded. It is understandable, then, that as the party battle continued with undiminished stridency the possibility of a compromise began to be mooted. When the home rule bill was in committee one of the liveliest members of the government, Winston Churchill, suggested to Redmond that since 'the opposition of three or four Ulster counties is the only obstacle which now stands in the way of home rule', the Irish nationalists should consider whether 'the characteristically protestant and Orange counties' ought not to be offered 'a moratorium' of several years before coming under the authority of a Dublin parliament.[48] Some liberal back-benchers also were uncomfortable about the way the Ulster problem had been ignored in the bill, and Agar-Robertes, an independent-minded young liberal member, when the bill was in committee moved that the four north-east counties of Ulster should be excluded from the operation of the bill. He described his amendment as 'an honest attempt to solve one of the most complex questions in connection with the government of Ireland', and it was grudgingly supported by the unionists on the ground that it would make the bill 'less bad'. The nationalists were indignant at the suggestion that Ireland should be divided, Redmond declaring that to attempt to cut off the protestants under the two nations theory, from the traditions of the Irish race 'sounds to many of us

[48] D. Gwynn, *Life of John Redmond* (1932), pp. 213–14.

something like sacrilege'.[49] Though the Government's majority was substantially reduced, the Agar-Robartes amendment was rejected. Later, during the report stage of the bill, Carson himself moved an amendment excluding the province of Ulster from its operation. He asked was the house prepared to drive the unionists of Ulster out of the constitution which they wanted to remain under and 'compel them to live under a constitution which they abhor and which is loathsome to them'. And he argued that the province should be the area chosen for exclusion on the ground that the whole of Ulster was 'bound up together in their business with the industries permeating out from the counties of Antrim and Belfast into the various towns around with Belfast practically the capital of the province'. Asquith pointed out that the exclusion of Ulster would render the bill practically unworkable, its whole finance for instance 'falling to the ground', and the amendment was rejected by a large majority.[50]

In the autumn of 1913 Loreburn, who had ceased to be lord chancellor only fifteen months before, demanded in a letter which filled three columns of *The Times*, that an effort should be made to arrive at an agreed settlement. Though, he said 'it would be a blunder', to take too tragically the prospect of a protestant rising, widespread rioting in the north of Ireland against home rule would be a calamity. On the other hand to drop the bill would inflame nationalist feeling in the south. He urged that an attempt should be made to find a solution through either a conference or direct communication between the party leaders. And he reminded political partisans who hesitated to abandon the traditional methods of party warfare that they had in Great Britain 'a more crowded population, more educated and more intolerant of preventible hardships and now fully possessed of power.[51] Coming from an able lawyer who had been a leading home ruler this was a weighty plea. Privately Loreburn, when challenged by Asquith to suggest a basis on which a conference could proceed with any hope of success, suggested that the four north-east counties might be turned into a legislative and administrative 'enclave'. The M.P.s from these counties, Loreburn suggested, could be given the power to veto

---

[49] *Hansard 5*, xxxix, 1087.
[50] *Hansard 5*, xlvi, 377–91.
[51] *The Times*, 11 Sept. 1913.

the application to the area of legislation passed by the Irish parliament (for the sake of equality the M.P.s from the other twenty-eight counties would have to be given similar power in respect to their area). Loreburn admitted this would be inconvenient but 'inconvenience is better than implacable hostility'. Moreover, to allay northern suspicions he was prepared to limit the taxing powers of the Irish parliament and to give the United Kingdom parliament power to appropriate between the areas the yield from Irish taxation.[52]

Herbert Samuel about the same time put forward two schemes for dealing with the Ulster problem. He first suggested that the representatives of Ulster (or a part of Ulster) in the Irish senate and house of commons should be constituted 'a third house' which could veto the application of legislation to Ulster. And if a select committee of this third house vetoed the application of a tax to the area, then the Irish parliament would not extend to it the benefits financed by the new tax. If it was found that the 'third house' had rarely to intervene, after some years 'it will be relegated to the museum of constitutional curiosities'. A couple of months later he suggested to the cabinet another plan. Defining Ulster for the purpose of his scheme as those counties which required differential treatment to the rest of Ireland, he proposed that the Ulster members in the Irish senate and house of commons should constitute an Ulster house of parliament which would sit in Belfast. Bills passed by the Ireland parliament would not apply to Ulster if vetoed by the Ulster parliament and that parliament could petition the imperial parliament to pass legislation for Ulster concerning matters normally within the province of the Irish parliament. The Ulster house would not have a veto over financial legislation but the yield from Ulster of any new tax imposed by the Irish parliament would have to be spent in the area. Ulster members would not be required to attend sittings of the Dublin parliament but they could do so if they wished, and Samuel hoped that in time 'a gradual process of amalgamation might take place'.[53]

---

[52] Lord Loreburne's memorandum, 17 Sept. 1913 (Cab. 37/116).

[53] Samuel, memorandum, A. Samuel to prime minister, 10 Oct. 1913 (Samuel papers, A/49/9,A/41/10); memorandum, 18 Dec. 1913 (Cab. 37/117/95).

With suggestions for a compromise in the air the party leaders began tentatively to see whether they could find the basis for a settlement. Crewe and Bonar Law played golf and talked at Balmoral. Churchill and Chamberlain went for a cruise together on the admiralty yacht. The prime minister and Bonar Law had a series of discreet meetings in London. And Asquith had talks with Carson. Asquith, the epitome of lucid rationality in politics, and Bonar Law, whose common sense in private contrasted strikingly with the rude assertiveness in public which he adopted at the outset of his career as the leader of the unionist party, made some progress in their talks. Bonar Law had long thought 'that it might be possible to leave Ulster as it was and grant some form of home rule to the rest of Ireland'. Asquith for his part was prepared to consider 'separate treatment' for Ulster. At the end of 1913 Asquith produced his basis for a compromise. Customs and the post office were to be removed from the jurisdiction of the Irish parliament. In a case where the Irish minority or a section of it alleged it had a grievance as a result of legislative or administrative action, the ultimate decision was to be given by judges imperially appointed. In 'statutory' Ulster (that is to say Ulster as defined for the purpose of the compromise), police and factory inspection were to remain under imperial control. If the Ulster M.P.s in the Irish parliament dissented from any legislation on certain enumerated subjects, it was not to take effect until the approval of the imperial parliament was obtained. These proposals were turned down by Bonar Law and Carson, the latter pointing out that he thought that when the exclusion of Ulster was discussed it clearly meant that Ulster should remain under the imperial parliament and that the Dublin parliament should have no powers in the excluded area.[54]

While the party leaders sought in private for the basis of a settlement, men of goodwill published a variety of suggestions for dealing with the Irish problem. Edward Clarke, an independent unionist, and Shirley Benn, a unionist M.P., both suggested there should be provincial assemblies in Ireland.

[54] J. A. Spender and C. Asquith, *Life of Henry Herbert Asquith* (1932), pp. 34–37, R. Blake, *The unknown prime minister* (1952), pp. 157, 166, I. Colvin, *Life of Lord Carson* (1936), ii, 266–7; A. Chamberlain, *Politics from the inside* (1936), pp. 572–3.

Clarke proposed that in addition to the assemblies, there should be an Irish parliament with limited powers and that the Irish M.P.s should be excluded from Westminster. Benn suggested that the Irish M.P.s at Westminster should form a standing committee to consider Irish bills.[55] Ridgeway, who had been under-secretary when Balfour was chief secretary, favoured the exemption from the rule of the Irish government, for a fixed period, of the north-east counties, the exempted area remaining under the imperial government. Ridgeway believed that Redmond would not want to be handicapped at the beginning of his administration by Ulster in revolt, and he was confident that before the fixed period came to an end the north-east would have decided to join the rest of Ireland.[56] Lord Mac-Donnell, who had also been under-secretary, advocated as a compromise, what he called 'home rule within home rule'. He suggested that an elected Ulster council of 52 members should be set up to aid the lord lieutenant in the exercise of his executive functions in Ulster in respect to certain services, for instance education, local government and agriculture and technical instruction. The aim of his scheme, he explained, would be to place under the control of the council the administration of all the Irish services which could be transferred.[57]

Henry Newbolt, writing as a liberal, proposed that Ulster or part of Ulster should be excluded for a definite number of years on the understanding that the excluded area should agree 'to come in without resistance whenever called upon to do so by a resolution of the house of commons'. Frederic Harrison, the well-known Positivist, who had stood as a home-rule candidate in 1886, suggested a solution which he called 'Ulster home-rule alongside Irish home-rule'. The Ulster M.P.s for a stated term should form a committee which would control matters affecting any part of Ulster, subject only to the king in council or the imperial parliament. At the end of the fixed period the position of Ulster could again be considered and might be settled by holding a plebiscite in the province.[58]

An ingenious solution was proposed by Sir Horace Plunkett,

[55] *The Times*, 9 Mar. 1914, 29 Oct. 1913.
[56] Ibid., 21 Feb. 1914.
[57] *Hansard 5 (Lords)*, xvi, 861–4.
[58] *The Times*, 1 Apr., 18 Feb. 1914.

the leader of the Irish co-operative movement, the virtual founder and first head of the Department of Agriculture and Technical Instruction, and, as he himself put it, 'a man of leisure and means' who had for quarter of a century occupied himself 'with the study of Irish life'. Plunkett suggested that it should be provided that at the end of a stated period after the home rule act came into operation, a defined area in the north should be allowed to decide by plebiscite whether or not it wished to continue under the authority of the Irish parliament. In other words unionist Ulster would at first be included in home rule Ireland with the option of exclusion after a fair trial. Shortly after producing his scheme Plunkett added the proviso that a competent and impartial tribunal should be constituted which 'would let Ulster out before the end of the agreed period if serious danger to her commercial and industrial interests or misbehaviour of any kind on the part of the Irish parliament should come to pass'. The tribunal, he suggested, might be composed of the lord chancellor of England, two 'eminent jurists or [men] of pro-consular type', and one or two Irish nationalist and unionist M.P.s. Plunkett explained to Asquith that this scheme would give the nationalists an opportunity of demonstrating that they could govern Belfast in 'a sane and sensible way' and lead to an all-party conference on the details of the home rule act. Moreover, if the scheme was accepted, Ulster businessmen, 'concerned to see that the experimental period was as little harmful as possible to their interests', would be eager to take part in such a conference. And Plunkett, it may be said at once, had a profound belief in the unifying effect of getting down to discussing points of practical detail.[59]

Lloyd George thought Plunkett's scheme provided an admirable solution 'on one condition . . . it should be accepted by the unionists of Ireland'. Asquith was pessimistic. He thought that compulsory inclusion at the start would be completely unacceptable to the Ulster unionists. Plunkett, always persuasive, secured for a moment an unexpected supporter who might have carried some weight in unionist circles – Lord Roberts. He called on the field-marshal and 'for imperial and

[59] Plunkett to Asquith, 4 Mar. 1914, Plunkett to Oliver, 12 Mar. 1914, Plunkett to Childers 9 Mar. 1914 (Plunkett papers), *The Times*, 10, 24 Feb. 1914.

especially Indian reasons' managed to persuade him to come out in favour of his scheme. But, as Plunkett sadly added, 'the dear old man' decided to consult Carson, 'and that was the end of his usefulness to me'.[60]

Plunkett was by no means alone in thinking that a conference of representative Irishmen might prove the best method of finding a solution for the Irish question. The idea had a surprising variety of advocates, ranging from Macara, the great cotton manufacturer, to Blakiston, the president of Trinity, Oxford. Macara, who after prolonged negotiations had managed to hammer out the agreement which for years governed relations between capital and labour in the cotton industry, emphasized how successful round-table conferences had proved in industry. Blakiston, when urging that a conference should be held, outlined a membership strikingly similar to that of the future 1917 convention. A strong conservative in national and academic affairs, he thought that when the conference got to work, 'it is most likely that the present union with some modifications . . . will be found better than any new constitution'.[61] Lang, archbishop of York, a politic churchman, argued that exclusion, though it might be necessary, certainly should not be the last word on the Irish question, and he suggested two conferences on the question, or as he himself put it, a statutory commission divided into two sections, an Irish and a British. The first section would consist of the party leaders and Irishmen such as MacDonnell, Dunraven and Horace Plunkett, with possibily Bryce as chairman. And its decisions would be referred to the other section which would then consider the question from the United Kingdom standpoint. When Lang put forward this suggestion in the house of lords it gained the support of a number of peers – Barrymore, the old leader of the southern unionist landlords (who urged that as a preliminary to a conference the government should tear up the home rule bill), Charwood, Dunraven, Meath, Shaftesbury, Sydenham, and Curzon, who went so far as to say he was prepared 'to stake everything I possess that a conference

---

[60] Lloyd George to Asquith, 23 Feb. 1914 (Asquith papers), Asquith to Plunkett, 16 Mar. 1914, Plunkett to Childers, 9 Mar. 1914 (Plunkett papers).

[61] *The Times*, 6 Mar., 2 June, 1914.

will come, that you will have to go to the men of Ireland and say, "meet together and tell us what you want and tell us what you are going to do". But that moment has not arrived yet.' Curzon's caution echoed the warning expressed more strongly by the learned and experienced Courtney, who pointed out that where a conference had been successful in reaching a constitutional settlement, 'all the parties had agreed the time had come they should work together'.[62]

It is perhaps worth noting that a number of the supporters of the conference approach to the Irish problem were federalists. Federalism was at this time fashionable in British politics. Acceptance of the federal principle had made possible the emergence of the great British dominions, Canada, Australia, South Africa, and, it was permissible for those who looked forward to an era when Anglo-American co-operation would be of the greatest importance in world affairs to add, the United States of America. Many keen imperialists also hoped that in the near future the British empire might be consolidated into closer union by the adoption of a federal constitution. With federalism so frequently coming up in discussion, it was almost inevitable that the application of federalism to the United Kingdom should be suggested. And of course the arguments for a federation of the British Isles, which would turn England, Ireland, Scotland and Wales (and possibly Ulster) into 'provinces' coincided to some extent with the arguments for a policy which the liberals favoured, devolution. And federalists who were unionists, such as Austen Chamberlain, an hereditary tariff reformer, and F. S. Oliver, whose biography of Alexander Hamilton is a brilliant federalist tract, saw advantages in tackling the Irish situation on federalist lines.[63] In a federal scheme the powers and status of the Irish parliament would be less than it would gain under home rule and, it need scarcely be added, the federalization of the British Isles would take some time.

At the beginning of the parliamentary session of 1914, the last session in which, under the provisions of the parliament act, the home rule bill had to pass the house of commons before becoming law, the cabinet had to decide what, if any, concessions it was going to offer to the unionist opposition. As has been

[62] *Hansard 5 (Lords)*, xvi, 555, 598, 647, 752.
[63] F. S. Oliver, *The alternatives to civil war* (1913), p. 1.

pointed out, from the start the government had been prepared to make special arrangements for Ulster if the situation seemed to demand it. This readiness to contemplate the possibility of a compromise was understandably disturbing to the government's allies, the Irish parliamentary party. Nationalists were dismayed at the prospect of a divided Ireland. Self-government for a united Ireland was a fundamental principle of their political faith. Their ideal, in Redmond's words, was 'a self-governing Ireland in the future when all her sons of all races and creeds within her shores will bring their tribute great or small to the great total of national enterprise and national statesmanship and national happiness'.[64] They were pained when it was borne in on them that the home rule bill, to them the legislative embodiment of a political absolute, was to a liberal cabinet an important and useful measure which might as a result of discussion be considerably amended so as to produce the maximum of happiness or the minimum of discontent. Redmond, while emphasizing his readiness to agree to safeguards which would meet the fears of the unionist minority, declared in the autumn of 1913: 'Irish nationalists can never be assenting parties to the multilation of the Irish nation; Ireland is a unit . . . The two-nation theory is to us an abomination and a blasphemy.'[65] But Asquith, Birrell and Lloyd George, by very correctly keeping him informed of the discussions between cabinet ministers and the leaders of the opposition, sympathetically and suavely brought home to him the liberals' scruples and fears over Ulster and their belief that a compromise was desirable.

In February 1914 Lloyd George, who was eager to get the Irish question out of the way, brought forward a bold plan which he felt the unionists would find difficult to turn down. He suggested that any Ulster county should be permitted by a plebiscite to contract out of home rule for six years. Under this scheme, he pointed out, the excluded Ulster counties would have an opportunity of laying their case before the British public at a general election, and they could scarcely rebel 'merely in anticipation of some act of oppression which could not possibly occur for years'. Lloyd George was convinced that the rejection of such an offer would put the unionists in the

[64] *Hansard 5*, xlvi, 406.
[65] D. Gwynn, *Life of John Redmond*, p. 232.

wrong with the British public. The Irish nationalist leaders, when the plan was submitted to them, though 'made conscious by innumerable communications from our own people we run enormous risks', reluctantly accepted it, 'as the price of peace'. They made plain, however, that their acquiescence was conditional. The offer, they said, must be the government's last word, and if it was not accepted by the opposition it was to lapse.[66]

The cabinet decided that Lloyd George's suggestions provided the basis for a conciliatory offer to the opposition. And at the beginning of March, Asquith informed the house of commons that the government 'had come to the conclusion that the fairest and simplest plan' was to permit each Ulster county to decide by plebiscite if it wished to be excluded and towards the end of June the government introduced the Government of Ireland Amendment Bill into the lords. It provided that, if in any Ulster county one-tenth of the parliamentary electors demanded it, a plebiscite should be held on the question whether or not the county should be excluded from the operation of the home rule act for six years.

To unionists the amending bill (as Lloyd George had foreseen) was something of a Greek gift. No doubt it represented a partial withdrawal by the government. But it also went a long way towards depriving the opposition of its most effective argument against home rule, that it involved the coercion of Ulster. Once British public opinion was convinced that Ulster was getting a fair deal, it would be futile for the conservatives to talk about using extraordinary methods to defeat home rule. They would be forced to restrict themselves to the conventional weapons of British political warfare, and the result would almost certainly be that by the summer of 1914 the amended home rule bill would be on the statute book.

One group was dismayed by this prospect, the southern unionists. During the controversy on the third home rule bill the southern unionists had expressed unstinted admiration for the northern unionists' stand, which, southern unionists emphasized, had put the government in the position of having only one course open to it, to hold a general election. Exclusion the southern unionists dismissed as unfair and impracticable. At the end of

[66] Ibid., pp. 256–8.

UNIVERSITY OF WINNIPEG
LIBRARY
515 Portage Avenue
Winnipeg, Manitoba R3B 2E9

1913, Lansdowne, the conservative leader in the lords and a great Kerry landlord, had frankly said in a public speech that the idea did not attract him. They had fought home rule because they were convinced it would weaken the empire and be grossly unfair to unionists all over Ireland. Privately, when agreeing that with certain conditions he would reluctantly accept home rule, he remarked: 'it would be a less bad thing both for Ireland and the rest of the United Kingdom if Ulster were *not* left out'.[67] And Arthur Godley, an elegant classicist, whose staunch unionism was expressed in letters to *The Times* and light verse, argued that home rule, if Ulster was left out, would not benefit anyone. In any event, he considered, nobody wanted home rule except some M.P.s, some ecclesiastics, and the ignorant peasantry of the south and west, who were 'duped and fleeced' by ecclesiastics and politicians. To Godley, it was clear that since the land question had been settled the driving force behind home rule had merely been 'the sentimental braggadocio of Celtic orators'.[68] Midleton, the leader of the southern unionists, asserted that to 'to set up an independent government on the basis of the present bill without Ulster is financially impossible and administratively absurd'.[69] And the *Irish Times*, the organ of 'sensible' southern unionism, declared that 'exclusion would be permanently fatal to every Irish hope and every Irish interest . . . it would condemn our country to an eternity of national weakness, industrial impotence and sectarian strife'.[70]

To southern unionists the logic of the situation clearly demanded the maintenance of the *status quo* in Ireland, and this they hoped would be ensured by a unionist victory at the general election which the opposition was asking for. But it had to be accepted that the government, with a majority in a parliament which had still over a year to run, might decide not to dissolve. And it is significant that in the summer of 1914 influential southern unionists began to mention the 'safeguards' they thought would be required by their section of the

---

[67] *The Times*, 19 Nov. 1913; A. Chamberlain, *Politics from the inside*, pp. 567–72.
[68] *The Times*, 17 Nov., 8 May, 1914
[69] *The Times*, 15 Apr. 1914.
[70] *Irish Times*, 19 Feb. 1914.

D   39

community if home rule came into force in the south and west. Midleton in the lords urged that the Irish judiciary should be appointed by the imperial government and that steps should be taken to prevent discriminatory taxation on land in Ireland and to ensure that the scales of graduated taxes in Ireland conformed to those in England. He also insisted that the imperial government should accept the responsibility of completing the operation of buying out the Irish landlords; otherwise, he said, 'you are going to lend yourself to a most gigantic act of robbery and spoliation'. Additional safeguards were suggested by Bryan Cooper, an intelligent young landlord, who had represented South Dublin for a year at Westminster and who later was to sit in the Dail. He suggested that the police should be a reserved service and that all government appointments should be on the results of a competitive examination.[71]

While the southern unionists were worrying about what would be their future under home rule with Ulster or part of Ulster excluded, the unionists were employing their majority in the lords to try to turn the government's offer of a compromise into a surrender. In moving the first reading of the bill, Crewe, the leader of the house, explained that the title of the bill had been drafted so as to 'afford the widest possible latitude for amendment'. The house took full advantage of this, drastically reshaping the bill in committee and excluding the whole province of Ulster from the operation of the home-rule bill indefinitely. A last desperate effort was made to find a compromise. The king summoned a small conference of the leaders of the four main groups involved, the liberals, the unionists, the Irish nationalists and the Ulster unionists, with the speaker as chairman.[72] They struggled with the problem for three successive days. It was agreed at the outset that there 'was no possibility, with any advantage, of discussing any settlement except on the lines of exclusion of some sort'. Carson began by demanding 'the clean cut', the exclusion of the whole province of Ulster, employing for the benefit of the nationalists the *argumentum ad hominem* that if the excluded area was smaller the reunion of Ireland would be delayed. In the end he seemed willing to reduce his demand to the six 'so-called plantation counties'. It

---

[71] *Hansard 5 (Lords)*, xvi, 633-4, *The Times*, 6 July 1914.
[72] Minutes of the conference, in Redmond papers.

was clear the nationalists would not accept either of his suggestions and Redmond mentioned county option as a possibility.

Asquith put forward two possible compromises – a division of
the province based on poor law unions and a division based on
parliamentary constituencies (making clear that in the latter
case West Belfast and Derry City though represented by
nationalists would be in the excluded area). Finally, with 'great
diffidence', he suggested that if agreement could be arrived at
on everything else Tyrone might be divided by an impartial
authority. This suggestion united Carson and Redmond. They
both pointed out that the problem had not been narrowed to
Tyrone and that the suggestion was in any event impracticable
unless there was agreement on the principles on which the impartial authority was to proceed. As a last resort the prime
minister appealed to the speaker to suggest a solution. According to the speaker, writing some years after the conference,
when the maps and statistics of Tyrone and Fermanagh were
inspected, the best line separating catholics and protestants was
obviously a contour line, the catholics tending to live on the
higher and protestants on the lower ground. Unfortunately, this
line was administratively impossible.[73] When appealed to by
the prime minister, the speaker suggested that Tyrone should be
excluded for a year or eighteen months, a plebiscite being taken
at the end of the period. If this plan were adopted, he explained,
Carson could claim that he had succeeded in having Tyrone
excluded long enough for its inhabitants to see the Irish parliament at work while Redmond could assure his followers that in
a year or eighteen months the county would undoubtedly vote
for inclusion. The conference rejected this compromise.

The reaction of Irish nationalists to the failure of the conference was to call on the government 'to carry out its programme under the parliament act' and enact the home-rule
bill.[74] The *Irish Times*, having complacently remarked that 'we
may now take it for granted that the last has been heard of
exclusion', went on to call for a general election as the alternative to civil war. The peace and safety of the empire, it said,
depend on 'an almost immediate dissolution of parliament'. *The
Times* also demanded a general election. The population of the

[73] Lowther, *A speaker's commentaries* (1925), ii, 163.
[74] *Irish Independent* and *Freeman's Journal*, 25 July 1914.

empire, it pointed out, amounted to 400 million, a quarter of the human race. And 'the whole of this vast and delicate structure was imperilled . . . because Mr Redmond wanted to get control of two counties in the north of Ireland with a population of 204,000'. Since the government would not stand up to him the only course was an election. Both *The Times* and the *Irish Times* abstained from saying that for a British government to win four general elections in succession would be a political miracle. But they were clearly not in complete agreement as to what should be the consequences of a unionist victory. The *Irish Times* seems to have hoped that home rule would be dropped. *The Times*, representative of moderate opinion in England, seems to have taken it for granted that the outcome would be home rule with six counties excluded.[75] But, very suddenly, stark violence obtruded on political argument and manoeuvre. The breakdown of the Buckingham Palace conference was announced on Friday, 24 July. On the next day the foreign secretary warned the cabinet that a grave crisis was impending in Europe. On Sunday, 26 July, the Irish Volunteers landed a cargo of arms at Howth, and the episode ended with a clash in the streets of Dublin between a military detachment and a crowd, which resulted in military and civilian casualties. On the day this tragedy occurred mobilization started in Europe. Within ten days, the United Kingdom was at war and all domestic issues abruptly declined in importance.

[75] *Irish Times, The Times*, 25 July 1914.

II

THE SUMMONING OF THE
CONVENTION

~~~~~~

WHEN IT WAS ADMITTED that the Buckingham palace conference had failed it was hard to see how the great crisis in
British politics created by the Irish problem could be solved.
But the conference had scarcely ended when the rush of events
swept the Irish question from the centre of the stage. On 30 July
the prime minister announced that the second reading of the
amending bill was being postponed because of the European
crisis; at midnight on 4 August Great Britain was at war with
Germany and for many Irishmen the question of Irish self-
government was immediately overshadowed by the great clash
of arms on the continent.

Irish unionists, needless to say, reacted as their fellow subjects
of the crown in Great Britain. And Redmond, in Lloyd George's
words, 'the leader of a section which has until recently for
historic reasons ostentatiously regarded the British empire with
an air of considerable detachment',[1] on 3 August, during the
tense debate which followed Grey's statement on the European
situation, declared that 'the democracy of Ireland will turn
with the utmost anxiety and sympathy to this country in every
trial and danger that may overtake it'. The government, he
added, might withdraw its troops from Ireland and protestants
and catholics would join in arms to defend their country.

[1] C. Petrie, *Life and Letters of Sir Austen Joseph Chamberlain* (1939), p. 3.

43

Redmond's declaration was in strict accordance with the principles of home rule. The home-rule bill had treated foreign affairs and defence as imperial responsibilities. But more than political logic was involved. Irish nationalist opinion was strongly influenced by the unprovoked invasion of Belgium, by the threat to Ireland's old ally, France, and, it is probably true to say, by innumerable ties with Great Britain.

With all energies being mustered for the war a provisional solution had to be found for the Irish question. Grey impressed on the cabinet that in view of the situation in the United States the home-rule bill should be placed on the statute book as soon as possible though it need not come immediately into operation.[2] So the government decided on 10–11 September that the bill, which had complied with the conditions prescribed by the parliament act, should receive the royal assent at the close of the session along with a short suspensory bill which enacted that the home rule act would not come into operation until the end of the war.

Unionists complained bitterly that placing the home rule bill on the statute book was a breach of the party truce. And private letters of Austen Chamberlain, a good-tempered man if a strong partisan, to Winston Churchill, complaining that the prime minister was 'trading on the patriotism of his opponents to carry a most controversial bill in its most controversial form', show how profoundly unionists felt over the issue. Chamberlain was unconvinced by Churchill's arguments – that the government's plan 'prevents anything being done, except the sentimental satisfaction of having an inoperative bill on the statute book, till the war and the election are both over' and that after the war 'the old party flags of the Victorian era' would be hung up and questions approached in a new spirit.[3] Nevertheless the Irish unionists gained a respite from home rule and could cherish the hope that the home rule act would be drastically amended before it came into operation.

The Irish parliamentary party on the other hand was in an unenviable position. It was pledged to the support of the war and many of its members were heartily behind the war effort,

[2] Report of Cabinet meeting, 10, 11 Dec. 1914 (Cab. 41/35)
[3] C. Petrie, *Life and letters of Sir Austen Joseph Chamberlain* (1939), ii, pp. 5–14.

but home rule was indefinitely deferred and the party left hovering on the threshold of success while their unionist opponents were recovering influence and power. In May 1915 Asquith was compelled to broaden the basis of his administration. A coalition ministry was formed, the unionists were included in the government, and Carson became attorney general. Redmond was offered office, but explained that 'the principles and history' of his party made it impossible for him to accept;[4] at the same time the nationalists resented the admission of Carson and other unionists to office. But their attitude was unlikely to win much sympathy from those who wanted political unity for the sake of winning the war.

Altogether the position of the constitutional nationalists was frustrating and difficult. Their attitude to the war to a large extent inhibited them from opposition, while they were still excluded from power. The awkwardness of their position was illustrated by a military issue which aroused intense bitterness. From the beginning of the war Redmond and his supporters had been very anxious that Ireland's efforts in the allied cause should be recognized. And they had been insistent that nationalist Ireland's contribution to the army should be embodied in distinct units, which it was hoped might be named the Irish brigade, a name redolent with historic memories. Soon there were complaints that the nationalists were not getting their fair share of commissions, that nationalist recruits were drafted to English regiments, that the southern Irish units were not being granted national emblems and that generally Irish nationalists, while being called upon to furnish recruits, were being snubbed and ignored.[5] That there should have been a lack of understanding between the military authorities and the nationalist leaders may have been unfortunate but it was almost inevitable. In the past the nationalists had had few contacts with the army. And from the time when Kitchener issued his call for 100,000 recruits, an administrative machine intended to handle a small regular army and staffed by men who were not noted for flexibility of outlook, found itself faced with the task of

[4] D. Gwynn, *Life of John Redmond*, p. 423.
[5] For the nationalist views about the way recruiting was handled see D. Gwynn, *John Redmond*, ch. xi.

building up a rapidly growing citizen army. When the mistakes which had been made in dealing with recruiting in Ireland were mentioned in 1918, Amery, a politician who was a student of war, exclaimed: 'Good heavens have there not been mistakes in abundance in England by officials in trying to bring the fabric of this peace-loving country to war conditions?'.[6] But Irish nationalists in the early years of the war were not in the mood to make allowances. The negligence or obtuseness of the military authorities aroused intense bitterness, besides bringing home to constitutional nationalists their powerlessness. And by the summer of 1915 irritation had reached the point that some of the younger members of the party were pressing their leaders to demand that the home-rule act be brought into operation immediately.[7]

The leaders of the parliamentary party had not only to reason with their restless younger followers. Always on the flank they had the more extreme nationalists, to whom home rule was a contemptible substitute for independence. The advanced nationalists urged that Ireland should be neutral, and at the outbreak of the war the National Volunteers had split, a large majority supporting Redmond, a small minority, which termed themselves the Irish Volunteers, declaring in favour of Irish neutrality. And the latter section was very active in denouncing the war and drilling and arming the Irish Volunteers.

The government was in a dilemma. As Hancock writing about the South African government in the latter half of 1914 has expressed it, if the government 'acted too mildly it would be accused of allowing the country to drift into civil war: if it acted too sternly it would be accused of provoking that same disaster'.[8] Birrell, the chief secretary, appreciating the dilemma, chose the former course. His aim was 'to avoid the shedding of Irish blood *in Ireland* during the war',[9] and he hoped that if the advanced nationalists were, as far as possible, left alone, they would content themselves with drilling and demonstrating. An amiable and fastidious sceptic, professing to be tired of politics – early in 1915 he remarked, 'I am only waiting for an oppor-

[6] *Hansard 5*, civ, 1937.
[7] *New Ireland*, 12, 19, 26, June 1915.
[8] W. K. Hancock, *Smuts* (1962), i, p 368.
[9] Birrell to ——, 23 May 1916 (Add. MS 49372).

tunity to bid the world of politics goodnight, but that opportunity never comes' – he was contemptuous of extremists.
When discussing some minor tory leaders, he regretted that
'their abilities are low as their tempers are high'. The Belfast
unionists leaders, were, he thought 'devilish clever fellows,
unsympathetic as a rhinoceros but splendid at doling out money
in the smallest possible sums'. One of the cleverist Irish anti-
war journals, Griffith's *Scissors and paste*, he pronounced 'not
worth powder and shot'. And the Irish Volunteers, he dismissed, as 'a play-acting business'.[10] In short Birrell, confusing
judgements based on taste with a political appreciation, underestimated the significance of what he considered silly. Moreover
the leaders of the parliamentary party, with whom Birrell and
his under-secretary Nathan were in touch, naturally tended to
favour a line of action (or inaction) which would avoid clashes
between the government and a vocal section of nationalist
opinion. Later, when, after the 1916 rising, his policy was in
ruins, Birrell wrote his own political epitaph. 'It is always
safest', he wrote, 'to do the obvious because whatever happens
you cannot be too much blamed then. If you refrain from doing
the obvious and things don't go too well you are defence-
less. The hum-drum is the safest and easiest in all human
affairs.'[11]

History shows that Birrell's policy might conceivably have
succeeded. Early in 1916 the leaders of the Irish volunteers
were divided over the expediency of rebellion. But the section
which believed that action in arms was called for prevailed,
and on Easter Monday a number of buildings in Dublin
were seized by armed volunteers and the Irish republic pro-
claimed. The rising was suppressed after a week of street fighting and though the casualties and devastation were small
compared to what was happening on the battlefields of Europe,
the effect on Irish feeling and British political opinion was considerable.

Immediately after the rebellion Wimborne, the lord lieutenant, and Birrell, the chief secretary, were recalled, and
Asquith went over to survey the situation and assess Irish

[10] Birrell to Le Fanu, 21 Feb. 1915 (Liverpool MS 81) Birrell to
Nathan, Oct., 21 Dec., 1914, 13 Jan., 3 Aug., 1915 (Nathan papers).
[11] Birrell to ——, 23 May 1916. (Add. MS 49372).

opinion on the spot. He stayed in Ireland a week, visiting Dublin, Belfast and Cork. At Cork he met a deputation of O'Brienites, who protested against anything in the nature of partition; in Belfast he met a number of 'hard-bitten Carsonite leaders'. 'Their genuine and inextinguishable hatred for the catholics of the south', whom they regarded as being idle and disloyal was, the prime minister thought, 'serious', and, he noticed, they made no distinction between Redmonites and Sinn Feiners. But he also noticed that these Ulster leaders and the nationalists whom he met during his Irish visit agreed in emphasizing that the Irish problem must be settled promptly. And he felt that the nationalists (except the O'Brienites) might for the time being at least accept the exclusion of Ulster. At the end of May Asquith summed up the situation in Ireland for his colleagues and the house of commons. The immediate duty of the government, he declared in a memorandum circulated to the cabinet, was to do everything in its power to force a general settlement, though, he added, the home-rule act, however amended, could not be brought into operation until the end of the war.[12] Speaking in the house of commons, he stated that he was convinced that the existing system of government in Ireland had broken down, that, though home rule was on the statute book, no one contemplated the coercion of one group of Irishmen by another, and that the time had arrived when a bold effort on fresh lines might lead to an agreed settlement.[13] These convictions, though they helped to define the problem, left it unsolved. But Asquith had his *deus ex machina*. Towards the end of May he announced that he had asked Lloyd George to try to settle the Irish question by negotiating with the Irish political parties. Lloyd George's dynamic force, determination to get things done, swiftness of apprehension, grasp of essentials and power of suggesting a warm sympathy with divergent points of view made him an admirable and successful negotiator. He was understandably reluctant to tackle the Irish problem. Success was likely to elude him and his duties as minister of munitions were onerous and exacting. But he was a patriot and an optimist, and he accepted the prime

[12] 'Ireland: the future'; memorandum by Asquith, 21 May 1916 (Cab. 37/148/18).
[13] *Hansard 5*, lxxxii, pp. 2309–12.

minister's commission. His decision, he later thankfully re-called, prevented him accompanying Kitchener on the *Hampshire*.[14]

Lloyd George set to work briskly. Before the end of May he had assembled six Irish leaders, four nationalists, Redmond, O'Connor, Devlin and Dillon, and two unionists, Carson and Craig in a room in the Ministry of Munitions. In Lloyd George's opinion they were all (with the exception of Dillon who 'found it hard to accommodate his ideas to the tyranny of facts') excellent negotiators, hard-fighting but realistic. Even so Lloyd George was surprised at the speed with which the discussion moved. Influenced by the crisis atmosphere, the Irish leaders agreed to accept as the basis for a settlement the proposals Lloyd George placed before them and left London with the intention of recommending them to their followers. Lloyd George's basis for a settlement was that the home-rule act of 1914, with some modifications, was to be brought into operation as soon as possible. The two most important modifications were that the act was not to apply to an excluded area comprising the six north-east counties, which were to be administered by a secretary of state directly responsible to the imperial parliament, and the number of Irish M.P.s at Westminister was to remain unaltered, instead of being reduced from 103 to 42. The act modifying the Government of Ireland Act was to remain in force for the continuance of the war and twelve months there-after. If by then parliament had not made permanent provision for the government of Ireland, the act was to be extended as long as necessary by order in council. And at the end of the war the permanent settlement of Ireland was to be considered by an imperial conference.[15] It is clear of course that Lloyd George, intent on securing a settlement, was postponing a major issue – for how long was Ulster to remain excluded. And there is no doubt some substance in the comments of two of Lloyd George's conservative critics. Referring to these negotiations, Walter Long complained that Lloyd George was asking an imperial conference to find a constitution for the United Kingdom. And

[14] For Lloyd George's account of the negotiations see D. Lloyd George, *War memoirs* (1936), ii, 699–708.
[15] *Headings of a settlement as to the government of Ireland*, [Cd 8310], H.C. 1916, xxii.

Midleton, generalizing on Lloyd George's technique as a negotiator, remarked that he had attained his successes by taking 'a very short view of life'.[16] Lloyd George might have retorted that a short-term settlement was an improvement on a prolonged crisis. In the future both parties might agree to accept the *status quo* or, inspired by the spirit of creative good will which was expected by many to sweep through public life at the end of the great conflict, they might achieve a settlement. It may be added that Devlin, the experienced leader of the northern nationalists, seems to have shared Lloyd George's predilection for imprecision on this occasion. Towards the end of June, referring to 'an apparent difference of opinion between Mr Redmond and Sir Edward Carson as to whether the exclusion (of the six counties) is permanent or temporary' Devlin, in private, remarked that the difference was more apparent than real, representing as it did two legitimate views of the proposals which could later be cleared up. Moreover, Devlin said he was against a statement on the proposals being made in the house of commons, because, if it were made, Carson might think it his duty to place a fresh interpretation upon the proposals and 'so lead the nationalists to believe that exclusion was in fact permanent'.[17]

Carson, having secured a short note from Lloyd George implying that the excluded counties would not at the end of the provisional period merge in the rest of Ireland, unless with their own consent, left for Belfast where he met the Ulster unionist council on 6 and 12 June. At these meetings he displayed to the full his ability to grasp the essentials of a situation and then to hammer home his case. He impressed on his followers that the cabinet wanted an immediate settlement of the Irish question for the sake of good relations with the United States on which victory largely depended. Then, having reminded them that the home-rule bill was now on the statute book, he argued that it would be a mistake to insist on the exclusion of nine counties because with the unionists amounting to only about 56 per cent of the population of Ulster, they would find the whole of Ulster

[16] Long, memorandum, 15 June 1916 (Chamberlain papers); *Hansard 5* (*Lords*) xxii, 504 (29 June 1917).

[17] W. H. Owen to Lloyd George, 20 June 1916 (Lloyd George papers, D14/3/21).

an unmanageable political unit. And, he stressed, if they refused an offer of exclusion for the six counties, an offer which left them 'clear and free under British government on Irish soil', they would forfeit British sympathy and Englishmen would ask them what they were fighting for. The majority of the Ulster unionist council were acutely conscious that the decision Carson advised them to make, which involved abandoning their fellow unionists and covenanters of Cavan, Donegal and Monaghan, was painful. But realism prevailed and they voted in favour of accepting the proposals.[18] Immediately after the second meeting of the Ulster Unionist Council Carson wrote to Bonar Law that he could see no alternative to recommending the Lloyd George scheme. 'I was told', he wrote, 'the necessities of the war imposed this duty upon me, and of course as the home rule act was on the statute book all I could do was to try and save something from the wreckage, once you had all agreed that a settlement must be come to. I feel very lonely in the whole matter, but I have confidence reposed in me in the north of Ireland which was, to say the least of it, refreshing.'[18A]

The nationalist leaders faced a hard task in asking their followers to accept the exclusion of the six counties. And Dillon was quick to notice that there was 'some confusion' over whether exclusion was temporary or permanent.[18B] Lloyd George who knew that Dillon had been greatly disturbed by the aftermath of the rising subjected him to an adroit mixture of persuasion and ruthless realism. Treating Dillon as an intimate, he emphasized the battle he was fighting on Ireland's behalf against his conservative colleagues. If Ireland, he argued, could not be governed with the assent of the Irish people, it would have to be governed by force. 'If things go badly', he declared, 'England will get angry, and as Ireland is already in an angry mood, you will have two angry and courageous people snarling at each other'. And Lloyd George tried to cheer Dillon by pointing out to him that Lansdowne and Long could be easily beaten if the

[18] R. McNeill, *Ulster's stand for Union* (1922), pp 246–9; I. Colvin, *Life of Lord Carson* (1936), iii, 116–70.
[18A] Carson to Bonar Law, 14 June 1916 (Bonar Law papers, 53/3/1).
[18B] W. H. Owen to Lloyd George, 13 June 1916 (Lloyd George papers, D14/2/37).

Irish party, the prime minister and Lloyd George himself joined forces.[18c]

In the event Dillon supported the proposals with tempered enthusiasm. Other nationalist leaders, especially Redmond and Devlin, fought hard for the compromise. There was the definite gain of home rule for three-quarters of Ireland, and, Devlin stressed, the ending of military rule, 'Hun-like' in its severity.[19] Admittedly the nationalist leaders emphasized that they would never accept a scheme which excluded the six counties as satisfactory. But, Redmond asked, if they possessed the power to coerce Ulster by force, would that give them a united Ireland? There was only one way, he declared, by which they could secure a united Ireland. That was by showing their opponents that their fears were 'unreasonable and unfounded'. If Lloyd George's proposals were accepted nationalist Ireland would have a wonderful opportunity to give an exhibition of sane government, wisdom, moderation and toleration. And while the twenty-six counties would be able to deal immediately with all their local problems, the six would be compelled to go to the over-worked imperial parliament to get permission for the simplest proposals for social reform or industrial development. And all the time they would be under strong pressure from the southern unionists to join the rest of Ireland. Thus union between the six and twenty-six counties was bound to come, and to come in such a way as would certainly appeal to protestant sentiment.[20]

It was probable that the strongest opposition to the proposed settlement would come from the nationalists in the six counties. An experienced political observer, Owen, who visited Belfast in June, reported that the majority of priests in the six counties were against exclusion but that Devlin's influence in Belfast and its vicinity would bring about fifty priests 'to conformity with the proposals'.[21] Devlin himself, at the beginning of June, seems to have generally agreed with this estimate of the position. He

[18c] Lloyd George to Dillon, 10 June 1916 (Lloyd George papers, D14/2/24).

[19] *Freeman's Journal*, 21 June 1916.

[20] *Irish Independent*, 24 June 1916.

[21] W. H. Owen to Lloyd George, 20 June 1920 (Lloyd George papers, D14/3/21).

told Redmond that the Belfast nationalists would accept the proposals but that nationalist opinion outside the city was thoroughly hostile. The bishop of Derry had contemptuously dismissed the proposals as 'rot' and O'Donnell, the bishop of Raphoe, who had considerable political experience, had said that the party could not support the scheme and survive. O'Donnell, after carefully considering the proposals, had pointed out that it would be impossible to exclude Tyrone, Fermanagh and Derry city without a plebiscite. 'The county vote,' he said, 'was rational, democratic and defensible.' And Cardinal Logue, the archbishop of Armagh, had also declared himself practically speaking averse to the proposals.[22]

Devlin, however, had plenty of political courage and he threw all his immense influence on the side of acceptance. About the middle of June, he persuaded a conference of Belfast nationalists to accept the proposals. But in spite of this success, he professed to be pessimistic concerning the outcome of the Ulster nationalist convention which was to follow on 23 June. To Owen, however, his pessimism appeared 'to be part of a good leader's desire that no stone should be left unturned'. The Ulster nationalist convention which met on 23 June was composed of a priest from each parish and representatives of the nationalist organizations, the Ancient Order of Hibernians and the Irish National Foresters. It was held in St Mary's Hall, and the meeting place, a bleak hall in a narrow street at the back of the city centre, reflected the political status of Ulster nationalism. There was a vehement debate, the anti-exclusionists arguing that to accept exclusion for a day was enough to put the unionists in an impregnable position. Redmond made a most powerful speech and Devlin and Dillon also spoke on behalf of the Lloyd George proposals, the latter emphasizing that it was not the time to indulge in heroics and that the rejection of the proposals meant the end of home rule. At the close of the debate the Lloyd George proposals were endorsed by 475 votes to 265. It was however pointed out by a member of the minority that

[22] Devlin to Redmond, 3 June 1916 (Redmond papers). About the same time MacVeagh assured Redmond that the bishops in the excluded area sympathized with him and suggested that he should press resolutely for a fixed period at the end of which a plebiscite should be taken in each county (MacVeagh to Redmond, n.d., Redmond papers).

of the 270 delegates from Fermanagh, Tyrone and Derry city who took part in the division, 183 voted against the proposals. And according to the *Independent* not only was the convention packed but the partitionists even spun out their speeches to prevent delegates who wanted to catch the last train home from voting.[23] These complaints might be expected from a defeated party. It is impossible to decide on their accuracy. What it is safe to say is that Devlin, who wrote and spoke persuasively in favour of the proposals, presumably at this crisis used all his knowledge of local politics and all his organizing powers.

Besides trying to get the Ulster question, temporarily at least, out of the way, Lloyd George attempted to render his proposals acceptable to that influential minority, the southern unionists. At the end of May he seems to have told a southern unionist deputation that there should be two southern unionists in the Dublin cabinet.[24] He repeated this suggestion to Carson, adding that for a provisional period twenty or thirty representatives of the unionist minority nominated by the government should sit in the representative chamber of the Dublin assembly. This, he argued, 'would be much more valuable than to pack these men into a separate chamber. When the time comes to consider the permanent settlement all this can be readjusted but I feel that the pressure of a powerful minority in the lower chamber would give the protestant unionists the greater confidence at this period.'[25]

As might be expected the southern unionists reacted unfavourably to the proposals. At the beginning of June the executive committee of the Irish unionist alliance declared that circumstances rendered it inopportune to make changes in the system of governing Ireland, and about a fortnight later it protested against the partition of Ireland, 'a country in itself too small as a political and economic unit'.[26] On 27 June a deputation representing the unionists of the south and west saw the prime minister and Lloyd George. It pointed out that if Lloyd George's proposals were put into effect 'members of the Sinn Fein movement will themselves usurp the power of government

[23] *Irish Independent*, 24 June, 6 July, 1916.
[24] Memorandum of interview, 29 May 1916 (Middlton papers).
[25] Lloyd George to Carson, 3 June 1916 (Carson papers).
[26] *Irish Times*, 9, 22, 28 June 1916.

in Ireland'. However, after the war, the deputation declared, the southern unionists would be prepared to attend an imperial conference 'with an open mind'.[26A]

About the same time a memorandum was presented to the cabinet on behalf of the unionists of the south and west. While emphasizing their opposition to the Lloyd George proposals it put forward a number of provisions which ought to be included in any settlement 'in the interests of justice and good government'. These were somewhat sweeping. There was to be an Irish senate, representing 'property, industry and commerce'. The imperial government was to have the right to veto Irish legislation which had received the assent of the lord lieutenant. Judges were to be appointed by the imperial government and there was to be a right of appeal from the Irish courts to the house of lords. Trinity College was to be one of the constituencies which was to continue to return members to Westminster. Land legislation, public loans and education were to be reserved services. The Irish parliament was to be debarred in a very comprehensive clause from imposing disabilities or granting advantages on religious grounds, and the law relating to malicious injuries was to be altered only by the imperial parliament. The Irish parliament when making laws regulating commerce or taxation was not to differentiate between any classes of persons or property; the powers of the Irish parliament over income tax were to be exercised only in respect of property in Ireland, and 'tacking' was to be strictly forbidden. Finally Irish government appointments were to be made on the results of competitive examinations.[27] The southern unionist memorandum was passed on to an expert parliamentary draftsman, Sir Arthur Thring, who brusquely characterized many of its proposals as absurd. He considered that some of them placed unreasonable restrictions on the already limited powers of the Irish parliament and he pointed out that it was impossible to impose taxation without differentiating between forms of property.[28]

The southern unionists also tried to put pressure on the

[26A] Statement made to the prime minister and Mr Lloyd George (Lloyd George papers, D15/1/20); *The Times*, 28 June 1916.

[27] Memorandum in convention papers, T.C.D., box 2.

[28] Cab. 37/152/10.

unionists in the cabinet. When Lloyd George announced his proposals George Stewart, a large land agent and leading southern unionist, at once took council with Barrymore, the old leader of the southern unionists. They both agreed that the proposals were unworkable and would satisfy the nationalists for only a short period, and they communicated their views to Long, the president of the local government board, an ex-chief secretary who had sat for some years as unionist M.P. for county Dublin.[29] At the beginning of June, Midleton, the leader of the southern unionists, offered to show Balfour the evidence which had reached him demonstrating the utter demoralization of the south of Ireland and of the Redmond party, 'to which Lloyd George proposed to confide the government *during the war*'.[30] Later in the month Midleton wrote to Bonar Law that the Lloyd George scheme would 'hand over Ireland to a government which cannot govern and open the country to German machinations at a most critical time.[30A] According to Lloyd George, Midleton at this time was urging every prominent unionist in the south of Ireland to write against the settlement to Long, Bonar Law, Lansdowne and probably Austen Chamberlain. 'Long', Lloyd George wrote, 'sends the letters on to me, and in the innocence of his heart he thinks it is all a spontaneous outburst of indignation'. He noticed that the letters all came from the old landlord class. 'So far', he wrote, 'there has been no exhibition of anxiety on the part of the big businessmen in the south. Stewart is the exception but I understand he is a considerable land agent.[31] But though Lloyd George was unimpressed by the alarm shown by the southern landed magnates, his unionist colleagues were likely to prove more susceptible.

The unionists in the cabinet seem to have thought that Lloyd George had been empowered merely to ascertain the opinions of the leaders of the Irish political parties.[32] According to a severe student of politics, F. S. Oliver, the unionist leaders 'knew that a

[29] G. F. Stewart to Long, 31 May 1916 (Asquith papers).

[30] Midleton to Balfour, 4 June 1916 (Add. MS 49721).

[30A] Midleton to Bonar Law, 19 June 1916 (Bonar Law papers, 53/3/3).

[31] Lloyd George to Carson, 3 June 1916 (Carson papers).

[32] That Lloyd George has been charged with the task of 'gathering up' opinions, was the way Lansdowne expressed it (Memorandum by Lansdowne, Cab. 37/150/11).

real settlement was impossible and *believed* that a settlement of *any kind* was impossible. They wanted to pose as moderate men and curry favour with the liberal papers, so they beamed and gave their blessing when Lloyd George was set on to try and arrive at something.'[33] Oliver, though he unsympathetically over-clarifies the attitude of busy men, was certainly right in saying that the unionist members of the cabinet were surprised by Lloyd George's speed and success as a negotiator and taken aback when they realized that what they regarded as exploratory talks were turning into a definite settlement involving immediate home-rule for three-quarters of Ireland.

As early as 30 May Walter Long, the quintessence of steady, limited toryism, tackled Lloyd George on his conduct of the Irish negotiations. Thirty years earlier Long had opposed the introduction of Gladstone's first home rule bill. Now, according to himself, he told Lloyd George that there were two points in his scheme which English and Irish unionists would never accept – a home-rule parliament in Ireland and the proposal that the exclusion of Ulster should be subject to revision at the end of the war. And a fortnight later he prepared a memorandum for the unionist members of the cabinet in which he declared that Lloyd George 'seems to me to have misunderstood his position from beginning to end and to have committed the cabinet to wholesale and drastic changes and to definite statements which are not in agreement with the facts'. On 1 June Lansdowne at a cabinet meeting declared his disapproval of Lloyd George's proposals. 'Is it the moment', he asked, 'for imposing upon the country in the guise of an interim arrangement a bold and startling scheme?' Lansdowne added that if home rule was going to be brought into operation he would prefer a measure applying to the whole of Ireland, with safeguards for the minority, to partition.[34]

By the middle of June a group of unionist ministers were seriously alarmed and began to insist that the implications of the proposals must be carefully considered in the light of the general situation. An argument which the unionists had often employed

[33] F. S. Oliver, *The anvil of war* (1936), p 150.
[34] Memorandum by Long, 23 June 1916 (Cab. 37/150/15); memorandum by Long, 15 June 1916 (Chamberlain papers); memorandum by Lansdowne (Cab. 37/150/11).

in quieter days, the strategic dangers inherent in Irish autonomy, had now developed overwhelming significance. In a powerful memorandum, Lord Robert Cecil, the minister of blockade, summed up his own and others' apprehensions. If a home-rule government were set up in the south and west of Ireland, it would, he pointed out, be headed by Redmond, Dillon and Devlin. Now Redmond, though loyal and straight-forward had no administrative ability. Dillon was the enemy of England and Devlin had shown himself ready to release the rebellion prisoners. Such a government, Cecil argued, would have as little prestige in Ireland as the Castle administration, and would be hard put to it to maintain its authority in the face of Sinn Fein, a large and growing movement, which was 'the latest expression of the ingrained Irish hatred for the British connection'. There might easily be another Irish rebellion aided by Germany, which would paralyse the war effort. And though, even with home rule operative, the imperial government could intervene, it would probably not be able to do so with the necessary promptitude. But, Cecil admitted, to withdraw the offer of home rule once it had been made would be very dangerous. Was there then, he asked, any way 'of reconciling the grant of home rule with withholding from the home-rule government executive power until after the war?'. He believed there was. It could be provided that, if home rule on the lines of the Lloyd George proposals was brought into operation immediately, the southern Irish parliament when it met in Dublin should merely elect a speaker and then adjourn until the end of the war. The setting up of a parliament would give nationalists a guarantee against any attempt to withdraw the offer of home rule while executive power would remain under the control of the imperial government for the duration of the war.[35]

On 17 June Cecil and Curzon on behalf of the unionist members of the cabinet explained to the prime minister that they had been placed in 'an unsatisfactory position' by Redmond's assertion that Lloyd George had made his proposals on behalf of the government. Asquith admitted there had been a misunderstanding. Apparently the discussions had moved much more smoothly and swiftly than had been expected. When he had suggested to the cabinet that Lloyd George should try to

[35] Memorandum by R. Cecil, 26 June 1916 (Cab. 37/150121).

settle the Irish question it had been on the assumption that home rule would not come into operation until the end of the war. But shortly after the negotiations started Lloyd George had reported that the nationalists would not be satisfied unless something was done at once. Asquith did not think an offer would make much difference, since Carson would certainly prove immovable. But Carson, to the surprise of both Asquith and Lloyd George, had been prepared to deal upon 'the basis of immediate delivery of the goods'. Having heard Asquith's explanation Curzon pressed for a public statement of the position which would prevent misapprehensions. Asquith agreed that a statement should be issued but pointed out he could do nothing until he had consulted Lloyd George.[36]

On 21 June the Irish question was discussed by the cabinet. It was rumoured, according to T. P. O'Connor who was in close touch with what was going on in London, that three cabinet ministers, Lansdowne, Long and Selborne, were going to resign. But before the cabinet met, Carson met its unionist members and with terrific vehemence defended the settlement. If it were not accepted, he declared, he would not be responsible for what might happen in Ulster and the rest of Ireland would be hell. In the event the cabinet seemed to have decided to stall. Lloyd George was to write to Redmond emphasizing that the proposals on which agreement had been reached had not been previously submitted to the cabinet which was as yet uncommitted. O'Connor cheerfully assured Redmond that this letter was intended to 'save faces' and that some even of the unionist ministers were lukewarm about sending it. Lloyd George immediately wrote to Redmond emphasizing that he had repeatedly said that opposition in the cabinet to the proposals was to be expected and that 'as you are aware the cabinet as a body has not yet considered any scheme for the government of Ireland and until they are agreed to by you and your friends these proposals will not be submitted to the cabinet for its sanction'.[37] Lloyd George no doubt stated the

[36] Memorandum by R. Cecil, 26 June 1916; Lansdowne to Chamberlain, 24 June 1916 (Chamberlain papers).
[37] A. Chamberlain to his wife, 21 June 1916 (Chamberlain papers); O'Connor to Redmond, 21 June 1916, Lloyd George to Redmond, 21 June 1916 (Redmond papers).

position correctly. But the momentum created by the success of the negotiations seems to have convinced Irish opinion in general that the proposals had the backing of the government.

One unionist minister, Selborne, did resign on the grounds that he was not prepared to bring home rule into operation during the war and on the 27th, the day in which he gave the reasons for his resignation in the lords, the cabinet had a thorough discussion of the proposals. Lansdowne, Long and Cecil all attacked the scheme as dangerous under existing conditions, and Curzon asked whether the Irish parliament, even if composed of the present Irish M.P.s, would be really Redmondite. On the other side Crewe and Grey supported the proposals, the latter stressing that their rejection would have a very bad effect on American opinion. Bonar Law thought that the rejection of the proposals would unite nationalist Ireland in hostility to England, and said that he was going to recommend their acceptance to the unionist party. If the party turned down his advice his position in the government would be an impossible one. 'The most effective pronouncement in this long conclave' was delivered by Balfour. Balfour had a fine mind, and the academic approach to political issues which he so often adopted enabled him either to give a sharp dialectical edge to crude partisanship or to place a problem in a new perspective.[38] It was common ground amongst the unionist members of the cabinet, Balfour now pointed out, that there could not be a complete reversal of policy on home rule. If some ministers wished to defer the application of home rule to the south and west of Ireland it was simply because they thought it dangerous to bring it into operation during the war. This Balfour doubted. If there was going to be further disorder in Ireland he would like to see a home-rule government responsible for its suppression. A Dublin parliament, he contended, would have both the means and strong incentives to act against the pro-German elements in Ireland. The Sinn Feiners were enemies not only of the empire but of the parliamentary party. And the constitutional nationalists' only hope of inducing Ulster to place itself voluntarily under a Dublin parliament, lay, Balfour pointed out, in demon-

[38] For Balfour's views on the Irish question at this time see his memorandum for the unionist members of the cabinet, 24 June 1916 (Cab. 37/150/17).

strating that a Dublin parliament in its foreign sympathies would be loyal and in its home government orderly. Finally, he explained, in a case of real necessity the imperial government, even if home rule was granted, would be able to take over control in Ireland.

After Balfour had spoken Lloyd George intervened to say that, if resignations could be prevented by adding to the proposals safeguards for imperial naval and military control in Ireland, he would do his best to devise such safeguards. And he suggested a small cabinet committee to consider the question. Curzon, Chamberlain and presumably Cecil agreed, but Lansdowne and Long remained obdurate. Then Asquith swung into the discussion with massive force. He said that resignations would probably mean the dissolution of the government, and this, at such a critical time, would be 'not a national calamity but a national crime'. It was then agreed (with Long dissenting but not resigning) that a small committee should be appointed to discuss what safeguards should be added to the arrangements already agreed to between Lloyd George and the Irish leaders.[39] And at a cabinet meeting the following week (5 July), Lansdowne declared that he had come to the conclusion that his and other resignations would mean political chaos and possibly even a general election. So, while heartily disliking the Lloyd George proposals he accepted them, subject to imperial control of order and matters relating to the war being maintained. Long, rather sullenly, associated himself with Lansdowne. His position, he complained, was 'a cruel one', and he believed that if he resigned he would carry with him a considerable section of the conservative party. But he was afraid of weakening the war effort. At the end of the meeting, Asquith wrote cheerfully to the king that the outcome of the discussion 'amply justifies the delay, which had obviated premature and precipitate decisions'.[40]

But those unionist members of the government who had reluctantly accepted the Lloyd George settlement were determined to render the amending bill as innocuous as possible. And Robert Cecil, who applied a rigorous logical intellect to political problems, drew up two powerful memoranda specifying

[39] Asquith to the king, 27 June 1916 (Cab. 37/150/23).
[40] Asquith to the king, 5 July 1916 (Cab. 37/151/8).

provisions which he was convinced should be incorporated in the amending bill. In the first memorandum, drafted at the end of June, he demanded that the paramount force in Ireland of legislation of the imperial parliament arising from the war was to be made absolutely clear. Furthermore the lord lieutenant was to be empowered to suspend any executive act or order of the Irish government which he considered to be prejudicial to public order or to the conduct of the war. The lord lieutenant was also to have power to appoint secret agents and an officer who would have access to the Dublin Metropolitan Police reports. And the lord lieutenant and the chief secretary were to be men acceptable to conservatives (Cecil helpfully suggested for the post of viceroy, Milner). In the second memorandum, drafted a fortnight later, Cecil recommended that Asquith's pledge that the excluded counties should not be included without their own consent, be incorporated in the amending bill, and that the Irish representation in the imperial parliament should be reduced – it being obviously highly undesirable to have such a large number of M.P.s at Westminster whose support would be given to whatever party was prepared to favour the extension of home rule to the excluded counties.[41]

At the time he drew up his first memorandum Cecil, along with Cave, drafted a clause for insertion into the amending bill which they thought would give complete executive control in Ireland for war purposes to the imperial government. This clause seemed to Chamberlain, who had disapproved of Lloyd George's proposals as precipitate, to be 'a real advance' and 'a great safeguard', and he pressed Lansdowne to insist that the clause be included in the amending bill. 'I believe', Chamberlain wrote to Lansdowne, 'you can secure that clause as the price of your remaining with us'.[42]

As the unionists stepped up their pressure the nationalists found themselves in a position of increasing embarrassment and difficulty. Recommending a compromise is usually a difficult task for a political party; if there is a more extreme party on its flank it becomes more difficult; if the terms of the compromise are disadvantageously changed it becomes almost impossible.

[41] Memorandum by R. Cecil, 30 June, 15 July, 1916 (Chamberlain papers 43, 47).
[42] Chamberlain to Lansdowne, 30 June 1916 (Chamberlain papers).

At the very end of June and again early in July Lansdowne, trying to cope with right-wing criticism of the government in the lords, made it clear that the cabinet when preparing the amending bill would certainly have in mind the 'precautions' required to prevent rebellion and disorder in Ireland. These speeches, coming from an old opponent and an Irish landlord, deeply annoyed the nationalists. Dillon on reading the first of them told Redmond that though he had suspected treachery all along he 'was never prepared for anything so treacherous'.[43] And Redmond pressed Lloyd George to insist that the prime minister when speaking in the commons on 10 July should make it quite clear that the settlement was a provisional one, that the six counties would not have a separate executive but remain under the home office, and that no new conditions were to be added to the scheme agreed to by the Irish leaders. 'Unless he is careful', Redmond wrote, 'he will raise Cain in Ireland'.[44] In his statement on the 10th the prime minister referred to the settlement as a provisional one, but Lansdowne the next day said that the coming bill would make 'permanent and enduring' alterations in the home rule act. Redmond at once issued a protest, emphasizing that the bill was temporary and provisional.

Of the three major amendments to the Lloyd George settlement which conservative critics demanded, one, the provision embodied in the Cave-Cecil clause, could be accepted by the nationalists since it was only an elaboration of a short phrase in the home-rule act itself. And indeed Redmond remarked to Dillon that he would not 'break off' on a set of proposals for enabling the imperial government to exercise emergency powers in Ireland similar to those suggested by Cecil in his first memorandum.[45] But the other two unionist demands, that the Irish representation at Westminster should be reduced and that it should be specifically laid down that the excluded counties should not be placed under the control of the parliament sitting in Dublin against their will, aroused nationalist indignation. On the latter issue Lloyd George had to contend not only with unionist pressure but with the technicalities of parliamentary

[43] Dillon to Redmond, 30 June 1916 (Redmond papers).
[44] Redmond to Lloyd George, 7 July 1916 (Lloyd George papers D14/3/40).
[45] Redmond to Dillon, 1 July 1916 (Redmond papers).

draftmanship. In his original proposals the future position of the six counties was left indefinite. The provision that the amending act might be extended by order in council introduced into the settlement a convenient element of vagueness. But as Lloyd George had to explain to the house of commons, it was impossible in an act of parliament to issue 'a mandatory order to the privy council'. Therefore to allay Ulster apprehensions that in default of an order in council the six counties would automatically slip under the jurisdiction of the Dublin parliament, it was necessary in the amending bill to provide that they should remain excluded until parliament should otherwise determine. Redmond with bitter clear-sightedness declared this 'permanent exclusion'. Carson, retorted that nothing parliament did was permanent. Lloyd George, emphasizing that it was generally agreed that the excluded counties should not be coerced, implored the nationalists not to wreck the settlement on what was 'purely a difference in the phraseology by which you carry out an agreed purpose'. Dillon replied that one of the issues involved was which counties should be excluded.[46] As soon as the nationalists realized that the Lloyd George proposals, when embodied in a bill, would be modified on the lines suggested by the unionist members of the cabinet they made it clear that they would not accept the proposed measure and about the middle of July Lloyd George's bid for a settlement collapsed.

With the failure of Lloyd George's attempt to hustle the Irish parties into an agreed settlement hopes of an early and relatively easy solution of the Irish question faded and the government was forced to deal with the immediate problem of how Ireland was to be provisionally administered until the end of the war or until a settlement could be arrived at. Asquith dismissed the proposal that a minister for Ireland should be appointed with an advisory council consisting of representatives of the different Irish parties, as attractive but impracticable. If the council had power to veto the minister's actions, Asquith pointed out, he would no longer be responsible to the house of commons; if it had not the power then 'it would become a debating society'. To Asquith the urgent need was to secure effective direction for the civil administration of Ireland. Therefore, he thought, the best thing to do was to appoint a chief secretary who would be a

[46] *Hansard 5*, lxxxiv, 61–2, 1427–43.

cabinet minister but who would spend most of his time in Ireland. As for the lord lieutenancy, it was, Asquith remarked, 'one of the most anomalous, and from the argumentative point of view, one of the most vulnerable institutions, in the whole world'. But it had its advantages. It was not unpopular in Ireland. 'It enables', he explained, 'gracious and well-mannered persons to discharge social and charitable functions to advantage and without, so far as I know, any drawback beyond the undoubted expense to which they patriotically put themselves'. Moreover the viceroy had definite powers under the home rule act, and therefore to abolish the office would throw everything into confusion. But, Asquith was constrained to add, it was difficult to get anyone to take the office, 'particularly a person who is qualified for it'.[47] The office of chief secretary was filled by the appointment of Duke, a unionist M.P. who had built up a reputation as a *nisi prius* advocate. Conscientious, conciliatory, decent and somewhat ponderous, he seems to have been selected partly because of his legal experience and partly on account of his success as a chairman of tribunals appointed to handle war-time problems. His speeches all suggest a fair-minded, unimaginative, well intentioned man. A week after he was appointed, it was announced that Wimbourne, a grand seigneur, who 'entered into politics, sport and art collecting with equal zest', had been reappointed lord lieutenant.[48]

To English liberals, indeed to all Englishmen brought up in the nineteenth century liberal tradition, the situation in Ireland in the autumn of 1916 was disturbing. A large section of the Irish people was deeply discontented; and the extent and depth of this discontent was being continually advertised by the dealings of the authorities, often acting under emergency legislation, with the more advanced nationalists who were defiantly displaying their sympathy for the insurgents of Easter week. As for the constitutional nationalists, the parliamentary party during the Lloyd George negotiations had, in an effort to secure immediate self-government, made an important concession which exposed them to damaging attacks from the more extreme nationalists. Understandably then, the breakdown of the negotiations left the party frustrated, shaken and

[47] *Hansard 5*, lxxxiv, 2134–47.
[48] *The Times*, 15 June 1939.

embittered. Its mood was starkly revealed in a series of debates which took place in the latter half of 1916. Between a debate on 24 July, which provided an acrimonious appendix to the Lloyd George negotiations, and the close of the year Irish issues were debated in the house of commons about half a dozen times, and members of the party with a masterly command of minute detail and intensive local knowledge castigated the government for its blundering, not to say criminal, handling of Irish problems. Some incidents of military misconduct during the fighting in Dublin, the detention without trial of the prisoners swept up after the rising, the working of the censorship, the prohibition of meetings, the general heavyhandedness of authority, were all vehemently criticized. The responsibility for the rebellion was largely, if not altogether logically, attributed to the government. Redmond, having dwelt at great length on the ineptitudes which had marked recruiting in Ireland, said that from the day the coalition had been formed the Sinn Fein party had largely increased. Devlin, in the course of a speech in which he too referred to the mistakes committed during the recruiting campaign and to 'ten years of liberal vacillation, of weakness' declared, 'the rebellion in Ireland had been your fault'. Dillon by an oratorical tour de force implied that many of the apparent rebels had not intended to rebel. 'It was', he said in the house of commons, 'perfectly notorious that of the thousands of men arrested in Ireland, hundreds, I should say far more than half, went out that Easter morning with no more idea of going into a rising than any honourable member of this house. They simply went out for a parade, a march, and before they knew where they were they found themselves involved in a rising. And being Irishmen they would not turn back.'[49]

Turning to future policy the party demanded that 'martial law' should be terminated, the internees released and persons sentenced to penal servitude after the rebellion treated as political prisoners. Most important of all, Redmond declared, 'let the government take their courage in both hands and trust the Irish people once and for all by putting the home rule into operation and resolutely on their own responsibility facing any problems that may entail'.[50] The Irish party and the govern-

[49] *Hansard 5*, lxxxiv, 2130, 2183–4; lxxxvi, 587.
[50] *Hansard 5*, lxxxvi, 593–4.

ment at this time could each complain that the other was by its attitude putting it in an impossible position. The Irish party was convinced that its hold on its following was being destroyed by its obvious failure to obtain anything from an intransigent administration. From the government's point of view it seemed that the Irish party was pressing it to adopt in the middle of a great war a policy which would compel it to cope certainly with a violently discontented Ulster and possibly with a disloyal administration in Dublin.

When they were addressing the house of commons during the latter months of 1916 the Irish nationalists often spoke as if they were facing a monolithic administration. In fact the cabinet was sorely divided and some of its members were losing confidence in the prime minister as a war leader. The year had proved a depressing one for the allies. In the east the great Russian attack in Galicia, after attaining a measure of success, had petered out and at the close of 1916 Russia was clearly feeling the strain and unable to arm adequately the huge masses it could muster. In the west the French had suffered appalling losses at Verdun and the British had gained very little ground on the Somme at a staggering cost in casualties. At sea Jutland had been a grave shock to those brought up in the Trafalgar tradition of total victory. In Great Britain there was a growing belief that the higher direction of the war was at fault, that there was a deficiency of drive, a lack of co-operation. Pressure on the government mounted and at the beginning of December 1916 Asquith was replaced as prime minister by Lloyd George, who immediately formed a small war cabinet.

Lloyd George was both a dynamic administrator and an exhilarating orator, and the public expected him to get things done, if necessary on unconventional lines. He himself, immediately after taking office, defined his task as being 'to complete and make even more effective the mobilization of all our national resources' and he believed that the 'removal of the misunderstanding between Great Britain and Ireland, which has for centuries been such a source of misery to the one and weakness to the other', would be a war measure of the greatest importance.[51]

But from the moment Lloyd George and his colleagues took

[51] *Hansard 5*, lxxxviii, 1338, 1353.

office they were under continuous pressure from a constant procession of problems, strategy, man power, munitions, food, shipping, inter-allied relations, all demanding swift and hard decisions. Yet when early in December 1916 Hankey surveyed the whole scene for the prime minister he emphasized that 'one of the greatest services that could be rendered to the allied cause would be a settlement of the Irish question', which would add 150,000 men to the Irish divisions, release the division then locked up in Ireland, facilitate recruiting in the dominions and favourably influence United States opinion.[52]

It was sometime however before the war cabinet got round to tackling the Irish problem. Other matters clamoured for immediate attention. In December there was an immense rush of work as the administration was reorganized on the higher levels, preparations made for inter-allied conferences and a reply drafted to President Wilson. At the end of the month Lloyd George (who had been fighting a heavy cold) received a group of French ministers. In January he attended a conference in Rome, in February he was over in France. When, in the middle of February, T. P. O'Connor had a talk with Duke, he discovered that 'Lloyd George had not given any serious attention to Ireland since he became prime minister' and that it was rather a misfortune for Ireland that, except in the July negotiations, he had never been brought into contact with Irish administration. Duke himself, however, was confident that 'honest and intelligent men can always agree on some solution for a question' and he suggested to O'Connor that the Irish question should be referred to a statutory commission. O'Connor was favourably impressed by this suggestion, especially as he hoped that, by the composition of the commission and 'by other understandings', it could be expected that the commission would come out in favour of county option, and this would give the nationalists Tyrone and Fermanagh.[53] O'Connor seems to have been convinced that this was the best they could hope for, and later, early in May, he even outlined a plan of campaign based on this conviction. Lloyd George, he thought, should begin by proposing the 'clean cut' (the exclusion of six counties), the nationalists should reject this, and then the ensuing debate

[52] Lord Hankey, *The supreme command*, pp 592–3.
[53] O'Connor to Devlin, 15, 16 Feb. 1917 (Redmond papers).

would show the Irish public that county option was not so easily obtained. In the end county option 'would be carried in the house of commons only the Orangemen and ourselves voting against it'.[54]

Various suggestion for settling the Irish questions were being made at this time. Northcliffe, who was at the height of his power and prominence and who was very eager to see 'the damnable business settled', exuberantly proposed as at least a partial solution 'the development of water by engineering', which would provide the power required to 'harness the Irish rivers, build up Irish industries, stop Irish emigration . . . and make Ireland a land of opportunities'.[55] Those who thought on more orthodox political lines urged that the Irish problem should be referred to an imperial conference. Statesmen from the dominions, it was argued, 'could bring to bear on an old stale subject the broad, downright, wide awake, fearless, independent, outspoken, practical form of mind that characterizes their countrymen'. To this a well-known Ulster unionist replied that the dominion leaders could scarcely avoid considering the Irish problem, 'the intimate and intricate factors of which they are wholly unfamiliar', in the light of colonial analogies 'which we do not admit to be valid'.[55A] In February Amery, an energetically minded conservative M.P., who was a member of the war cabinet secretariat, in a powerful memorandum argued that the Irish problem would be solved only if a determined effort was made 'to fit Ireland with a complete working plant of a modern civilization', and if the responsibility of finding a workable form of government for Ireland within a federalized United Kingdom was placed on Irishmen themselves. And he suggested that a convention should be nominated composed of home rulers, unionists and a few Irishmen who had experience of working in federal systems.[56] About a month later, towards the end of March, Bernard, the magisterial anglican archbishop of Dublin, pressed for a conference of the Irish leaders and other

[54] O'Connor to Redmond, 10 May 1917 (Redmond papers).

[55] *The Times*, 19 Mar. 1917. R. Pound and G. Harmsworth, *Northcliffe* (1959), p. 501.

[55A] Ibid., 10, 12, 17 Mar. 1917.

[56] Memorandum by L.S.A., 18 Feb. 1917 (Lloyd George papers, F 66/3/1).

representatives of Irish opinion to consider any plan for the government of Ireland which accepted that Ireland was to remain part of the British empire and that defence and foreign policy would remain reserved subjects.[56A] And the suggestion that there should be a conference of representative Irishmen was also strongly sponsored by an *ad hoc* organization, the Irish conference committee, composed of liberal nationalists, very moderate unionists and university dons, which in April sent a deputation to the chief secretary.[57]

At the beginning of March, O'Connor decided to force the Irish question on the government's attention by proposing in the house of commons that it was essential to confer on Ireland, without further delay, the free institutions long promised. While the debate on this resolution was impending, the war cabinet, with Carson in attendance, twice discussed the Irish question and a few days before the debate Lloyd George had a long meeting with O'Connor. The prime minister explained that he was quite ready to agree to the suggestion of a statutory commission but that Ulster blocked the way, Carson's following objecting to putting their rights at the mercy of a commission. Lloyd George then sketched the speech he would make in the debate, declaring his determination to bring home rule into operation the very first moment conditions permitted. O'Connor frankly told him that a speech on these lines would be disastrous and Lloyd George remarked 'I can see that of course – derisive cheers from the Irish benches'. They then got down to working out another 'line of escape'. They decided that a series of speeches could be organized 'which would become one long appeal for an Irish settlement, these speeches being delivered, if possible, alternatively by tories and liberals'. And the debate would be followed by a tremendous chorus in the press in favour of a settlement. O'Connor both informed Redmond of his talk with Lloyd George and told Asquith about the plan, suggesting that during the debate he should make a plea for settlement.[58]

Early in the debate on O'Connor's motion, which was held on 7 and 22 March, Lloyd George defined the government's

[56A] *The Times*, 21 Mar. 1917.
[57] Ibid., 13 Apr. 1917.
[58] Minutes of the war cabinet, 2, 7 Mar. 1917 (Cab. 23/2); O'Connor to Redmond, 5 Mar. 1917 (Redmond papers).

attitude by stating that Great Britain was prepared to confer self-government on those parts of Ireland which unmistakeably demanded it but would not agree to put the population of the north-east area under a government with which they would be completely out of sympathy. Both Lloyd George and Asquith suggested that the Irish problem might be tackled by either a conference of all the Irish parties or by a commission. Asquith, enlarging on the latter suggestion, explained that the commission's decision would be subject to parliamentary approval and that it might include statesmen from the dominions, where 'the problem of local autonomy has presented itself in different forms and has been solved in different ways'. Redmond, answering the prime minister, declared that after his experiences in the summer of 1916 he would not enter again into negotiations, and he ended his speech by asking the prime minister to agree to a proposal, which 'he knows will be accepted by the whole of Ireland', and put home rule into operation, with 'such additions, amendments and changes', as altered circumstances required. At the close of his speech, he left the house, followed by the members of the Irish party. The party then held a meeting in a committee room and approved of an address to President Wilson.[59]

The debate, however, continued, taking an unusual and significant turn. A number of British backbenchers implored the government 'to lift the question out of the rut it has got into'. Pemberton Billing, an eccentric apostle of the grandiose in politics, even remarked that a hundred million would be well spent in compensating those who would not live in Ireland under home rule. But most speakers dwelt on the potentialities of a conference or commission, though, characteristically, Hugh Cecil warned the house that the Irish question could not be solved merely by getting people into a conciliatory humour. Bonar Law, closing the debate, declared that the government were going to make another attempt to settle the question, adding that he wished to heaven someone would indicate what steps it should take.

On the same day as Bonar Law gave this undertaking the war cabinet discussed the Irish problem. After taking into account the increasingly serious nature of the Sinn Fein movement and

[59] *The Times*, 8, 9 Mar. 1917.

the widespread desire in Great Britain for a settlement, it decided that the question should be referred to a commission. The commission was to inquire how far the home rule act should be modified to permit its application to Ireland at the earliest possible moment, and the colonial secretary was authorized to sound the representatives of the dominions on the possibility of their taking part in the work of the commission.[60] But the dominion premiers refused to join the commission since their own countries were divided over the Irish issue.[61]

About this time Carson made an effort to produce a solution to the Irish problem. He began the memorandum he prepared by indicating 'two broad factors', that Ulster insisted on exclusion and that the nationalist party refused to agree to it. He saw however a possibility of reconciling these two contradictory propositions. If it were agreed that Ulster was not going to be forced to accept home rule, then, if the Irish parliament proved successful, they might contemplate the ultimate reunion of Ireland. He insisted, however, that, in the event of home rule extending over the whole island, arrangements should be made to guarantee Ulster fair treatment in economic matters, education and taxation. His most striking suggestion was that, assuming exclusion, there should be set up a national consultative assembly of Ireland which would meet annually in alternate years in Dublin and Belfast. It would be composed of the Ulster M.P.s at Westminster and of a delegation from the Dublin parliament. By agreement between the two delegations it could frame legislative measures for the whole of Ireland, which, he explained, could be brought into operation in the excluded area by orders in council. Carson did not know how far his scheme would be acceptable to Ulster but he was prepared to press it on his supporters.[62] The scheme was a sensible and sincere attempt at a solution, though Carson, an experienced negotiator, did not fail to begin by embodying in his eirenicon an important concession to his own party.

Lloyd George must have had Carson's memorandum in mind when, at the end of March, T. P. O'Connor and Devlin had an interview with him. For, in the course of the discussion,

[60] Minutes of war cabinet, 22 Mar. 1917 (Cab. 23/2).
[61] H. Spender to Redmond, 27 Mar. 1917 (Redmond papers).
[62] I. Colvin, *Life of Lord Carson*, iii, 224–6.

he emphasised the concessions he had won from the Orange-men, referring specifically to their willingness to agree to meetings of delegates from both areas, a practice which Lloyd George was convinced would ultimately end exclusion. O'Connor retorted that this scheme 'would not make much appeal to the Irish imagination'. According to O'Connor, when they were talking about the northern unionists, the two Irish leaders told the prime minister that 'he ought to defy them' but 'he says he could not'. On the same day O'Connor and Devlin had a talk with the lord lieutenant. Wimborne suggested there be 'a delimitation' of Ulster which would give the unionists a politically homogeneous block (apparently in-cluding Tyrone). The Irish leaders displayed no enthusiasm for the idea.[63]

At the end of the Easter recess, in the middle of April, the war cabinet was abruptly forced by a parliamentary emergency to again turn its attention to Ireland. On 17 April a bill pro-longing the life of the existing parliament was to come up for its second reading, and it looked as if the Irish party was going to oppose it. The prospect of an opposition conducted by past-masters in the art of obstruction was alarming, and the war cabinet found itself faced with two unattractive alternatives, an immediate general election or trying to force the bill through against the resistance of the Irish party, which might easily become a focus for opposition from other quarters of the house. It was finally decided to go ahead with the bill, while simul-taneously formulating a policy for settling the Irish question.[64]

In the event the second-reading debate on the Parliament and Local Elections bill was unexciting. The Irish party did oppose the bill and were ridiculed by Healy, who told them that the tories would be delighted to have a general election in which they would smash the liberals. Equally embarrassing was the support of Hugh Cecil, who thought that the country should have an early opportunity of pronouncing on Welsh disestab-lishment. The second reading was carried by 286 to 52. But by then the war cabinet had discussed the Irish problem at length. Before attempting to formulate a policy the cabinet agreed that four facts greatly influenced the situation: that the home-rule

[63] O'Connor to Redmond, 29 Mar. 1917 (Redmond papers).
[64] Minutes of war cabinet, 16 Apr. 1917 (Cab. 23/2).

act was in some respects out of date; that the government was committed to making an attempt to settle the question; that the Irish party would not enter into negotiations; and that, while nobody supported the permanent partition of Ireland, any attempt in the immediate future to include Ulster in a home-rule scheme would end in failure. These points having been accepted, the idea of setting up a commission to deal with the problem was ruled out. It was agreed that it would not be acceptable to any of the parties, and parliament would not be prepared to cede its rights by providing that the decisions of such a commission should have statutory authority. Another proposal which was considered was to go ahead with home rule for twenty-six counties, excluding the six northern counties until the end of the war on the ground that many of the electors in those counties were with the colours. At the end of the war a plebiscite would be held in each of the six counties, it being laid down that no county should be included in the home-rule area unless 55 per cent of the voters were in favour. However, this scheme was ruled out because the unionists 'regarded the risk as too great and the nationalists regarded it as an expedient to exclude Tyrone and Fermanagh'.

At last the war cabinet worked out a procedure for dealing with the question. A bill to amend the home-rule act was to be introduced as 'an earnest' of the government's desire to reach a settlement, but it would not be forced through if opposed by the Irish M.P.s. Between the second reading and the committee stage, the bill along with the home-rule act would be referred to a committee of peers and M.P.s representing the political parties in proportion to their numbers in the house of commons. It could hear all parties involved and make recommendations to parliament.

The task of preparing a draft bill was referred to a small committee, Curzon, Duke and Addison, the minister for munitions. This committee was instructed by the war cabinet to provide that each of the six northern counties should have the option of staying out and would not be included in the home-rule area unless 55 per cent of the electors voting in each county desired it. The committee was also instructed to include in the bill arrangements for the periodic meetings of delegations from the home-rule parliament and the Ulster M.P.s to consider, and if agreement was reached, legislate on, matters affecting the whole of Ireland. When the drafting committee got to work it decided that to require a 55 per cent majority in the county plebiscites was open to criticism, as being 'an apparently trifling departure from ordinary constitutional procedure for the transparent purpose of enabling a minority in Tyrone and Fermanagh to decide the issue in these counties'. The committee therefore decided that a bare majority in each county would suffice. It balanced this decision by a remarkable suggestion. If Tyrone or Fermanagh voted for inclusion, then, until the excluded area ceased to exist, any inhabitant of either of those counties would for all civil and criminal purposes be entitled to be treated as if he lived in the excluded area, any case in which he was involved going to a court in the excluded area. In practice this would have meant that the unionists in Tyrone and Fermanagh would, if their counties accepted home rule, have been able to claim extra-territorial status.[65]

At the end of March the government's proposals for an Irish settlement had not been announced (in fact they had not been formulated), and at the beginning of April parliamentary activity was suspended for a fortnight by the Easter recess. April 1917 was one of the most critical months in the war. From the close of 1916 the German submarine campaign had been inflicting steadily growing losses on British shipping and the possibility was looming up that the necessary movements of men and supplies might be seriously – even disastrously – threatened. During April, with tremendous energy, inspired by a frightening sense of urgency, Lloyd George forced on the admiralty the convoy policy, in the process first brushing aside the first lord, Carson, and then removing him by promotion to the war cabinet.

On 1 May, when Bonar Law was asked in the house of commons about the scheme for an Irish settlement, he had to say that a statement would be delayed for a short time because the prime minister had left for the continent. A week later there had to be a fresh postponement so that Redmond could be present to hear the statement. On 15 May Devlin complained that the Irish M.P.s were getting impatient, and Bonar Law

[65] Minutes of war cabinet, 16 Apr. 1917 (Cab. 23/2); cabinet paper, 29 Sept. 1919 (Cab. 24/89).

assured him that the leaders of the Irish party and the Ulster unionists would hear from the prime minister the next day. The following day Redmond stated that no communication had reached him, and Bonar Law rather tartly replied that he would receive one that afternoon.[66]

In the letter which he sent to the leaders of the Irish parties on 16 May the prime minister put forward two solutions for the Irish question, either of which the government was prepared to adopt. The first was that home rule should immediately come into force with the six counties excluded from its operation, the question of their exclusion being reconsidered by parliament after five years. There was to be a council of Ireland, composed of delegations from each of the two areas, responsible for certain common problems, its decisions to be approved by a majority of each delegation. And the prime minister promised that the financial provisions of the home-rule act should be revised in Ireland's favour. The alternative plan, which he suggested as 'a last resort', was 'a convention of Irishmen of all parties for the purpose of producing a scheme of Irish self-government'.[67]

The text of Lloyd George's letter, with its emphasis on home rule with exclusion, implied that this was the course favoured by the government. And other evidence shows that the suggestion of a convention was a last minute addendum to the original proposals. On 15 May Redmond at the banquet to Smuts in the gallery of the House of Lords heard from Crewe, who was sitting beside him, that Lloyd George was going to offer him home-rule with the exclusion of the six counties. Redmond replied that this offer was unacceptable and that no scheme sent over from London had a chance of being accepted in Dublin. He then, possibly inspired by the presence of Smuts, went on to ask Crewe whether he thought 'it would be the right course to copy what had been done in the dominions and leave the constitutional question to a convention entirely Irish'. Crewe seems to have sympathized with the suggestion, and drawing on his memories of the South African convention he pointed out 'it would be hopeless to give any enacting power to an Irish body because a quarrel would start at once on the representation'. Later that evening Crewe, in his own words 'an honest broker',

[66] *Hansard 5*, xciii, 192, 1062, 1487, 1612.
[67] *The Times*, 17 May 1917.

went to Downing Street and suggested to Lloyd George that the government should refrain from making proposals for an Irish settlement and instead offer to refer the question to a convention. Carson was in favour of including in the prime minister's letter both the proposals and the offer of a convention, and when the war cabinet finally settled the terms of the letter on the 16th, this course was adopted.[68]

The replies of the Irish party leaders to the prime minister's letter were generally speaking cautious but encouraging. Midleton, speaking for representative unionists in the south and west, declared that the proposed home-rule scheme involved grave dangers as the Sinn Fein movement had been growing since the rebellion. But, he went on, the southern unionists, while convinced that 'the union was the only form of government to which the control of Ireland could with safety be committed', were prepared to take part in a convention. Lonsdale, the leader of the Ulster unionist group in the commons, said he would lay the prime minister's letter before the Ulster unionist council; Redmond, while rejecting the proposed home rule scheme, stated that he was strongly in favour of a convention and William O'Brien, the leader of a small group of dissentient nationalist M.P.s from county Cork, agreed with him. Having received these replies, the prime minister on 21 May announced in the house of commons that the government had decided that 'Ireland should try her hand at hammering out an instrument of government for her own people', and intended to summon a convention of representative Irishmen which would prepare and submit to parliament a scheme of the government of Ireland within the empire. The convention was to be representative of 'all leading interests, classes, creeds and phases of thought in Ireland', and Lloyd George promised that the government would take all the necessary steps to give legislative effect to the convention's conclusions if 'substantial agreement' was reached within the convention on the character of the proposed constitution. When referring to 'substantial agreement', perhaps instinctively realizing that he was at a very delicate point in his statement, he made a parliamentary joke. He remarked that he must of course protect the treasury, since 'Irishmen have a knack of being wonderfully unanimous'

[68] Crewe to Asquith, 16 May 1917 (Asquith papers).

whenever it was a question of making a demand on the imperial treasury. A few days later, when he was asked to say what was meant by 'substantial agreement', Bonar Law said it was rather difficult to define and had better be left to 'the common sense of the government'.[69]

The summoning of a convention being decided on, it was necessary to determine its composition and recruit its members. By 21 May Redmond had already transmitted to the war cabinet a plan for the composition of the convention. It was to include representatives of the Irish parliamentary party, the unionists, the O'Brienites, Sinn Fein, the churches, local authorities, the Irish peers, chambers of commerce, trade unions, the universities and of secondary and national teachers associations. All these, along with 30 persons nominated by the government, would give a total membership of 171. The war cabinet was anxious to leave the procedure of the convention as far as possible to Irishmen, but since it thought the suggested membership far too large for the effective transaction of business it asked the chief secretary to sound the Irish leaders on the matter.[70] The next day Duke reported that Redmond and Dillon, 'though not wedded to Mr Redmond's scheme . . . considered it difficult otherwise to include all the different interests'. The war cabinet, convinced that public opinion was opposed to a large assembly, spent the next meeting trying 'to frame a smaller convention'. Carson pointed out that the scheme would be more acceptable to the Ulster unionists if the representatives were to be nominated by the political parties. 'In Ireland', he explained, 'every man was a politician, so that on whatever principles its membership was chosen, the convention would in fact be composed of members of one or other of the Irish political parties'. But the general opinion of the war cabinet was that the best chance of securing a settlement was by introducing into the convention 'an element of a non-political character'.[71] Finally there was considerable discussion on an important and delicate point, the weight which each political party should have in the convention, it being pointed out that if the Irish nationalist party had not a bare majority the other parties

[69] *Hansard 5*, xcliii, 1995–2000, 2473.
[70] Minutes of war cabinet, 21 May 1917 (Cab. 23/2).
[71] Minutes of war cabinet, 22 May 1917 (Cab. 23/2).

might unite against it. From calculations which O'Connor sent to Redmond it is obvious that the nationalist leaders were not unaware of this problem, and in fact, when the convention met, just over half its members were probably supporters of the Irish parliamentary party.[72]

At the end of the war cabinet's meeting on 22 May the chief secretary was again directed to see the Irish leaders and to tell them that the war cabinet thought the membership of the convention should not exceed 70 or 80, and that Carson thought the Ulster unionist council was more likely to agree to taking part in the convention if assured that there would be in it a compact body of Irish unionists. Duke reported back that Dillon still favoured a membership of 170, but that Devlin thought a smaller number would do and that Dr Kelly, the bishop of Ross, one of the nationalist party's financial experts, had drawn up a memorandum advocating a convention of 50, sitting *de die in diem*. The bishop, incidentally, was strongly opposed to any association of teachers being invited to send representatives. On 24 May the war cabinet decided that the prime minister, Curzon and Duke should draw up two schemes for a convention of 60 and 85 members respectively.[73] The scheme for a convention with a membership of 60 was conveyed to O'Connor, who said that Redmond and Dillon had telegrammed to say it was 'absolutely inacceptable'. In fact Dillon described it as 'absolutely fatal', and that the proposed assembly would be denounced as 'packed and absolutely unfair'. The prime minister told O'Connor he was surprised that the Irish leaders were not in London.[74] However a few days later, at the very end of May, Professor W. G. S. Adams, a member of the war-cabinet secretariat who early in his career had been a civil servant in Ireland, was able to inform the cabinet that a compromise had been arrived at – a convention of 101. But he had to add that Dillon expected that the nominated members would be selected by the political parties.[75]

[72] O'Connor to Redmond, 29 May 1917 (Redmond papers).
[73] Minutes of war cabinet, 22 May 1917 (Cab. 23/2).
[74] Minutes of war cabinet, 24 May 1917 (Cab. 23/2); Minutes of war cabinet, 25 May 1917 (Cab. 23/2); Dillon, telegram, 25 May 1917 (Convention papers, State Paper Office), Dillon to Redmond, 26 May 1917 (Redmond papers).
[75] Minutes of war cabinet, 31 May 1917 (Cab. 23/2).

On 1 June the Irish Unionist Alliance met in Dublin and resolved that, though they deprecated the reopening of the Irish question during the war, they were prepared to take part in a convention of representative Irishmen. And Midleton, referring to this meeting, told Lloyd George that the southern unionists would enter the convention provided they were given adequate representation and it was understood that the convention was limited to discussing a constitution within the empire.[76]

The Ulster unionists took longer to make up their minds, 'many of the stalwarts' taking the line that they would have nothing to do with the convention. Fellenburg Montgomery, for instance, told Carson that as there was not a reasonable possibility that a majority of the convention would agree to the exclusion of the six counties, the Ulster representatives would at some stage have to withdraw, and 'we shall get as much blame for this as for not sending any at all'. But another leading Ulster unionist, Sir James Stronge, for many years grand master of the Orange order, was in favour of Ulster sending a delegation to the convention on the clear understanding they were not bound to accept the convention's decisions. He was convinced that any home-rule plan put forward by the nationalists would be demonstrably injurious to Great Britain and the empire. He hoped that the convention would split over military and commercial questions, and he urged that the Ulster delegation should insist that defence – naval and military – should be under the control of the United Kingdom government and that there should be free trade between Great Britain and Ireland. Stronge's neighbour, the archbishop of Armagh, argued that the home-rule bill being on the statute book 'gives an overwhelming advantage to the enemy and makes it absolutely necessary for us to attend'. And one of his suffragens, D'Arcy, bishop of Down, a distinguished academic philosopher, pointed out 'if only the Redmondites attended, some scheme which will seem plausible to England will be produced', and both English parties would combine to force it on Ulster. He suggested that the Ulster unionist council should announce that, if Ireland accepted conscription, the Ulster unionists would go into the convention with real good-will and a desire for a settlement.

[76] *Irish Times*, 2 June 1917; Midleton to Lloyd George, 12 July 1917 (Midleton papers).

Otherwise they would attend in order to protect imperial interests and safeguard the Irish unionists.[77]

What was bound to be decisive was that Carson was in favour of the Ulster unionists attending the convention. He was quite clear why. 'Above all things', he wrote, 'it must be remembered that under the home-rule act Ulster is "included" and remains so until some compromise is agreed and carried through parliament'. The functions of the Ulster delegates, he laid down, should therefore be to secure a position for Ulster compatible with the principles for which they stood, to obtain safeguards for the unionist minority that would be under the Irish parliament, and to endeavour to secure that the form of home rule which would be put into operation would be the best possible, taking into account the interests of Ireland, Great Britain and the empire.[78]

On the 8 June 350 delegates to the Ulster Unionist Council assembled in Belfast and resolved, with only four dissentients, that since the convention would consider every scheme and since no party would be bound by its decisions, they would send a delegation.[79] They then set up a committee to select their representatives and to keep in touch with the delegation while the convention was sitting. If the Ulster delegates were to be exposed to the winds of alien doctrine within the convention, like Antaeus they were to be reinvigorated by contact with their home ground.

The advisory committee, composed of county, farmer and trade union representatives, was a strong one, its membership including J. M. Andrews, later prime minister of Northern Ireland, Sir James Stronge and Fellenburg Montgomery.[80] The delegates met the advisory committee at intervals during the convention, and in October Barrie, the leader of the delegation, told the advisory committee that the Ulster unionist group in the convention would do 'nothing in any way binding . . .

[77] A. Duffin to ——, 14 June 1917 (Duffin papers), Montgomery to [Darcy], 4 June 1917, Stronge to Montgomery, 3 June 1917, Crozier to Montgomery, 2 June 1917, D'Arcy to Montgomery 6 June 1917 (Montgomery papers, 430).

[78] Carson to Montgomery, 28 May 1917 (Montgomery papers).

[79] *Irish Times*, 9 June 1917.

[80] Minute book of Ulster delegation to the convention gives names of advisory committee.

without consultation with the Ulster people'.[81] When the advisory committee first met, Montgomery was delighted to discover that most of the members thought it would be nothing short of treason to agree to setting-up any form of home rule in any part of Ireland,[82] and of course the committee remained safely insulated from the play of argument which occupied the convention during the following eight months.

The government was anxious that the convention should include representatives not only of the unionist groups and of the constitutional nationalists but also of advanced nationalist opinion and of labour. But it soon became clear that it was not going to be easy to secure spokesmen for these sections of Irish political life. A few days after the prime minister made his offer, Edward O'Dwyer, the bishop of Limerick, who some months before had had a public dispute with General Maxwell, asked in a letter to the press whether the convention was to be freely elected and whether it would have the power to implement a settlement. His letter indicated the line the more extreme nationalists were about to follow. A week later the executive council of Sinn Fein, with Arthur Griffith in the chair, declined to participate in the convention unless it was elected by adult suffrage and had power to declare Ireland independent. Moreover Sinn Fein demanded that the British government should pledge itself to the United States and the European powers to ratify the decision arrived at by a majority of the convention.[83] And a few weeks before the convention assembled Mr Eamon de Valera, standing as Sinn Fein candidate in Clare, implicitly condemned it by declaring there were only two courses Irishmen could follow 'with a certain amount of logic'. 'The unionists of the north', he said, 'were consistent in their desire to remain part of the British Empire; the only other position was the Sinn Fein position completely independent and separate from England. How then could they have conciliation?'[84]

The Sinn Fein attitude to the proposed convention might have been expected. The reaction of William O'Brien, the leader of a small but articulate group of nationalist M.P.s was,

[81] Minute book of Ulster delegation, 10 Oct. 1917.
[82] Montgomery to Crozier, 23 July 1917 (Montgomery papers, 430).
[83] *Irish Times*, 19, 24 May 1917.
[84] Ibid., 6 July 1917.

as always, not easily predictable. O'Brien, a man of strong emotions, a powerful orator and a fluent journalist, had been for nearly forty years a restless force in Irish politics. A vehement leader in the land war, he had taken part in the conference of 1902 which had led to Wyndham's great land act, and this experience had helped to convince him that Irish problems were to be solved by round-table discussion, compromise, conciliation and co-operation amongst all sections of Irishmen. Soon he was vehemently urging his party to adopt this approach, and, a belligerent, if generous, advocate of conciliation, he soon broke with the parliamentary party. His small group usually tended to outbid the official nationalist party, and by 1917 it was showing itself rather more sympathetic to Sinn Fein.

About the middle of June, O'Brien announced that his group would not send a delegation to the convention on the ground that it was wrongly constituted. The Ulster unionists he (incorrectly) assumed would have a third of its voting power, while the local government representatives would be largely men chosen by the United Irish League and the Ancient Order of Hibernians (organizations closely linked with the parliamentary party). Such a body, O'Brien prophesied, would arrive at 'a hateful bargain for the partition of the country under a plausible disguise'. What was needed was not a 'heterogeneous assembly' but a small round-table conference of representative Irishmen.[85]

With the approval of the chief secretary, Plunkett and Mounteagle, a well-intentioned ex-unionist peer, strove to get the five seats in the convention offered to Sinn Fein filled. Though at the start Mounteagle realized that 'all representative bodies of the left', including Sinn Fein and the Gaelic league, had denounced the convention, he hoped at the beginning of July that the right wing of Sinn Fein and William O'Brien might modify their attitude to the convention 'if referendum principle is conceded'. In the end, after rushing between Great Britain and Ireland, he thought he had found some independent nationalists willing to serve in the convention. In addition, he was, he said, able to ask some men whose names were known to the public to sponsor them. But he warned the government: 'some sponsors may

[85] Ibid., 21 June 1917.

83

hesitate *if names published*.[86] Another peer, Lord MacDonnell, a sometime under secretary, told Hopwood that Mrs Stopford Green, the widow of the historian, had suggested that Douglas, a Quaker businessman and Barton, 'an officer in the army', might be nominated as representatives of the Sinn Fein point of view.[86A] 'It would seem', Hopwood wrote, 'she herself would be prepared to accept the third place. It touches one's imagination to have a woman representative!'[87]

In the event three independent nationalists, William Martin Murphy, George Russell (A. E.), and Edward MacLysaght, accepted invitations from the government to serve in the convention. Murphy was a friend of Healy's and a close political associate of O'Brien's; Russell had shown himself sympathetic to Sinn Fein, and MacLysaght, a young farmer and publisher, was 'an advocate of everything the Gaelic League stood for, from speaking the language to wearing Irish made clothes'. Before accepting the nomination, MacLysaght made sure that the Sinn Fein leaders approved of his doing so. They agreed that it was desirable there should be someone in the convention in touch with Sinn Fein, who could act 'as a sort of liaison member but still could not be regarded in any sense a representative of the party'. And so long as he was in the convention, MacLysaght met almost daily Eoin and James MacNeill, Bulmer Hobson, and James Douglas and discussed convention problems with them.[87A] About the end of July, just after the convention started work, it was suggested that the vacant places which had been offered to the Sinn Feiners might be filled by the convention co-opting suitable persons. After discussing the question with Mac-Lysaght, the Sinn Fein leaders decided that Douglas, James MacNeill, Barton and Mrs Green, the historian, might be co-opted. William Magennis was considered, but not agreed on, and Colonel Moore, who incidentally had been asked by the chief secretary to get in touch with 'the extreme party' and find out would they accept places in the convention was considered

[86] Plunkett diary, 21 May, 2 June, 1917; Monteagle telegrams to the Chief Secretary in Convention papers, S.P.O.

[86A] Robert Childers Barton, a County Wicklow country gentleman was to be one of the Irish delegation to London at the close of 1921.

[87] Hopwood to Adams, 17 July 1917 (Lloyd George papers, F 65/1/11).

[87A] MacLysaght, Autobiography and Diary.

but turned down. Plunkett, the chairman of the convention, Devlin, and the lord mayor of Dublin were favourable to the suggestion of co-option. But when, during the lunch interval on 16 August, MacLysaght mentioned the suggestion to Barrie (the leader of the Ulster unionists) and Midleton (the southern unionist leader), it met with a cool reception. 'Barrie's crowd turned it down and Midleton after consideration did not seem well disposed'. So MacLysaght decided not to press the matter.[88]

Two representative labour bodies also refused to participate. The Dublin Trades Council, which at the end of May had resolved that it would not accept any scheme for the government of Ireland produced by a conference not elected by adult suffrage, in June refused to nominate a delegate, its chairman, William O'Brien, declaring that the convention was a political dodge to deceive the people of Russia, the U.S.A. and other countries and a plausible pretext to evade putting into practice at home 'the principles of the right of small nationalities'. The Cork Trade and Labour Council also refused to nominate a delegate to the convention; 'one member said that where the bishops led they need not fear to follow, but this found no favour with the meeting'.[89]

By the end of June the chief secretary was getting anxious about the absence of labour representatives, and Houlihan, the secretary to the insurance commissioners, was sent to Belfast to make contact with organized labour in the north.[90] His mission was a success and representatives of the shipyards workers, the building trades and the Belfast Trades Council were chosen. The shipyard workers representatives were John Hanna, 'a stalwart in the loyalist cause,'[91] who in the convention worked closely with the Ulster unionist group, and Charles McKay, who later was chairman of a Belfast district committee of the Workers' Federation during the industrial troubles of 1919.[92]

[88] MacLysaght, Diary under 13, 17 Aug. 1917; Moore to Plunkett, 28 July 1917 (Plunkett papers).

[89] Dublin Trade Council minutes, 21 May, 25 June, 1917; *Irish Independent*, 13, 22, June 1917.

[90] Chief Secretary to under secretary 27 June 1917 (Convention papers P.R.O. 1).

[91] *Belfast Newsletter*, 30 Apr. 1914.

[92] Ibid., 3 Feb. 1919.

The building trades were represented by Robert Waugh, district secretary of the Amalgamated Society of Carpenters and Joiners and the Trades Council by Henry Whitley, a member of the Typographical Association. Houlihan thought that Whitley was a capable and unassuming man but he was afraid that some other members of the Trades Council, 'though by no means as capable as representatives as Mr Whitley', might 'in their desire to be in the limelight afforded by the convention', get themselves elected. So he suggested that the government, when asking the Trades Council for a nomination should 'with an air of simplicity' remark that Mr Whitley's name had been mentioned.[93] In any event Whitley was unanimously chosen. Houlihan also considered that Londonderry labour should be represented and Alderman James McCarron, whose name he mentioned, a home ruler who was an official of the Amalgamated Society of Tailors, and who had been several times president of the Irish T.U.C., accepted an invitation to be a member of the convention.[94]

It was more difficult to secure representation of southern labour in the convention. However John Murphy, a member of the Kingsbridge branch of the National Union of Railwaymen, became a member of the convention, though apparently the branch was quite unaware of how he secured his nomination. And the Land and Labour Association, a loosely organized body whose membership included agricultural labourers and unskilled men in country towns, which was closely connected with the parliamentary party, nominated Thomas Lundon, a nationalist M.P. and party organizer.

The Irish parliamentary party was represented by a strong, well-balanced team, consisting of John Redmond, Joseph Devlin, Stephen Gwynn, Clancy and Harbison. Redmond, who had been an M.P. for thirty-five years, was outstanding amongst the members of the convention in experience and status. A devoted follower of Parnell, he had after Parnell's death led the small Parnellite group at Westminster until in 1903 he was chosen to be the leader of the reunited party. With a sturdy, close-

[93] J. Houlihan, report on visit to Belfast (Convention papers, S.P.O. 1).

[94] It was stated in the press that McCarron had accepted an invitation from the premier (*Derry Standard, Irish Independent*, 23 July 1917).

knit figure, a pugnacious face illuminated at times with a genial smile, he looked the happy political warrior. But his appearance was deceptive. He hankered after solitude, retiring when he could to his shooting lodge, deep in the Wicklow hills. Sensitive, generous and fair-minded, he found it hard to comprehend why his opponents would not meet him at what he regarded as a reasonable point. By 1917 he was a tired man in failing health whose prestige had slumped heavily. Nevertheless he was an able and assured parliamentarian, and still, when he mustered his powers, a magnificent orator with poetic fire and imagination. Devlin, a younger man, had tremenduous vitality and a remarkable grasp of the mechanics of Irish political life. He was a most powerful speaker, capable of both superb rhetoric and good-humoured but devastating banter, and having begun his working life as a pot-boy in a Belfast public house, he unlike many nationalist politicians possessed an acute and sympathetic awareness of the problems of urban working-class life. Stephen Gwynn had a very different background. A protestant, educated at St Columba's College, Rathfarnham, and Brasenose, a member of a distinguished academic family, connected with the southern landed gentry, a poet and a man of letters, who wrote gracefully on a wide range of subjects, he had been a schoolmaster and a journalist who had, as he said himself, 'drifted rather into book writing'. Becoming a home ruler at Oxford, 'under the stimulus of hearing my country abused', in 1905 he was adopted as candidate for West Clare and returned in spite of the feeling that he 'was too cultured for Clare' (later, one of his critics, Gwynn wrote, 'admitted very candidly that I was not so cultured as he thought'). Tall, with striking acquiline features, Gwynn was intellectually and physically fearless. He was always outspoken and in 1915 though over forty he joined the Leinsters as a private, was commissioned, and was serving in France when recalled for the convention.[95] John Joseph Clancy was the party's expert on public finance. Thomas Harbison, a solicitor in Cookstown, was suggested by Devlin when Dillon made up his mind not to go to the convention. Harbison, Devlin pointed out, had been opposed to Redmond and himself over the Lloyd George proposals but

[95] *Who's Who*, and S. Gwynn, *Experiences of a literary Man* (1927), pp 33, 274–5.

he would both represent Tyrone and be a thoroughly loyal colleague.[96]

The southern unionist representatives were Midleton; Henry Blake, a retired colonial civil servant who had recently ended his official career as governor of Ceylon and who in the eighties had written a series of intelligent studies of Irish life; Andrew Jameson, the head of the great firm of distillers; G. F. Stewart, a land agent on a large scale and a director of the Bank of Ireland; and John Powell, a catholic barrister who had begun his career as a solicitor, and, it was rumoured, a Parnellite. A man of fine presence and great legal ability, he was placed on the bench in 1918. Midleton, the leader of the southern unionist group, a modest but self-assurred man, was not, he himself wrote, one of those politicians whose name was a household word. Nevertheless he had had a successful political career, measured in terms of office, having held successively three junior ministerial posts and the secretaryships of state for war and India. An Irish landlord and a strong unionist, who at the outset of his parliamentary career had aroused nationalist fury by referring to the Irish as 'a garrulous and impecunious race', in 1909 he had been elected chairman of the Irish Unionist Alliance. He had already noticed that the southern unionists were generally speaking lacking in political drive, and that 'while the sympathy of Great Britain with the north was steadily increasing, leading politicians in England regarded the south as a losing game'. In 1916 the growing strength of Sinn Fein was forcibly brought home to him by the Dublin rising and the threat of disturbances in Munster. At the end of April, hurrying from the south of Ireland to England, he persuaded Asquith to send military reinforcements to Cork, and crossing on a transport he played a vigorous part in persuading the lord mayor to urge the local volunteers 'not to make the south a shambles'.[97] By May 1917 he was prepared to accept a local assembly for Ireland with limited powers, emphasizing however that no settlement would be lasting 'except one that carries the whole of Ireland and gives a predominating majority to the loyal element' – which included 'the best nationalists'. He seems to have thought such a settlement was possible if Ulster, 'aware

[96] Devlin to Redmond, 25 June 1917 (Redmond papers).
[97] Middleton, *Records and reactions* (1939), pp ix, 221–34.

of the revolutionary feeling going on all over Europe', came in, and Redmond, realizing his own weakness, accepted the fact that, like Lloyd George in England, he was dependent on unionist support.[98]

When the Ulster unionists decided to be represented at the convention, an influential member of the advisory committee appointed at the beginning of June indicated the sort of delegation Ulster should send. It should, he wrote, include 'two or three men of first-rate ability with a wide as well as a practical knowledge of industry and commerce who will be able to flatten out clever, plausible gasbags like the Roman Catholic bishop of Ross, Father Finlay and AE who pose as "economists". The rest of our men should, I think, be chosen for character.'[99] The Ulster unionist representatives were Hugh Barrie, a Scotsman who had built up a grain and produce business in County Londonderry, George Clarke, a linen merchant and bank director who had been an M.P., Knight a solicitor from the border county of Monaghan, Robert Hugh Wallace, who had commanded the 5th R.I.R. (the South Down Militia) in South Africa and was Grand Master of the Orange order, and the marquess of Londonderry, who had served in France and was to become a cabinet minister in the thirties and make a contribution of some importance to the building up of British air power. Londonderry was one of the youngest members of the convention, and on hearing him speak, Plunkett remarked that 'he had all the charm of his father and a good share of his mother's brains. He seemed to belong a little more to the later nineteenth and earlier twentieth century than either of his parents.'[100] Barrie was the leader of the delegation. Lucid and blunt, he made no attempt to give an impression of flexibility, though prepared to negotiate within narrow limits. On economic questions he was ably seconded by Pollock, the representative of the Belfast chamber of commerce, a shipbroker and flour importer who later was the first minister of finance in Northern Ireland. Plunkett thought him 'an extremely able exponent of

[98] Midleton to Bernard, 22 Mar., 12, 23 May 1917 (Add. MS 52781).

[99] Montgomery to Herdman, 16 June 1917 (Montgomery papers 430).

[100] *Confidential report*, p 12.

the views of himself and his business associates in Belfast but he has no special gift for appreciating other points of view'.[101]

The catholic hierarchy was represented by Dr John Harty, the archbishop of Cashel, and the bishops of Down, Raphoe and Ross, the Church of Ireland by the archbishops of Armagh and Dublin, the presbyterian church by the moderator, Dr John Irwin. O'Donnell, the bishop of Raphoe, was a man of princely presence and gracious manners who had for years played a leading part in the counsels of the nationalist party. An able debater with a quick intellect, he was able to deal both with broad issues and minute detail. Dr Joseph MacRory, the bishop of Down, was a forcible exponent of the northern nationalist point of view. Dr Denis Kelly, the bishop of Ross, was an expert in Irish economic and fiscal matters and had been a member of the Primrose committee. By the summer of 1917 he was very conscious that 'Ireland was travelling frightfully fast . . . The younger population have no moorings and the old generation are rapidly losing theirs'. The bishop feared 'universal collapse and shipwreck' if the coming convention did not agree on 'a strong measure of home rule for all Ireland'.[101A]

The archbishop of Armagh, Crozier, had great dignity, exquisite manners and abundant good-will, but his dual position as the senior prelate of the Church of Ireland and bishop of a diocese in the Ulster unionist zone put him in an awkward position. And after the convention had been sitting for six weeks, Fellenburg Montgomery told him bluntly that the Ulster group were getting 'uneasy and suspicious about you'. Montgomery went on to say that he had explained to them that the archbishop was 'quite staunch', but that his position obliged him to take a detached attitude. Nevertheless he felt constrained to point out to the archbishop himself that the idea that a citadel could best be defended by placing the outworks in the hands of the enemy was not in accordance with the principles of modern warfare nor of the Enniskillen men.[102] The archbishop of Dublin, Dr John Henry Bernard, before being placed on the bench had been a fellow of Trinity and a divinity professor.

---

[101] Plunkett to McDowell, 27 Nov. 1917 (Plunkett letters).

[101A] The bishop of Ross to Adams, 15 July 1917 (Lloyd George papers, F 66/1/40).

[102] Montgomery to Crozier, 6 Sept. 1917 (Montgomery papers 430).

Bernard was not only a scholar who covered a wide range of learning with calm competence, but from an early age had impressed his contemporaries by his gifts as an organizer. His patience, lucidity and decisiveness, his massive common sense allied to intellectual alertness, his 'gravitas', inspired confidence and gave him immense weight in council. Neither the archbishop of Cashel nor the moderator played a conspicuous part in the convention; the former belonged to the nationalist, the latter to the Ulster unionist group.

The Irish peers were represented by Lord Oranmore and Browne, a vigorous unionist debater in the lords and by the earl of Mayo, a man of wide interests as is illustrated by the subjects of two of his books – Irish land law and sport in Abyssinia. The chambers of commerce of Dublin, Belfast and Cork were each represented by a protestant businessman. Pollock, the Belfast representative has already been mentioned. Dublin was represented by Edward Andrews, a wine, spirits and tea merchant, Cork by Alfred MacMullan, a flour miller. Andrews acted with the southern unionists in the convention, MacMullan with the nationalists. At the close of the convention Andrews and MacMullan each signed two reports, the southern unionist and the moderate nationalist. When the chairman explained to them that this implied support of contradictory views on the taxing powers of an Irish parliament and that such 'a conflict of opinion would be hard to explain', Andrews withdrew his signature from the nationalist, and MacMullan his from the unionist, report.[103]

The largest group of members in the convention was formed by the representatives of the local authorities. It comprised 32 chairmen of county councils (only Kerry did not accept an invitation),[103A] the lord mayors and mayors from six county boroughs, and eight representatives selected by the chairmen of urban district councils – 46 in all. The group was naturally largely composed of businessmen and farmers, but it included a duke (the duke of Abercorn, who on one occasion 'spoke for the small farmers and farm labourers of his part of Ulster'),[104] a

[103] Plunkett to MacMullan, 7 Apr. 1918 (Plunkett letters).

[103A] There are of course thirty two counties, but the north and south riddings of Tipperary each had its own county council.

[104] *Confidential report*, p 23.

dentist (the lord mayor of Cork), a doctor, two solicitors, two M.P.s, Fitzgibbon, a trustee of the nationalist party and O'Dowd, a farmer and the author of *Lays of south Sligo*, and four landlords or ex-landlords. Three of this last named group were Ulster unionists, the fourth was MacMurrough Kavanagh from Carlow, the head of one of the oldest Irish families. The son of a conservative M.P. and a protestant, he had sat for a couple of years as a nationalist M.P. In the autumn before the convention met, Kavanagh poured out his political feelings to Bernard. The majority of nationalists, he wrote, were not working for or expecting 'independence'. 'All the same', he added, 'you must not take away from us our dreams, our ideals. They are the best part of us. Have you never in youth or middle age built castles in the air, without really any hope or expectation of these fancies being realized? And if so, were you the worse for those dreams, but rather I suggest the better? . . . Nationality is not a bad dream.' And he ended his letter by lamenting: 'there is no moral courage in Ireland. I speak personally, I have little or none of it but it is better to remain and guide rather than break away.'[105]

The county councillors and urban representatives who had been elected before the outbreak of the war were as a body less distinguished than most of the other members of the convention. And one of them at least displayed an amiable weakness associated with democratic local administration when he wrote to the chairman of the convention asking him to use his influence to secure for a friend of the writer promotion in the postal service. The country councillor ended his letter with the significant phrase: 'I hope to have the pleasure of thanking you personally at the reassembling of the convention'. The chairman caught the hint and writing to the secretary of the post office remarked that 'it would assist matters in the convention' if the request were granted.[106] Nevertheless the representatives of the local authorities, as Lloyd George said, reflected the everyday life of the country.[107] They were in their own neighbourhoods men of light and leading, and Southborough, the

---

[105] Kavanagh to Bernard, 9 Oct. 1916 (Add. MS 52782).

[106] John McHugh to Plunkett, 1 Feb. 1918, Plunkett to secretary of the Post Office, 4 Feb. 1918 (Plunkett letters).

[107] *Hansard 5*, xciv, 613–4.

secretary of the convention, a very experienced civil servant, was greatly impressed by how well many of them spoke.

The fifteen members nominated by the government included four peers (Desart, Dunraven, Granard, MacDonnell), three holders of academic posts (John Pentland Mahaffy, Bertram Windle and William Whitla), three men closely connected with the business life of Belfast (Patrick Dempsey, McCullagh and Alexander McDowell),[107A] two leading Dublin businessmen (William Goulding and Murphy), two literary men who could express the views of the more extreme nationalists (Edward MacLysaght and George Russell) and Horace Plunkett. Desart, an Irish landowner, after serving as a midshipman in the navy had been called to the bar, and entering the civil service had held the office of director of public prosecutions for fifteen years. He blended a high sense of public duty with ironic humour. Dunraven was an admirable Crichton, a soldier, a journalist, an author, an explorer, a yachtsman, a popular land-lord, a crusading politician and a successful racehorse owner. Unfortunately he had neither 'the equipment nor the tempera-ment of an orator',[108] and by 1917, being well over seventy, he could at times be testy. Granard, also a leading racing man, had been a junior minister in Campbell-Bannerman's and Asquith's administrations and his approach to Irish politics was character-ized by breezy common-sense, MacDonnell, 'a poor man's son in Connaught', on leaving Queen's College, Galway, had secured a place in the Indian civil service, and rising rapidly 'had proved himself a governor as imperious and as capable, as beneficient, as India has known since the Laurences'.[109] A superb administrator, unsparing of himself and his subordinates, after leaving India, he had become chief secretary for Ireland and was a moderate home-ruler. Adapt at marshalling argu-ments and at devising administrative expedients, he could display pro-consular authority and eloquence, and at times a

[107A] Redmond had hoped that Lord Pirrie, the chairman of Harland and Wolff, the great Belfast shipbuilding firm, who was a strong liberal, would be a government nominee. But Lloyd George felt that Pirrie, who was helping the government in dealing with the vital problem of shipping, could not be spared (Lloyd George to Pirrie, 19 July 1917, Lloyd George papers, F 42/9/I).

[108] *D.N.B.*

[109] S. Gwynn, *Connaught* (1912), pp 8–9.

touch of pro-consular irritability. Windle, the president of University College, Cork, was a Trinity, Dublin, graduate, who as a young man had become a catholic and a home ruler. He was an able scientist and had played a big part in building up the Birmingham medical school. Accepting membership of the convention, he remarked, 'knocks the bottom out of my holiday, which I shall spend gassing and being gassed'. However, he added, he had never refused to do anything he could in connection with the war, and he believed that the convention, 'a wonderfully representative body', would enable 'a great body of sensible, moderate opinion in this country which has never become articulate' to express itself.[109A] Whitla, a medical professor at Queen's university, Belfast, and the author of well known text books, was later to be a unionist M.P. at Westminster. Mahaffy, the provost of Trinity, was by 1917 well into his seventies and already a semi-legend. A regal don, he was a distinguished classical scholar, a historian, a pioneer in papyriology, a musician, a sportsman, a cricketer and a conversationalist. Proud of being an Anglo-Irish protestant, by the time the convention met he had become a disillusioned unionist, driven into being a home ruler, he explained, by the proven incapacity of British politicians to govern Ireland. Birrell had allowed the country to drift into rebellion; Duke had let loose a pack of convicted criminals. Mahaffy prided himself on his independence, which he thought enabled him to take an unbiased view of the Irish situation, and, as he pointed out, ensured that his opinion carried 'no weight whatever in the counsels of the nation'.[110] There perhaps was another reason why his political influence was in inverse ratio to his intellectual reputation. Mahaffy on his feet in public strove to be epigramatic and obviously enjoyed startling his audience by displays of intellectual audacity. A fellow member of the convention, Stephen Gwynn, explained that, when the convention met, 'we were ardently desirous to be on our good behaviour and avoid causes of offence – all of us but Mahaffy. He let himself go when he felt like it. "Patriotism" he said, "is like alcohol; taken in moderation, it is healthful, stimulating and agreeable; taken in excess, it is a deadly poison, which corrupts the character". That is a

[109A] M. Taylor, *Sir Bertram Windle: a memoir* (1932), pp 256–7.
[110] *Blackwood's Magazine*, cc, 548–55.

mild example; but one day, when he had been speaking his mind on the shortcomings of the Roman Catholic faith, I asked one of my friends how the mass of the assembly, mostly chairmen of county councils, were standing it. The answer I got was, "Sure it's only the provost, and nobody minds him".'[111]

McDowell, a Belfast solicitor, had a great reputation as a negotiator, gained in handling labour problems and intercompany relations. Crawford McCullagh, a draper was a leading figure in the municipal life of Belfast. Patrick Dempsey, chairman of the Belfast Whiskey Company, which controlled a number of public houses in Belfast, was a leading nationalist, active in charitable and municipal affairs. According to a unionist, being 'a constitutional nationalist of the old school', Dempsey was 'broad minded and tolerant.'[112] Goulding was chairman of an expanding company with eight factories in the south of Ireland, manufacturing fertilizers. He was also a steward of the Turf Club and had been one of the first Irish rugby internationalists. William Martin Murphy was one of the most outstanding businessmen in Ireland. Beginning as a contractor, he had built railways and tramways at home and abroad (including the railway system of the Gold Coast). Amongst his many enterprises was the *Irish Independent*, which under his management had become one of the most successful newspapers in Ireland, noted for its news coverage, its outspokenness on political issues, its photography, and for being the first halfpenny morning newspaper in the British Isles. A generous, and with many a popular employer, Murphy, *The Times* remarked in 1919, had 'ideas of discipline which now perhaps would be considered old fashioned',[113] and in the great Dublin labour disputes of 1913 he had been the stern and unbending leader of the employers. The same severe integrity characterized him in politics. He had been a nationalist M.P. from 1885 to 1892. But he had broken with the party, and by the time the convention met he regarded the parliamentary party as a group thirsting for power, place and patronage.[114] Believing that Ireland should have complete control over its finances, he thought the

[111] S. Gwynn, *Dublin old and new* (1938), pp. 125–6.
[112] *Belfast Newsletter*, 5 Dec. 1922.
[113] *The Times*, 27 June 1919.
[114] Murphy to L. Murphy, 22 Jan., 2 Mar., 1918 (Murphy papers).

home-rule bill 'not one to enthuse over'.[115] When Lloyd George became prime minister, Murphy pressed him 'to bring about a broad, far-reaching and, as far as human foresight can provide, final, settlement of the Irish question'. Murphy suggested that Ireland should have the same fiscal and commercial freedom as the self-governing colonies, but not control over its armed forces, and he was ready to allow the Irish protestants, 'undoubtedly as a whole the most progressive people and best industrial element in the country', half the seats in the Irish house of commons.[116] Neat and upright in bearing, cool and intransigent, with the immeasurable, mysterious power which contemporaries attributed to a successful newspaper proprietor, Murphy was a formidable figure.

Strangely enough, when the convention started work, Murphy found that he had a strong ally in George Russell, who had been, Murphy remarked, 'a Larkinite in 1913'.[117] Russell (better known as A.E) was a poet, a painter, a mystic, aware of divine forces at work in Ireland, an able journalist and a co-operative organizer, who in his time had travelled over Ireland, encouraging local co-operative societies, inquiring into the prices of pigs and the properties of manure, and living in Irish country hotels, 'a thing apart from "the wholesome, cheerful life of man" because I won't get drunk'.[118] Shortly before the convention met he published two works on Irish politics, *The national being: some thoughts on an Irish policy* and *Thoughts for a convention*. The first of these expounded his general political philosophy. The task confronting Irishmen was 'to truly democratize their civilization . . . to spread in the widest commonalty culture, comfort, intelligence and happiness'. And this, he believed, could be done by a wide extension of co-operation to Irish economic life, agricultural and industrial. But though the foundation on which Irish life would rest would be co-operation, other elements, 'the socialist, the syndicalist, the capitalist, the individualist' would make their contributions. In the community which Russell visualized, a democratic organization of life would bring to the fore those 'vivid and original personali-

[115] *Irish Independent*, 12 Apr. 1912.
[116] Murphy to Lloyd George, 21 Dec. 1916 (Murphy papers).
[117] Murphy to L. Murphy, 22 Dec. 1917 (Murphy papers).
[118] A. Denison (ed.), *Letters of A.E.* (London 1961), pp 25, 28–9.

ties' who 'quicken and vivify the mass' and a tolerant harmony would allow the best to prevail. Russell devoted only a few pages in passing to political machinery. He thought there should be a national assembly to supervise matters of general interest and councils representing special classes which would control the departments of state concerned with their spheres of interest. The *Thoughts for a convention* put into shape the ideas of a group, whose members, Russell wrote, represented all extremes of Irish opinion. In fact the unionists in the group would be more accurately described as ex-unionists. In this work Russell exhorted Irishmen to give due weight to one another's opinions and if possible arrive at a compromise which would save their country from chaos. And he pointed out 'that it is the traditional Irish way which we have too often forgotten to notice the good in the opponent before battling with what is evil'. Having sympathetically outlined the views of the main Irish sections he urged the adoption of a scheme which would give Ireland self-government with complete control of taxation and trade, while reserving defence to Great Britain and providing for an imperial contribution and safeguards against oppression for Ulster.

For twenty years Russell had worked for and admired Horace Plunkett, one of the most remarkable Irishmen of his day. The younger son of a family well established in County Meath for centuries, Plunkett, being threatened with consumption after coming down from Oxford, had emigrated to the middle west of America. A frail young aristocrat, flung into a rough pioneering world, he quickly made a fortune which assured him financial independence. He then turned to what became his lifelong task, trying to raise the standard of living of the rural world by the development of agricultural co-operation. While engaged in this he was appointed the first vice-president (and for practical purposes head) of the newly founded Irish Department of Agriculture and Technical Instruction, which under his direction soon became one of the most efficient, and undoubtedly the most popular, branch of the Irish administration.

Plunkett combined high ideals, imaginative vision and creative energy with a capacity to work hard and steadily, often in dreary and discouraging circumstances. He was a crusader, but unlike many other self-sacrificing workers for good causes, he had elegance of bearing, worldly awareness, and a keen sense of humour. He was a delightful and persuasive conversationalist and his writings are frequently enlivened by epigram and unexpected argument. And though he contemplated life with an ironic if gentle melancholy, he remained remarkably optimistic. His position in Irish politics was unusual not to say unique. He had been returned as a unionist M.P. for South County Dublin in 1892. His management of the Department of Agriculture and Technical Instruction cost him the support of the more extreme unionists in his constituency and in 1900 he lost his seat. By 1914 he was a very moderate home ruler, and, an idealist, he was ceaselessly urging his fellow countrymen to think in practical terms of social and economic welfare.[119]

Plunkett was so generous, tolerant, candid and witty that it seems ungracious to dwell on his weaknesses. But as they had some influence on the convention, it is necessary to indicate them. At a time when Irishmen prided themselves on their oratorical prowess he was a wretched speaker, inaudible and obviously unhappy. Fertile in ideas he talked too much, quick-minded and friendly, he was indiscreet. Believing that men of goodwill could by rational discussion reach agreement, he failed to appreciate that methods of persuasion which were effective when it came to enlisting men in a good cause might fail when it was a question of getting adversaries to modify their convictions for the sake of a settlement.

His virtues and defects are strikingly illustrated by his confidential report on the convention's proceedings which he wrote for the king. It is lively and penetrating with a flair for the well-turned phrase, and it displays an informed awareness of the complexities of Irish political life, a ready sympathy for all sorts and conditions of Irish public men, remarkable fairness and a sense of the dramatic. But throughout the report the reader is conscious of Plunkett's determination to achieve a settlement, his amusement at the idiosyncrasies of some members and his impatience at the obstinacy of others – especially the Ulster unionists. As one critic of the report not altogether unfairly put it, 'all the speeches of Horace's friends, A.E. etc., were soul inspired, an Ulster unionist speech per contra was poor stuff'. The report was prepared in sections at intervals while the convention was in being, and Plunkett, with pardonable pride in

[119] M. Digby, *Horace Plunkett: an Anglo-American Irishman* (1949).

his work, had a number of copies printed. Not only did the king, who, in Southborough's opinion,[120] was the one person who did not read it, get a copy but a number of politicians and publicists were able to read Plunkett's frank comments. Plunkett himself suddenly realized that Carson, who as a member of the war cabinet would probably see the report, might resent some passages, 'though', Plunkett optimistically reflected, 'I doubt this as he is pretty broadminded'. But he admitted he was afraid that if Carson let his Ulster friends know the general tenor of the report 'there would be an ugly row in the convention'.[121]

Once the convention was summoned there was a distinct possibility that Plunkett might be asked to act as chairman. At the beginning of June he discussed with Duke the qualities required in a chairman. He should, Plunkett thought, possess skill in presiding, constitutional knowledge, and 'intimacy' with Irish opinions and personnel. Lowther and Balfour, who were mentioned as possible chairmen, would both lack this intimacy, but Balfour, Plunkett was confident, would nevertheless be able to get 'in rapport' with the convention.[122] A few days later he heard that he himself had been considered for chairman but had been turned down by the persons consulted – he suspected Carson and T. P. O'Connor.[124] A fortnight later, writing to an intelligent northern unionist, Adam Duffin, he returned to the question of the qualities required by a chairman. He should, Plunkett wrote, be an Irishman, aware of Irish currents of opinion, who would know what a speaker was trying to say or 'what he has to say or why'. 'With this knowledge', Plunkett remarked, 'speakers are easily controlled, without it an omnium gatherum of Irishmen soon gets out of hand'. Duffin in reply suggested that Arthur Balfour would make a good chairman, a candid expression of opinion which implied that Plunkett was not the obvious choice in the minds of northern unionists.[124]

From what has been said it is clear that taking the convention as a whole it undoubtedly contained a remarkable number of

[120] Southborough to Midleton, 7 Dec. 1929 (Midleton papers).
[121] Plunkett to Duke, 24 Aug. 1917 (Plunkett letters).
[122] Plunkett, Diary, 2, 5, June 1917.
[123] Plunkett to Duffin, 18 June 9117, Duffin to Plunkett, 20 June (Plunkett letters).

men of ability and personality. Politically speaking the 95 members who accepted invitations were divided as follows: 52 were nationalists (two of whom, MacLysaght and Russell, were in advance of the others), two were liberals (Granard and Mac-Donnell), six were labour, nine were southern unionists, twenty-four were Ulster unionists, Mahaffy is hard to label, and Plunkett, as will be seen, strove to be detached. Grouping the members theologically – which many Irishmen at this time would almost automatically attempt to do – there seem to have been 53 catholics and 42 protestants.

III

THE CONVENTION, 1917

BY THE MIDDLE OF JULY 1917 the arrangements for launching the convention were nearly completed. Most of the invitations had been accepted, the question of a chairman was temporarily settled, a secretary had been designated and a meeting place secured. A number of possible chairmen were mentioned – Plunkett, Balfour, Bernard, and James Campbell, the chief justice. Redmond remarked that Carson would make an excellent chairman, and it was suggested that the speaker, James Lowther might preside.[1] But Lowther, who was having a most successful tenure of the speaker's chair, pointed out that attending the convention might keep him away from Westminster for months; also that it would be highly undesirable that an Englishman should preside over an assembly of Irishmen discussing their own affairs.[1A] So it was decided that the chief secretary should take the chair at the first meeting. The government selected as secretary Sir Francis Hopwood, then a civil lord of the admiralty, who in November 1917 was created a peer, taking the title Southborough. Hopwood had not only been permanent head of two important departments (the board of trade and the colonial office), but he had taken part in the creation of the union of South Africa. Two meeting places were

---

[1] Hopwood to Adams, 17 July 1917 (Lloyd George papers, F 65/1/11) and Monteagle to Adams 17 July 1917 (Lloyd George papers, F 66/1/43).
[1A] *A speaker's commentaries*, 11, 213.

suggested, the College of Surgeons or Trinity College. Both Plunkett and Hopwood thought that the College of Surgeons was the better suited for the purpose (though Hopwood complained that 'busts and pictures of departed medics diagnosed you from every stair and wall').[1B] But Plunkett and Hopwood both agreed that the College was situated 'in a very Sinn Fein locality',[2] and John Dillon strongly urged that Trinity should be the meeting place, 'as a symbol of the common union of hearts'. To choose the College of Surgeons, he said, would be to suggest that Ireland was on the dissecting table.[2B] Finally, the offer of accommodation in Trinity was accepted. The college placed at the disposal of the convention for its meetings the Regent House, a large finely-proportioned room over the front gate, noted for its good plaster work and bad acoustics. The college also set apart a number of rooms round the front gate for the use of the delegates and secretariat.

The government tried to ensure that the convention would start in an atmosphere of harmony and good-will by releasing in June 1917 the prisoners convicted of offences connected with the rebellion. This decision dismayed southern unionists. 'We should not be honest', the *Irish Times* declared, 'if we did not express our grave doubts of the efficacy and wisdom of this experiment'.[3] Apparently it would have been even more critical of the government's behaviour if Plunkett had not got hold of the proprietor and editor in the Kildare Street Club and persuaded them 'to modify a very unfortunate presentation of the government's action'.[4] Midleton told Curzon that the decision to release the prisoners would be fatal to the convention, since it would antagonise the loyalists and encourage the extreme nationalists to 'trade on the weakness of the government'. Curzon, who could not have forgotten his catastrophic dispute with Midleton twelve years earlier, replied that the decision to which Midleton took exception had been made by the war cabinet, with other ministers present, after a full dis-

---

[1B] Hopwood to Adams 11 June 1917 (Lloyd George papers, F 65/1/15).
[2] Plunkett, Diary, 11 July 1917.
[2B] Bishop of Ross to Adams, 8 July 1917 (Lloyd George papers, F 66/1/ 38).
[3] *Irish Times*, 16 June 1917.
[4] Plunkett to Adams, 16 June 1917 (Plunkett letters).

cussion.[5] The prisoners on their return from England were given an enthusiastic reception which in Dublin and Cork ended in rioting, and the *Irish Times* remarked that the Sinn Fein flags displayed during the celebrations on the ruins of the Post Office represented 'the triumph of violence over law in the capital of Ireland'.[6]

The first meeting of the convention was fixed for 25 July. Ominously, the night before the opening meeting there was a misunderstanding between the Ulster and the southern unionists. The Ulster unionists, a closely-knit, well-organized group had taken a house in Merrion Square for their head-quarters during the convention. And they suggested that the southern unionists should meet them there on the the the evening of the 24th. The southern unionists thought the meeting was to be at 8 p.m. and left a dinner party at Lord Iveagh's early to be in time. When they arrived at Merrion Square they were kept waiting for an hour; when the northern unionists arrived the southerners discovered that the object of the meeting was to arrange that both groups should agree not to support for the post of chairman any person connected with the government of Ireland, or the administration of the law there. This resolution, Midleton believed, probably correctly, was aimed at Campbell, the chief justice who, it was rumoured in the north, was both hoping to be chairman and weakening in his unionism.[7]

On 25 July the convention met for the first time. A silent crowd round the gates of Trinity watched the delegates walk in. A faint cheer greeted Devlin when he got out of his motor car. Duke avoided the photographers by driving through the back gate, and when the delegates left in the afternoon a group of Blackrock councillors tried unsuccessfully to raise a cheer for Redmond, who was followed to the Gresham by a crowd of hostile youths.[8] Duke took the chair and 'with consumate tact'[9] in a portentous speech persuaded the assembly to choose a

[5] Midleton to Curzon, 22 June; Curzon to Midleton, 24 June 1917 (Midleton papers).

[6] *Irish Times*, 21 June 1917.

[7] Minutes of Ulster unionist delegation; Midleton, *Records and reactions* (1939), pp 236–7; Montgomery to Stronge, 29 June 1917 (Montgomery papers 430).

[8] *Irish Times, Irish Independent*, 26 June 1917.

[9] *Confidential report*, p. 5.

committee of ten to select a chairman. When the committee met, Midleton suggested Southborough for chairman of the convention, pointing out that 'as his mother was an Irishwoman, the trouble of race did not arise'. Midleton secured a majority of six to four for his candidate, but George Russell, whose name had been put forward for the committee by MacLysaght on the ground that 'independent nationalism, though the weakest element in the convention, was the strongest in the country', declared that if the committee did not select Plunkett he would raise the question on the floor of the convention. In the end, Redmond, who had at first agreed to Southborough, asked Midleton to withdraw his name. Midleton, protesting that 'it was astonishing to ask a man in a majority of two to one to give way to the minority', did so, and Plunkett was chosen.[10] The committee then reported to the convention and Duke vacated the chair. His valedictory speech was composed of amiable commonplaces but his closing remarks electrified his audience. He ended by declaiming in 'his most weighty tones: "Gentlemen, one thing I have learned in the course of my experiences, *never despair of the republic*". A faint titter went through the room . . . the southern unionists looked aghast'.[11]

Southborough was elected secretary and during a two-weeks adjournment a secretariat was rapidly recruited. One of the main duties of this body, in Plunkett's opinion, was to supply the members of the convention with constitutional and economic information. He wanted it therefore to be composed of men who would possess both specialized knowledge and the ability to make it 'interesting and easy of assimilation'. Moreover they would have to be aware of 'all the main currents of political thought in Ireland, where what may appear to be a mere abstraction or even a truism, may arouse a storm of controversy.'[12] The secretariat was certainly varied in experience and outlook. It included Walter Callan, an R.M and a moderate nationalist,[13] Captain Richard Shaw, who had been secretary of the Irish

---

[10] Midleton, *Records and reactions*, pp 237–8; MacLysaght, Diary; Plunkett to Adams, 25 Aug. 1917 (Plunkett letters), Hopwood to Adams, 25 July 1917 (Lloyd George papers, F 65/1/12).

[11] MacLysaght, Diary.

[12] *Confidential report*, p 6.

[13] Callan to O'Donnell, 3 Oct. 1917 (Logue 17).

Unionist Alliance and a member of *The Times*' staff, Roland Venables Vernon, a civil servant who was having a successful career in the colonial office, Erskine Childers, a keen proponent of financial autonomy who was serving in the navy, Thomas Moles, later an Ulster unionist M.P., Shan Bullock, a dramatist and civil servant, very knowledgeable about Ulster rural life, and Dermot Coffey, a young barrister and historian from Trinity who sympathized with Sinn Fein.

During the adjournment Plunkett went over to London and lunched with the prime minister. Lloyd George was 'as nice as possible', Plunkett wrote, 'about my appointment and thought it the very best that could be made; he could not make it on account of Dillon. He was for a very liberal settlement of the Irish question.'[14] A few days after Plunkett's return the convention met again, adopted a list of standing orders, and approved of a grand committee of twenty to assist the chairman, nominated by the committee of ten which had been appointed to select a chairman.

The committee of twenty then met to settle the procedure the convention should follow. Plunkett had already worked out a procedure through which the convention might attain its objective, an agreed settlement. He believed 'that anyone who really understands Ireland can get the most antagonistic elements to combine once they consent to meet'. He wanted the members of the convention to begin by getting to know one another and their subject, Ireland, thoroughly. The first stage of the convention's proceedings should be a general debate in which all points of view could be freely expressed. During the next stage resolutions on definite points could be tabled and probably a drafting committee constituted.[15] The *Irish Times* had already in a burst of unusual optimism sketched what might happen if the convention adopted such a procedure. If the convention, an editorial explained, began by discussing for some weeks a number of plans for the future government of Ireland, at the end of that time 'all the members would have received a liberal education in Irish affairs, would have come to understand one another's points of view . . . and to realize

[14] Plunkett, Diary, 2 Aug. 1917.
[15] Plunkett to Adams, 22 May 1917; Plunkett to Duffin, 18 June 1917 (Plunkett letters).

that, as Irishmen the things in agreement between them were not less vital then the things in dispute'. Then, 'when this unconscious conversion had been achieved, the chairman might say, "Now let us get back to partition"', and a solution might emerge.[16]

Plunkett therefore wanted the convention to start with a series of debates, 'a talk about anything and everything with an apparent discussion of definite proposals'.[17] 'The more', he explained to Redmond, 'we fight over controversial issues under absolutely non-committal conditions the quicker we shall move in the negotiations stage which must follow'.[18] And Southborough seems to have agreed with this approach, his aim, it was said, being to put off as long as possible a debate on a definite issue, in the hope that 'personal intercourse might wear the Ulstermen's feelings down'.[19]

Another course of procedure was suggested. It was proposed that the convention should begin by setting up committees to tackle concrete issues – trade, tariffs, education, electoral systems – as a preliminary to a general discussion. The southern unionists supported this course. 'My great difficulty', Plunkett wrote, 'is with the "high brows" (Midleton leading them), who want to get down at once to business and have little patience with the manoeuvring for position of the different groups'.[20] The southern unionists fought hard for the procedural course they favoured, but the chairman (somewhat embarrassed by finding himself at loggerheads with the party to which he had once belonged) prevailed and it was decided the convention should start work by holding a series of debates. Then the question arose, what were the debates to be about. Three possibilities were considered: a general discussion of the existing system of Irish government and the best methods of improving it; a discussion on a series of resolutions raising the main questions of principle on which agreement had to be reached; or a discussion of all the proposals for the better government of Ireland which the grand committee should submit to the house.

[16] *Irish Times*, 1 June 1917.
[17] Plunkett to Oliver, 30 Aug. 1917 (Plunkett letters).
[18] Plunkett to Redmond, 25 Aug. 1917 (Plunkett letters).
[19] Murphy to W. L. Murphy, 5 Aug. 1917 (Murphy papers).
[20] Plunkett to Oliver, 30 Aug. 1917 (Plunkett letters).

The first two plans Plunkett dismissed as leading to 'lean and profitless debate' or to 'a blind alley'. And he advocated the adoption of the third course, in the hope that the debate would be 'argumentative and conversational rather than declamatory and impassioned'. 'No man', he added, 'should hesitate to express his views because he has difficulty at first in finding the appropriate phraseology which is familiar to few besides members of parliament and lawyers. I speak feelingly when I say the utmost indulgence should be extended to bad speakers.' It was again agreed to accept the procedure recommended by the chairman, and Plunkett wrote a long letter to the members explaining how he expected the first stage of their proceedings to develop. The day before he wrote the letter he had to go and see Byrne, the under-secretary who, he was horrified to hear, was trying to arrest de Valera. Plunkett had heard that if de Valera was arrested several county councils would at once withdraw their representatives from the convention, and he was able to get Byrne, who fortunately had not been able to catch de Valera, to promise to leave him alone for the immediate future.[22]

The grand committee submitted to the conventions seven plans for the better government of Ireland, drafted respectively by McDonnell, Murphy, 'Two Irishmen', Alexander Moles, Vesey Knox, Dunraven, and the provost. Four of these authors were members of the convention. The pseudonym, 'Two Irishmen' stood for two members of the secretariat, Cruise O'Brien, Plunkett's devoted if at times irreverent secretary and Dermot Coffey,[23] Vesey Knox was a member of a well known Ulster landed family, a chancery barrister and fellow of All Souls who had been for some years a home rule M.P. and Alexander Moles, a businessman, apparently working in the north of England, who wrote of himself as being 'an Ulsterman and an Irishman to whom the question of Irish self-government is a question of all absorbing interest'.[24]

The first six plans all followed the same general pattern by providing that there should be a lord lieutenant appointed by the

[21] *Confidential report*, pp 8–11.
[22] Plunkett, Diary, 15, 16 Aug. 1917.
[23] Plunkett to Rolleston, 7 Sept. 1917 (Plunkett letters).
[24] Moles to Plunkett, 4 July 1917 (Plunkett letters)

crown, an Irish parliament with two houses, and cabinet govern-ment.[24A] McDonnell, who frankly admitted that his scheme was based on Childers's *The framework of home rule*, stated that it gave Ireland full executive, legislative and financial autonomy, reserving to the imperial parliament defence, foreign affairs, treaties (except commercial treaties), postal services, coinage and copyright. Moles, broadly speaking, reserved to the imperial parliament the same functions as McDonnell listed. Murphy declared that Ireland should have the powers of 'a self-governing colony'; the 'Two Irishmen' and Knox wanted Ireland to have dominion self-government. These last three schemes left only defence reserved to the imperial parliament. Dunraven gave the Irish parliament power to make laws on all matters exclusively relating to Ireland. All the schemes, with the exception of Moles's, gave Ireland control over customs and excise. Five of the schemes implied that Ireland might make an imperial contribution, MacDonnell for instance being prepared to agree to an imperial contribution to the expenses of the United Kingdom when Ireland's taxable capacity reached one twenty-fifth of Great Britain's. Murphy was unenthusiastic about an imperial contribution. In a blunt explanatory note he said that the question was no longer 'how much can Ireland get out of the British treasury but how little if anything should Ireland contribute towards the common expenditure of the United Kingdom'. His view was that Ireland should take over all the financial obligations which had been reserved to Great Britain in the 1914 home-rule act, and then, if Ireland was to pay an imperial contribution, it should be reduced by the cost to Ireland of these obligations (which implied that Ireland would pay little or nothing).

Only two of the schemes, Dunraven's and Moles's, provided for continued Irish representation at Westminster. Dunraven indeed hoped that his scheme would not only give the fullest possible measure of self-government to Ireland, but that it would fit into 'the future complete federalization of the United Kingdom' and form 'a consistent link in the chain that may lead up to some form of constitutional synthesis for the whole empire'. Naturally then, he favoured Irish representation at Westminster. And, having a streak of romanticism in his

[24A] The plans are in the convention papers, T.C.D.

political planning, he suggested that the Irish parliament should occupy the building in Dublin which had housed the pre-union parliament and that the king should be requested to open its sessions.

All these schemes (except MacDonnell's) had provisions for dealing with minority problems. MacDonnell simply said that, if, after agreeing on a far-reaching scheme, they found themselves faced with an Ulster difficulty, a remedy could 'easily be superimposed on a dominion scheme'. Murphy brushed aside 'fancy schemes' for setting up two parliaments in Ireland as not being practical politics. As for provincial parliaments, he remarked, that the Irish county councils already possessed almost the same powers as provincial assemblies in Canada or Australia. But he suggested that in the three southern provinces each constituency should return two M.P.s, one elected by the electors on the parliamentary register, the other by the electors on a special register, based on a valuation of £20 or £30 per annum. The 'Two Irishmen' suggested that there should be two provincial councils, one for Ulster, the other for Leinster, Munster and Connaught. Each of these provincial councils would make ordinances for its province in relation to direct taxation for provincial purposes, education, hospitals, local government, public works and police. If an act of the Irish parliament was rejected by a two-thirds majority of a provincial council it would not be operative in the province. The provincial council could refuse to allow a tax to be levied in the province, but in the event of doing so, it would be obliged from local taxation (the rates) to pay to the Irish exchequer a sum equivalent to the calculated yield of the tax in the province. Moles empowered provincial assemblies to deal with all matters not specifically designated as being within the jurisdiction of the Irish parliament. Knox laid down that in the Irish parliament the Ulster M.P.s and the M.P.s from the rest of Ireland could sit separately. Each group could send to the upper house a bill relating to its own area. If in a joint session a vote by provinces was demanded, the question would be deemed to have been carried only if there was a majority in its favour in each group. There were to be three executives, one for the whole of Ireland and one for each area. Each executive was to be elected for the term of a parliament and would continue in office for that term, notwithstanding an adverse vote. In each executive, the minority, in Ireland or the area, was to be represented. The two local executives would be empowered to deal with licensing, local government, public works, police, justice, agriculture, fisheries and technical instruction. Dunraven proposed that in the Irish house of commons the M.P.s for any province could constitute themselves a grand committee, and by a majority of two-thirds resolve that any bill, in so far as it referred to the province, should be considered by the grand committee and not by a committee of the house. Moreover any area, being not less than four contiguous counties, not less than three years after the new constitution came into force could, by a majority of two-thirds of the electors voting in each county, exclude itself from the jurisdiction of the Irish parliament. The excluded area would then have the same relationship with the United Kingdom as the rest of Ireland possessed.

The six schemes which have been mentioned proposed to give Ireland a considerably greater degree of autonomy than had been granted by the home-rule act of 1914. Only two of them seem to have been discussed at any length during what Plunkett called 'the presentation stage'. This lasted for eighteen sittings of the convention, of which three were in Belfast and three in Cork. The reason for visiting Belfast was to give the convention 'a clear and concrete idea of the fine achievement in industry and commerce of the north-east corner of our country'. The members of the convention were shown Gallaher's tobacco factory, the Belfast rope-works, the docks and the shipyards, where the shipwrights decorated the ships' sides with mottoes such as 'the somewhat unnecessary assurance on a torpedoed cruiser, 'No pope here'''.[25] Plunkett, who was staying with Sharman Crawford, found his hostess 'the most bitter Ulsterite I have met for some time', and while he was impressed by the efficiency of the arrangements made for the convention in the Belfast City Hall, he was overwhelmed by the civic state, by which, as chairman, he was accompanied. 'Whenever I moved outside my private room', he wrote, 'I was preceded by two awful, top-hatted, brass-bounded mace-bearers, who would not move until they got into step with one another'.[26] The proceed-

[25] *Confidential report*, p. 20.
[26] Plunkett, Diary, 3, 4 Sept. 1917.

ings in Belfast were enlivened by Mahaffy, who insisted on introducing his scheme. On hearing that Mahaffy intended to intervene in the discussions at Belfast, McDowell remarked to Plunkett: 'for God's sake keep him till the last day, for it would play the mischief if it got out we were not serious on the first or second day'.[27] Mahaffy's speech was in part arrogant – he spoke of himself as coming down from 'a purer atmosphere' to the region of politics – and tactless: elaborating a metaphor based on classical mythology he referred to the Goddess Pallas Athena as being as great a jobber as the most experienced member of the convention, 'Mr John Fitzgibbon could not hold a candle to her.' But he emphasized forcibly and intelligently the political difficulties created by denominational feeling. 'We protestants', he said, 'fear the very same injustices which the Roman Catholics had to suffer, I will not say under penal laws, but under the rule of the tory gentry and their party all through the early nineteenth century, even after the emancipation act of 1829. We want to protect ourselves from the same treatment as they suffered even in the later and more humane days of the protestant ascendancy.' And he cited as a recent example of administrative injustice, 'making the dying and unpracticable Irish language or rather a smattering of it, of no value to anyone' a condition for the reward of a county council scholarship, with the aim, Mahaffy believed, of excluding the protestant schools from competing for scholarships.[28]

After its return to Dublin from Belfast the convention paid a visit to Guinness's brewery, 'to show the northerners that industrial organizing with welfare was possible in the south'.[29] The following week the convention went down to Cork. There the members were magnificently entertained and a great effort was made to impress the convention with the industrial potentialities of the region. The members were told about the new Ford factory which was going to be started on the banks of the Lee and they were taken out on a boat to see 'the ancient custom' of throwing the dart – the mayor of Cork as admiral of the port claiming jurisdiction over the surrounding waters by

[27] Plunkett to Redmond, 1 Sept. 1917 (Plunkett letters).
[28] There is a printed copy of the provost's speech in the convention papers, T.C.D.
[29] Plunkett, Diary, 20 Sept. 1917.

throwing a silver dart into the sea. The excursion was a most convivial one but the boat had to turn abruptly back when it was rumoured that a German submarine was in the harbour. Mr Devlin when landing at Cork was also very nearly thrown into the water by some Sinn Fein sympathizers, who followed him singing the Soldier's Song. But, 'excited and warlike', he pluckily turned on the crowd and was rescued by a party of friendly cattle drovers.[30]

The entertainments in Belfast and Cork were part of the active and varied social life which developed round the convention and which, it was hoped, would break down the isolation of the Irish political groups and promote acquaintanceships and understanding. The dinner and the garden party were expected to prove useful accessories to the technique of negotiation. Lady Granard, a great London hostess, entertained with pre-war magnificence in Ely House, and Lord Iveagh gave a garden party which had a soothing effect after a warm August meeting. Lady Diana Manners, who paid a short visit to Dublin in the late summer of 1917, gives a vivid impression of this side of the convention's life. 'I went straight up to dinner at the Viceregal Lodge in grandest *tenue* and alone. Perfect I thought – don't believe a word said against it. Forty to dinner – convention men, labour ones and peers – red ties, diamond studs and stars. The table and its pleasures a treat – all gold and wine and choicest fruit. One conventioner said he had never tasted a peach before (I don't believe him). The footmen too, such beauties, battling with their silver cords, blinded by powder. After dinner, talking to the conventioners, some of them a bit unintelligible and smoking gift cigars. One said of Lord Oranmore, who looks as prosperous as he is: "Sure he's as stout as the Lamb of God".'[31] Political puritans sometimes condemn inter-party sociability as enervating to principle. During the convention, however, the members by relaxing and chatting together certainly gained a new respect for one another's views and personalities, without making many concessions.

Considerable frankness and fairness and some real eloquence characterized the debates during the 'presentation stage'.

[30] *Irish Independent* and *Irish Times*, 27 Sept. 1917.
[31] Plunkett, Diary, Aug. 1917; D. Cooper, *The rainbow comes and goes* (1958), pp 154–5.

Spokesmen for the parliamentary party, the southern unionists and the Ulster unionists stated their standpoints. At least three labourmen from the north spoke, two of them, Whitley and McKay, representing the working men of Belfast and McCarron from Londonderry. McCarron made a moderate nationalist speech. Whitley asked why wages were not higher in Belfast and McKay complained that religion was being used to hoodwink labour. 'Take away religion', he declared, 'and Belfast will be all right'.[32] At the end of August, Granard noted that the Ulster unionists had received a severe blow from the labour group, its leader (probably Whitley) saying 'that owing to home rule being continually before the country there had been no room for labour'.[33] MacLysaght, in a speech which Plunkett described as 'a ten-minute shocker', emphasized the strength of Sinn Fein but declared that 'Sinn Fein can be won if it can be persuaded that national freedom is possible within the empire'. Bernard rebuked MacLysaght for threatening the assembly and privately referred to him as a whippersnapper. The other advanced nationalist in the convention, Russell, attacked the Ulster unionists for indulging in economic complacency when the population of the province had fallen. He emphasized that the different parties in Ireland needed one another and that a sound system of education was essential. 'A far less costly police force and a more efficient if more costly education would be among the chief reforms of the Irish government'.[35]

There were dull patches in the debate. Fitzgibbon made a long speech about the congested districts; Blake 'bored but did not offend' by giving a survey of the constitutional systems of the colonies in which he had served; and one morning eight county councillors spoke, 'a demonstration', Plunkett noted, 'of the bad composition of the convention'.[36] But there were many vigorous and intelligent speeches (an oratorical tradition rooted in the eighteenth century was still alive in Ireland), and Plunkett felt that a sense of creative responsibility was being encouraged. 'The discussion had been really fruitful', he wrote, 'in hardening the heart of the south and softening the head of

[32] *Confidential report*, pp 18–19.
[33] Granard to Asquith, 31 Aug. 1917 (Asquith papers, 37).
[35] *Confidential report*, pp 15–16.
[36] Plunkett, Diary, 21, 28 Aug., 19 Sept. 1917.

the north'.[37] Feeling that an atmosphere favourable to a settlement was growing he revelled in the play of ideas. Anxious to see barriers collapsing, he was pleased and amused by 'a delightful little comedy' which he labelled 'the sword versus the crozier'. Colonel Wallace, the grand master of the Orange order, 'looking every inch a grand master', raised the subject of two recent papal announcements, *Ne Temere* and *Quantavis diligentia*. 'His complete avoidance of anything which could be called tact in dealing with so delicate a subject', Plunkett reported, was thoroughly enjoyed, and O'Donnell, the bishop of Raphoe answered him with dialectal skill, minimizing the significance of the decrees. The discussion was closed by Barrie relentlessly pointing out that if the Irish catholic bishops were to ask the pope to withdraw the decrees it would make a settlement much easier.

From Plunkett's own account of the debates it is clear that, while goodwill was generated, little or no progress was made towards formulating a detailed agreed scheme or even towards reaching agreement over the principles on which it should be based. Admittedly the southern unionists, who naturally emphasized their satisfaction with the status quo, by dwelling on the safeguards for imperial and minority interests which must be included in a home-rule scheme, at least hinted at the possibility of agreement on such a scheme. And towards the end of August the northern unionists were highly annoyed to discover that a southern unionist, Powell, had handed in anonymously a scheme which provided for two provincial legislatures, one for the six, the other for the twenty-six, counties, each with an executive responsible to it, along with an Irish senate which would also have an executive responsible to it. 'Our southern friends', Barrie wrote, 'did not like the situation in which they found themselves and Powell was evidently deputed to see me and get matters agreed. I said in the light of what had happened I preferred not to discuss matters with individuals but if his group appointed three we could meet them.' Shortly afterwards, Barrie, Londonderry and McDowell met Midleton, Desart and Jameson. The southern delegates expressed regret that the scheme had been put forward, and Barrie gave them a firm

[37] Plunkett to Balfour, 28 Sept. 1917; Plunkett to Bryce, 13 Sept. 1917 (Plunkett letters).

talking to, telling them that an official expression of regret should be conveyed to the Ulster group and that their own group should be properly organized. The southern unionists in a very polite letter stated they wished to co-operate with the Ulster group as much as possible and would not put forward any scheme without consulting it in advance.[38] At the very time this awkward incident occurred, Montgomery, suspicious and intransigent, reported to Barrie that the southern unionists were saying that Ulster should accept home rule with power to manage its local affairs, and that he had heard the archbishop of Armagh, with 'his usual caution' talking on these lines in the University Club. 'I am sorry', Montgomery added, 'that the cause of the southern unionists has fallen into bad hands as many of them are very staunch fellows with whom it would be a pleasure and an advantage to work, but you are quite right to keep your team separate from people who have shown they are not thoroughly to be trusted'.[39] And a couple of days after Montgomery expressed these opinions, another member of the advisory committee wrote to him: 'No doubt we *did not* wish for separation. But we have grown to think that we might be better off if we were no longer part of the distressful country. In fact (like Great Britain) we long to be rid of the Irish question.'[40] On the other hand Midleton a little earlier had told Montgomery, 'the bulk of the southern unionists will never think of partition which will hand them over to the enemy'. If recently the southern unionists had taken a line which was 'not quite on all fours' with Ulster unionist policy, it was because for three years the Ulstermen had 'cut us out of all their councils'.[41]

If in private discussion a cleavage was developing between the southern and the Ulster unionists, in the convention debates the gap between the Ulster unionists and the official nationalists was if anything widening. Redmond, discussing MacDonnell's and Murphy's plans, expressed his pleasure that they both gave the Irish parliament far more power than had been conceded to

[38] Barrie to Montgomery, 25 Aug. 1917 (Montgomery papers, 430); Midleton to Barrie, 22 Aug. 1917 (Minutes of the Ulster delegation); Minutes of the Ulster delegation, 22 Aug. 1917.
[39] Montgomery to Barrie, 18 Aug. 1917 (Montgomery papers 430);
[40] Sronge to Montgomery, 20 Aug. 1917 (Montgomery papers 430).
[41] Midleton to Montgomery, 12 May 1917 (Montgomery papers 431).

it by the 1914 home rule act, though he added that he was ready to support almost any scheme which was agreed to by a substantial majority of the convention. On the other hand the Ulster unionists emphasized how their area had thriven under the union and asked the nationalists 'to direct your arguments to our intellect not to our passions and show us how the material interests of Ireland will be bettered by your proposals, and we will talk of change'. Were the industries of the north, Pollock asked, to be injured by a series of tariff wrangles with Great Britain? Turning to taxation, he pointed out that if Great Britain, as was certainly possible, adopted prohibition, Ulster would follow her example, and, assuming that the rest of Ireland remained 'wet', 'Irish finances would be in a hopeless muddle'. If however all Ireland went 'dry', the Irish farmers would use their political power to prevent agriculture being taxed to make up the resultant deficiency. Instead 'the northern industrialists would be overwhelmed by income and excess profits tax'.[42]

Understandably the Ulster unionists made no suggestions for constitutional change. But their unconstructive silence was exasperating. Twice about mid-September Lord MacDonnell's temper snapped. On the first occasion in a tone which Plunkett thought highly provocative, he appealed directly to the Ulstermen. 'In God's name', he said, 'declare your mind to us and with the help of God you will find us not unwilling to meet you'. Some sittings later, stung by their continued silence, he 'almost intimated they had come not to help but to wreck the convention'. This brought Barrie to his feet to state firmly that the Ulster delegation genuinely wanted to arrive at an agreement which 'they could honestly tell their people at home was likely to secure good government and prosperity for Ireland'.[43]

By the middle of September the debate was showing signs of flagging in spite of the presentation of Dunraven's and Moles's schemes, and a spirited letter from the chairman suggesting seven questions on which further discussion was desirable – for instance 'should Ireland be represented in the imperial parliament'. Members were becoming impatient. Towards the end of September Murphy felt that while the long-winded discussion had elicited opinions and got men acquainted with one another, it

[42] *Confidential report*, pp 13–14.
[43] Ibid. pp 25, 27.

had exhausted itself and that the time had come to find out if the 'Ulster extremists' were prepared to agree to anything. Midleton complained to the chairman that several members had told him that the delay was 'dissipating the atmosphere of the convention'.[44] And on 25 September the convention adopted a new procedure by instructing the grand committee to meet in October and frame a scheme which would 'meet the views and difficulties expressed by various speakers during the course of the debates'.

Plunkett was on the whole satisfied by the way things had gone during September. Before the middle of the month he reflected 'the convention is getting tired which is just what I want and I am working for. In another few weeks it will gladly adjourn and let a few of us get to work.' At the end of the month he felt that after the meetings in Cork the Ulster delegates were a little nearer to a settlement.[45] Another member of the convention, with a rather different standpoint, tended to agree with him. At the beginning of October, MacLysaght considered that the Ulster unionists had reached the point of being willing to 'come in' if there was fiscal unity with Great Britain and Irish representation at Westminster,[46] MacLysaght was convinced that 'these conditions are as bad for them as for us . . . so we may be able to break them down on these points'. And he circulated a memorandum in which he pointed out that at the end of the war the British national debt would amount to about £6,000 million, which would mean income tax at a rate ruinous to Ireland. He also argued in this memorandum that after the war Great Britain would probably adopt protection, which might easily lead to an increase in the price of steel adversely affecting Belfast shipbuilding. Irish agriculture on the other hand would not be encouraged by protection, the doctrine of a free breakfast table being deeply engrained in British fiscal policy.[47] George Russell thought the memorandum 'splendid', 'the best statement of the Irish case on the business side made by anyone in the convention'.[48]

[44] Murphy to W. L. Murphy, 23 Sept. 1917 (Murphy papers), Midleton to Plunkett (Plunkett letters).

[45] Plunkett, Diary, 13, 27 Sept. 1917.

[46] MacLysaght, Diary, 8 Oct. 1917.

[47] *Self-government and business interests: a memorandum* (1918). It seems to have been circulated in October 1917.

[48] A. Denison, *Letters of A.E.*, p 30.

But it made no impression on the Ulster unionists. In fact a member of their advisory committee, Duffin, in a slim pamphlet published in the summer of 1917, had to some extent answered MacLysaght in advance. 'With a nationalist government based upon shirking Irish responsibility to contribute her quota in men, money and work for the defence of liberty and the very life of the empire', Duffin wrote, Ulster, 'will have nothing to do'.[49] And some days before Plunkett and MacLysaght recorded their opinions on the Ulster unionist attitude, Barrie, the leader of the Ulster delegation, had defined his position in a confidential talk with Midleton. Barrie said he had come to the conclusion that 'no time so favourable for a settlement would ever recur as the present'. Though he admitted that he did not know how far he could carry his followers. He thought Ulster's interests would be better protected by a disproportionately large share in the representative body to be set up rather than by paper safeguards, and he emphasized that the control of customs by the imperial parliament and Irish representation at Westminster were a *sine qua non*. In conclusion, while wondering how far Redmond's demands for a parliament could be met, he expressed his determination to try to meet them.[50]

Barrie was obviously anxious in his talk with Midleton to be concilatory but his remarks show how wide was the gap between the Ulster group and the nationalists. And at the beginning of October Plunkett's optimism was temporarily dashed by a talk he had in London with Carson. Ulster's principal demand, Carson said, was that the Irish executive, in so far as it operated in Ulster, must not be controlled by a parliament sitting in Dublin. Plunkett strove to get from him a clear statement as to how this was to be arranged. But, he ruefully wrote, 'all I did succeed in getting admitted was that it was up to Ulster to answer these questions'.[51]

A few days before he met Carson, Plunkett received an ominous letter from a different quarter. Murphy wrote to tell him that, at the coming meeting of the grand committee, he

[49] A. Duffin *Thoughts and facts for the consideration of the Irish convention* (Belfast, 1917).

[50] Memorandum of interview with Barrie, 25 Sept. 1917 (Midleton papers).

[51] Plunkett to Cruise O'Brien, 5 Oct. 1917 (Plunkett letters).

was going to submit two resolutions. These enunciated that any scheme of self-government must apply to all Ireland and that the Irish parliament should be the only taxing authority for Ireland. 'I cannot see', Murphy explained, 'how the business of drafting a bill could be entered on with any degree of satisfaction . . . unless those who are entrusted with the task have some principles to guide them'. Plunkett must have seen that a discussion on Murphy's resolutions would irreparably divide the committee before it started one what he trusted would prove the consolidating activity of constitution-making. So he explained to Murphy that the best course would be to have a scheme which embodied Murphy's conditions tabled in the grand committee. And he tried to cheer Murphy by assuring him that the trouble with the Ulster delegates was 'not . . . disinclination on their part to make pretty large concessions but a genuine fear that it should get out prematurely in Sandy Row that they have made concessions at all'. Murphy recommended Russell as the best man to draft a scheme but at the same time forwarded his resolutions. So Plunkett in the end had on procedural grounds to refuse to put them on the grand committee's agenda. It was for the committee, he explained, to decide how it would proceed.[52]

When the grand committee did meet on 11 October in Trinity College, McDowell, 'pushing Barrie and Londonderry aside', declared that further debating over a scheme would be a sheer waste of time. He proposed therefore that a small sub-committee should be appointed 'for the purpose of negotiation between the leaders on the vital issues in dispute'. 'A few vital issues frankly faced, a little give and take and the rest was plain sailing'.[52A] Midleton, Redmond and Barrie were asked to choose the small sub-committee. They chose five nationalists, one southern unionist and three Ulster unionists.[53] And though the labour men on the grand committee 'kicked up a great row about the overlooking of labour it was agreed that these nine

[52] Murphy to Plunkett, 29 Sept., 1 Oct. 1917; Plunkett to Murphy, 30 Sept., 5 Oct. 1917 (Plunkett letters).
[52A] *Confidential report*, pp. 37–8; Plunkett to Desart, 14 Oct. 1917 (Plunkett letters).
[53] The members of the sub-committee were Redmond, Devlin, the bishop of Raphoe, W. M. Murphy, George Russell, Lord Londondarry, Barrie, Sir Alexander McDowell, and Lord Midleton. Sir Alexander McDowell, who was too ill to attend, was replaced by Pollock.

nominees should form the sub-committee. Plunkett was not placed on the sub-committee.[54] Midleton and Barrie, he wrote, 'both gave me hints which I took to mean my room would be preferable to my company'.[55] However, when the membership of the sub-committee of nine was announced to the grand committee, it was suggested that the chairman would be ex-officio a member of the sub-committee. Plunkett wisely said that he would rather not attend as he had so much to do. But after lunch the question was again raised in the grand committee and the discussion ended in Midleton 'saying in his most tactful way "we have considered the matter very carefully and were unanimous in *not* desiring the presence of the chairman at our deliberations"'.[56]

The next day there was 'a buzz of excitement in the convention premises, everyone talking about "the insult to the chairman"'.[57] But Plunkett was not the sort of man to allow resentment over a snub to interfere with his work. And almost immediately he was fortunately able by energetic intervention to save the convention from what he conceived to be an awkward contretemps. The sub-committee after being selected decided to adjourn for a fortnight and then meet in London. The delay and the transfer of the venue for a meeting to London dismayed Plunkett who thought they would provide material for the critics of the convention.[58] He at once summoned a fresh meeting of the grand committee. None of the Ulster delegates came, but eleven members attended and Plunkett persuaded them to set up three small sub-committees which would sit in Dublin to consider respectively the franchise and electoral systems, land purchase and local defence (including the Royal Irish Constabulary and the Dublin Metropolitan Police).

The first meeting of the sub-committee of nine, which was held after lunch on the day it was appointed, was not very fruitful. Murphy 'found the Ulstermen as far away as ever from showing any prospect of agreeing to anything, even the first

[54] MacLysaght, Diary, 10, 11 Oct. 1917.
[55] Plunkett to Desart, 14 Oct. 1917 (Plunkett letters).
[56] Granard to Asquith, 20 Oct. 1917 (Asquith papers 37).
[57] MacLysaght, Diary, 15 Oct. 1917.
[58] Plunkett to Bryce, 19 Oct. 1917, Plunkett to O'Donnell, 13 Oct. 1917 (Plunkett letters).

proposition that there should be a parliament in Dublin for the whole of Ireland'.[59] But when the sub-committee met a fortnight later for a couple of days in London at the Langham Hotel, after it was settled that 'provisional agreements arrived at during the debates were not to bind anybody' unless agreement upon a draft constitution was arrived at, the discussion began to advance. The establishment of an Irish parliament having been accepted as 'the basis of deliberation' or 'as a working hypothesis', the sub-committee got down to considering a home-rule scheme drafted by the bishop of Raphoe. During the two days it sat, fast progress was made. It was decided to tackle the composition of the Irish parliament before defining its powers. And on this subject the nationalists made considerable concessions. (It is scarcely necessary to say that under home rule the composition of the Irish parliament would probably have proved a more easily variable factor than its powers.) The elected senate provided in the home rule act of 1914 was replaced, in Plunkett's words, by a second chamber 'in which the church, the peerage, the privy council and organized commerce provided all the elements of stability or, as the unitiated might say, of reaction'. While as a concession 'to modern ideas', 'a decorative feature' was added – four representatives of labour. Moreover this very conservative senate was empowered to insist on a joint sitting with the lower house for a final decision on money bills as well as other measures.[60]

It was also agreed the unionists must be adequately represented in the lower house. According to Murphy, 'Barrie declared that unionist Ireland (i.e. protestant Ireland) would require half of the representation in the commons, adding that " he gave no heed to the protection of the upper house". At the same time Barrie pronounced himself to be a democrat . . . and that he was opposed to nominated members.' Proportional representation was mentioned as a possible solution, only to be rejected, as Plunkett acidly remarked, 'for the sufficient reason that disproportionate representation was the essential of compromise'. In the end it was decided that the unionists should be given 'by effective means' forty per cent of the membership of the house of commons, it being estimated that at a joint session

[59] Murphy to W. L. Murphy, 13 Oct. 1917 (Murphy papers).
[60] *Confidential report*, pp. 41–2.

of the two houses they would command half the votes. Murphy was not at all averse to Barrie's suggestion that the unionists should have extra seats in the commons, assuming that the arrangement was to last for a limited number of years (say ten). The unionists, he thought, if offered half the seats in the lower house could not object to the Irish parliament having ample powers. Moreover if the proposal was genuine it was the first hopeful sign of an agreed solution coming from the convention. However, he was quite prepared to find 'the Ulstermen in a nebulous condition when we meet again'.[61]

When the sub-committee met in Dublin at the end of October and at the beginning of November the nationalists reluctantly agreed to the Ulster demand that Ireland should be represented at Westminster. Then, when the sub-committee arrived at the financial clauses of the bishop of Raphoe's scheme, a deadlock ensued. The bishop's scheme gave the Irish parliament complete control over fiscal matters including of course customs and excise. A joint commission was to try to arrange a postal and customs union between Great Britain and Ireland. Failing agreement on any tariff question, the most-favoured-nation terms were to operate between the two countries. The Ulstermen insisted that these proposals were quite unacceptable. Murphy, a keen fiscal autonomist, sensed that if he were not on the sub-committee Redmond and Devlin might have made concessions, and he wrote that he 'got a kind of message, with what authority I don't know, wanting to know whether if they agreed to customs and excise being retained at Westminster I would refrain from attacking them'.[62]

Russell, apparently speaking for his fellow nationalists on the sub-committee, strongly supported the bishop's proposals. Then Hopwood, who Murphy thought 'most tactful and patient', made two attempts to produce an acceptable compromise. His aim, Plunkett explained, was 'to reconcile three apparently irreconcilable propositions: that Ireland should have complete fiscal autonomy, that she should maintain free trade with Great Britain, and that she should have power to protect her industries from unfair British competition. First he made 'a gallant attempt to square the circle' by granting the

[61] Murphy to W. L. Murphy, 28 Oct. 1917 (Murphy papers).
[62] Murphy to W. L. Murphy, 25 Nov. 1917 (Murphy papers).

Irish parliament full powers over customs and excise and then whittling down those powers by provisions guaranteeing free trade between the two islands by prohibiting either country from imposing duties on goods produced by the other. This scheme proving inacceptable to the Ulstermen, he tried another approach. He suggested that the imperial contribution that Ireland should make should be charged against the customs. This would make it convenient to keep customs under imperial control, but to render this palatable to nationalists he proposed that, if the yield from customs duties fell below the figure at which the imperial contribution should be fixed, the deficit should be irrecoverable, but that if there was a surplus the Irish exchequer should receive it.[63] The nationalists refused to discuss this scheme unless the Ulstermen intimated that they regarded it as a basis for discussion. The Ulstermen did not respond.

Meanwhile Plunkett himself intervened in an highly original manner. He decided to present the nine disputatious members of the sub-committee with an examination paper the answers to which, he hoped, would reveal the 'precise cause of their inability to subordinate their differences of economic faith to the supreme need of their distracted country'. Plunkett asked Pigou, the celebrated Cambridge economist who was staying with him, to draft the questions and he himself wrote a covering letter emphasizing that he wanted the fiscal question to be 'threshed out in its purely business aspects and that it should be assumed that the Irish parliament in its economic policy would be guided by common sense'.[64]

The examination paper consisting of ten questions was divided into two sections, the first to be answered by the Ulster representatives, the second by the nationalists. The questions for the Ulstermen were designed to discover what they feared from fiscal autonomy and how could their fears be met by a guarantee of free trade between Great Britain and Ireland, by a limitation of the expenditure permissible on bounties to industries, by special representation in the lower house or by a provincial veto. The second part of the paper aimed at eliciting

[63] *Report on the proceedings of the Irish convention*, p. 63; *Confidential report*, pp. 42–3, 51.
[64] *Confidential report*, p. 43.

from the nationalists what disadvantages they saw in fiscal union and what degree of fiscal autonomy they would be satisfied with – Irish control over direct taxation, or Irish control over direct taxation and excise but not customs, or over the rates of customs duties but not the selection of articles to be charged.[65] 'My Socratic method', Plunkett remarked to Bernard Shaw just after preparing the paper, 'has at least postponed the crisis but heaven only knows what is going to happen'. A couple of days later Shaw replied, 'I do not believe that the deadlock on the fiscal question can be got over as long as the minds of the parties contain nothing but stale tariff-reform twaddle. Their stock and trade must be enlarged by the notion that Ireland, in consideration of accepting federation with the other island, should insist on the pooling of certain services such as the postal and telegraph services and of the rent nationalized by supertaxation.' Shaw incidentally had tried to secure nomination to the convention, but according to himself this suggestion 'brought the British government and the Irish convention nearer to unanimity than was supposed possible'.[66]

Four of the nationalists, the bishop of Raphoe, Redmond, Devlin and Russell, drafted a reply in which they stated that to leave customs and excise under the control of the imperial parliament would give it a degree of control over direct taxation, deny Ireland responsibility for part of its own government, and remove trade and social policy, in so far as they could be influenced by these duties, from the control of the Irish parliament. Moreover, they were afraid that England, when deciding on its future fiscal policy, might not consider Ireland's interests. England might adopt industrial protection while retaining free trade in food, so that Ireland might find itself buying manufactured goods in a protected market and trying to sell its agricultural produce in the face of foreign competition. To meet the objections of their critics they suggested than an arrangement might be made to encourage free trade between Great Britain and Ireland. The fifth nationalist member of the sub-committee, Murphy, acting on his own, put in a laconic paper. If England

[65] *Report on the proceedings of the Irish convention*, pp. 44–5.

[66] Plunkett to Shaw, 7 Nov. 1917, Shaw to Plunkett, 9 Nov. 1917 (Add. MS 50547); G. B. Shaw, *How to settle the Irish question* (1917), pp. 5–6.

turned protectionist no attention would be paid to Irish interests. 'No British budget', Murphy pointed out, 'was ever directly affected by anything that could be done by Irish M.P.s'. Without fiscal autonomy Ireland could do little or nothing to encourage new industries. Partial fiscal autonomy would take away every incentive to economy.[67]

Plunkett was so impressed by 'the severely practical answers' the four nationalists gave to his 'severely practical questions' that he asked them to send a copy of their replies to the Ulster representatives on the sub-committee, since he was sure that 'the businessmen of Ulster could not have failed to be impressed by such an unexpected demonstration of economic sense in the dreamy agricultural south'. Before transmitting their replies to the Ulstermen the nationalists added a memorandum strongly defending fiscal autonomy as an important attribute of nationality. Ireland, they declared, was as a nation an economic entity. 'No nation', they asserted, 'with self-respect could accept the idea that, while its citizens were regarded as capable of creating wealth, they were regarded as incompetent to regulate the manner in which the taxation of that wealth should be arranged, and that another country should have the power of levying and collecting taxes, the taxed country being placed in the position of a person of infirm mind whose affairs are regulated by trustees'. And this vigorous doctrinaire defence of fiscal autonomy was forwarded to the Ulster representatives before the chairman had an opportunity to see it.[67A]

Having seen the nationalists' document, the Ulster unionists sent their reply to the chairman's examination paper in the form of a letter, composed of nine short, blunt paragraphs, signed by Barrie and Londonderry. They began by pointing out that the deadlock on the fiscal question rested 'on points of principle and not of detail'. Fiscal autonomy, they asserted, implied that Ireland would 'except for the sovereignty occupy the position of an independent nation'. This meant that in the 'welter of economic trouble' which would follow the war Ireland would be 'cut adrift' from the strongest economic power in the world. They were convinced that Ireland's interests could 'be best furthered in full community with the economic

[67] *Report of the proceedings of the Irish convention*, pp. 65–8.
[67A] *Confidential report*, pp. 46–8.

life of the great industrial people with whom we have so much in common and from whom we refuse to be divorced'. Plunkett thought the letter was 'so preposterous, in its misrepresentations, implications and pretensions that they cannot possibly stand over it, nor I think, would it be fair to the community they represent to treat it as final'.[68]

On 15 November, with this letter before them, the sub-committee of nine started to prepare a bleak report for the grand committee which was to meet on the 22nd. Unexpectedly the secretary of the Ulster group, Londonderry, suggested a line of approach which afforded a little hope. He offered to table a federal scheme at the next and last meeting of the sub-committee on the 21st.[69] Federalism was still in the air, the war having stimulated in England interest in schemes for strengthening imperial co-operation; Selborne, an ex-conservative minister with wide imperial experience, and Plunkett's friend, F. S. Oliver, had produced a pamphlet outlining a federal scheme for the British Isles in which Ireland would be one or two units. And immediately after Londonderry announced his intention of proposing a scheme, Plunkett forwarded a copy of this pamphlet to Barrie, remarking, 'I think you will find that when the federal as well as the dominion way of looking at the controversy has been put into the minds of the contestants, the atmosphere will be immensely improved'.[70]

Londonderry's move alarmed his associates and an influential member of the advisory committee, Adam Duffin, at once wrote to him at length. Duffin admitted that he was impressed by Londonderry's and Barrie's opinion that it was desirable that the Ulster unionists in the convention, while breaking with the nationalists over the demand for fiscal autonomy, should show 'readiness to consider if not initiate some alternative constitutional policy'. But he impressed upon Londonderry that any federal scheme should be expressed in the most general terms and should make 'large reservations' for Ulster (e.g. judiciary and education). He concluded his letter by suggesting that it was scarcely the time to be working on a new Irish constitution. All their energies ought to be absorbed by the war and it

[68] Plunkett to O'Donnell, 24 Nov. 1917 (Plunkett letters).
[69] *Confidential report*, p. 51.
[70] Plunkett to Barrie, 15 Nov. 1917 (Plunkett letters).

would be wise to wait and see if Sinn Fein is as the nationalists contended a passing phase'. However he quickly added, that the Ulster delegation had better not suggest the suspension of the convention as it might indicate weakness on their part.[71] Duffin's view prevailed. When the sub-committee met on 21 November Barrie announced that the Ulster group had decided that 'Londonderry's proposals should not be presented, as they did not think that such a course would ease the situation'.[72]

At this stage the southern unionists began to intervene energetically. Up to November 1917 they had played a relatively inconspicuous part in the convention. This was not because they were not concerned about the outcome of its deliberations. Conscious of their great traditions, of the value of their contribution to the community and of their political weakness, they were desperately anxious to secure a compromise which would go some way towards satisfying Irish national aspirations, maintain the connection between Ireland and Great Britain, preserve the unity of Ireland, and protect minorities. Though they represented a comparatively small section of the community they had the self-confidence bred by generations of governing, and their leaders, Midleton and Bernard, obviously believed that by a well-timed display of authoritive common-sense they could decisively influence the convention's proceedings.

When the convention met, the southern unionists seem to have hoped that they would be able to work with the Ulster delegation. But by the autumn they were striving to find common ground with the nationalists (or to try to get the nationalists to modify their position). Early in October Midleton and Bernard privately met Devlin in a house in Fitzwilliam Square. Midleton, having dwelt on the growth of the Sinn Fein movement, explained that the southern unionists, being anxious for 'the re-establishment of the law in Ireland', wanted a new chief secretary. 'Did Mr Devlin', Midleton asked, 'hold out any prospect of his being able to work side by side with the unionist forces in the struggle against Sinn Fein and in the maintenance of public order?' Devlin, after remarking that if the convention

[71] Duffin to Londonderry, 16 Nov. 1917 (Duffin papers).
[72] *Confidential report*, p. 52.

failed he would probably leave public life, replied to Midleton's question by saying that 'he hated Sinn Fein . . . but he was a home ruler, first of all, and he would not fight on behalf of any British rule in Ireland'. He would have nothing to do with coercive measures sponsored by Dublin Castle, but, believing time to be ripe for 'a dramatic stroke', he suggested that the convention should be entrusted with the government of Ireland. It was an assembly of Irishmen and he would support any executive it nominated. Neither Midleton nor Bernard welcomed this suggestion. Midleton argued that, if Redmond and his party put themselves at the head of all the stable forces in Ireland, 'a large number of so-called Sinn Feiners would rally to them'. Devlin, who clearly was not prepared to support any chief secretary, in a burst of realism said that if there was an immediate general election his party was finished. The unionist leaders considered that the interview 'was not very satisfactory although quite frank and friendly'. They thought that Devlin was obviously afraid that, if his party supported measures against Sinn Fein, it would be accused of having gone over to the unionists, and, naturally enough, they felt that he did not appreciate the sacrifices the unionists would have to make if they co-operated with the nationalists.[73]

Ten days later the parliamentary party took a course which the southern unionists must have deplored; they strongly attacked Duke in the house of commons for the measures he was taking to check the activities of the advanced nationalists. And Asquith to some extent supported the attack, remarking that he had noticed that there had always been in Ireland 'a good deal of what I may call rhetorical and contingent rebellion', which need not be taken very seriously. The unfortunate Duke, scarified by the nationalists and described by a conservative M.P. as an 'elderly lawyer politician' of the Birrell type, explained that he could not permit preparations for armed rebellion to go forward unimpeded.

In spite of this debate, at the beginning of November Midleton proposed to Bernard that they should try to have an interview with Redmond and the bishop of Raphoe. He suggested they should begin by pointing out that 'face saving', while it kept discussion going in the convention, would achieve

[73] Memorandum on meeting, 12 Oct. 1917 (Add. MS 52782).

nothing. They should then go on to press the nationalists to agree to Irish representation at Westminster and the control of customs duties by the imperial parliament. The control of excise could be left open to discussion. Bernard endorsed the letter in which Midleton outlined his suggestion: 'Refused to take part as unlikely to lead to result'.[74]

But three weeks later Bernard himself intervened energetically and effectively. When the grand committee met on 22 November and began to discuss the deadlock which had halted the work of the sub-committee, Barrie asserted that he saw no half-way house between the Ulster position on the fiscal question and the nationalists' demands; and Pollock, backing him up, declared there were 'insurmountable obstacles to any compromise'. Bernard however 'insisted that a mere *non possumus* would not do'. He won widespread support, and, yielding to the general feeling in the committee, Pollock and the bishop of Raphoe remarshalled their familiar arguments. A general discussion developed in which Redmond expressed his readiness to listen to suggestions for a compromise, and Barrie went so far as to admit that an Irish parliament must have some taxing power and that there must be a responsible financial authority in Ireland. Finally Lord Midleton 'took the plunge' and produced his basis for a compromise. He proposed that the Irish parliament should have control of internal taxation, including excise duties, but that customs duties should remain under the control of the imperial parliament.[75]

The Midleton scheme was defended in 'a memorandum on fiscal autonomy' circulated by the southern unionists at the end of November. In it they declared that they had entered the convention with the object of discovering what concessions could be made to the nationalists 'with safety to the empire, security for the minority, and if possible the participation of all sections in Irish government'. They had assumed from the outset that the Irish parliament would be genuinely subordinate to the British, but the discussions on fiscal autonomy had opened up 'a new vista of Irish aims which was wholly unexpected by us'. Fiscal autonomy meant that Ireland would be free 'to play her own hand' in foreign affairs. In short 'a government on the

[74] Midleton to Bernard, 4 Nov. 1917 (Add. MS 52781).
[75] *Confidential report*, p. 55.

colonial model' would be set up only a few miles from the shores of Great Britain. The southern unionists were prepared to allow the Irish parliament to control internal taxation, the administration of the country, the judicature and the police. On these lines, they believed, 'all legitimate national aspirations will be satisfied'. 'We are not prepared', they added, 'to jeopardise the imperial connection by conceding more extreme demands. . . . We have gone, we believe, to the extreme limit of safety from the imperial standpoint.'[76] The evening after this memorandum was circulated, the Ulster unionist delegates and members of their advisory committee had what Duffin described as 'a very interesting pow-wow with the southern unionist lot'. 'They want', he wrote indignantly, 'to capitulate and make terms with the enemy lest a worse thing befall them. They are a cowardly crew and stupid to boot . . . We shall do all we can to stiffen them and keep them in our ranks and they may be driven to reconsider their position.'[77]

The southern unionists met with a better reception in London when, early in December, Midleton and Bernard had an interview with Lloyd George and Curzon. Just before this interview Southborough wrote to Adams expressing the hope that the prime minister 'will make much of the southern unionists. We have got them with blood and tears.' Southern unionist support for a settlement, Southborough argued, 'should enable the government to differentiate between the old and new position' and to push through a home rule bill, with the southern unionists holding 'a watching brief for reasonable Ulster'. Having dealt with issues of major policy Southborough begged Adams not to allow Lloyd George 'to call Bernard "Dr Bernard", as he does not like it; "Archbishop" is the thing'.[78]

When they met Lloyd George and Curzon, the southern unionist leaders suggested that Ulster, if pressed by the government, might be willing to acquiesce in a settlement which granted administrative autonomy to the northern area. The only chance of moving Ulster from its *non possumus* position was

---

[76] *Report on the proceedings of the Irish convention*, pp. 83–4.
[77] Duffin to ———, 28 Nov. 1917 (Duffin papers).
[78] Southborough to Adams, 4 Dec. 1917 (Lloyd George papers, F 65/1/21).

by 'suggesting she would probably fare worse in the future when the next parliament was in being'. The prime minister praised the memorandum as 'statesmanlike', and agreed that Ulster by clinging to its old policy was running risks. 'But', Bernard noted, 'he did not say (and did not promise) that she would be forced into a settlement'. Midleton suggested that the lord lieutenant and the chief secretary might be replaced by five lords justices, chosen to represent the main political groups. Bernard expressed no opinions on this suggestion, simply stressing the growing danger from Sinn Fein and the determination of the southern unionists never to agree to the division of Ireland.[79]

A week later, shortly before the convention again assembled, Bernard and Midleton had an inconclusive conference with Redmond at Iveagh House. Midleton began by asking could conscription be applied to Ireland. Redmond, though anxious that Ireland should do its duty in the war, replied that an attempt to extend conscription to Ireland would wreck any hope of a settlement. Fear of conscription was, he believed, the main force behind Sinn Fein. 'The young men in the country', he said, 'to show that they were not cowards, had joined the Sinn Fein forces, but their real motive was to avoid enlistment for service in the British army'. When they got down to discussing the work of the convention, Redmond thought a compromise could be formulated by fusing the southern unionists' memorandum and Southborough's suggestions. He himself would have supported such a compromise if he still had the power he had possessed eighteen months earlier, but now, he added sadly, he could not answer for the country. He also said that Lloyd George had told him that, if the nationalists agreed to the southern unionists' terms, he would accept them, 'giving Ulster the go bye'. Finally Midleton again mentioned his scheme for the government of Ireland by five lords justices representing the parties. The archbishop said that it would not work, Redmond said it would be unconstitutional. The conference ended with Redmond assuring the unionists that, if the convention reached agreement, the catholic bishops would strongly support the settlement and forbid the clergy to oppose it. Midleton emphasized that the points to which the southern

[79] Memorandum, 5 Dec. 1917 (Add. MS 52781).

unionists attached supreme importance were the war and the restoration of order in Ireland.[80]

At the same time Midleton tried to make his position absolutely clear to Plunkett. Writing to him as an old friend, he said frankly that he had not thought that a 'general exploration' of schemes and subjects would have led to agreement. And in fact, as the discussions had gone on, the contending parties had hardened. Now a crisis had come and Midleton, having put his cards on the table, was not prepared to spend his time talking about other issues unless the customs and excise question was settled. If the fiscal difficulty was not immediately faced he would not take part in the discussion in the grand committee. Nothing, he thought, would bring the Ulstermen and Redmond to accept a settlement except the prospect of the convention failing. Plunkett by return of post gave a soft answer. He assured Midleton that 'we see eye to eye' on the next move. The time had come to ask the Ulster unionists to say on what terms they would come into an Irish parliament. If their reply was '"on no terms whatsoever" we are entitled to say and every impartial outsider will say "you have no right to come into the convention and conceal so long your intentions".' On the other hand, if Ulster stated obviously impossible terms, the next step would have to be carefully considered. What Plunkett perceived as a possibility with immense potentialities for good was an alliance between the southern unionists and the nationalists, an alliance which could put pressure on the northern unionists. And he suggested there should be a conference between the southern unionists and the nationalists. 'If perchance', he wrote to Midleton, 'Redmond and you were completely agreed upon the terms of compromise to be offered to Ulster, it is not at all improbable that Ulster's *non possumus* would be reconsidered'. Dunraven, Plunkett was sure, would support Midleton, and Plunkett thought that Dunraven had considerable influence over MacDonnell and Murphy (though, Plunkett added, with an unusual touch of pessimism, hardly as much as was required in the case of Murphy). Midleton replied by return, registering that he was not quite in agreement with Plunkett as to the next step. Plunkett had suggested a conference between the southern

[80] Two memoranda referring to the meeting, dated 12 and 13 Dec. 1917 (Add. MS 52782).

unionists and the nationalists. But this, Midleton pointed out, implied that it would be possible 'to make a bridge between our terms and theirs'. This, he said was 'out of the question'. He was, he explained, quite prepared to help the chairman to bring pressure on both the Ulster unionists and the nationalists. 'But', he wrote to Plunkett, 'you must please realize, and make the nationalists realize, that I am not going to give way one step further. As it is I doubt if I can carry many of my friends on this side.'[81]

At the time he was conducting this correspondence with Midleton, Plunkett had a very depressing meeting with Redmond at the house of commons. Redmond, Plunkett wrote, 'laid himself bare. He, I am afraid, will not stick to his guns and fight for a settlement. He sticks to the customs, admitting that the popular clamour is so ignorant that many people believe the dispute is whether a sum of 6 or 7 millions is to go into English or Irish pockets'.[82]

By the beginning of December the convention had not met for over two months, and some of the members were getting restive. So the chairman summoned a meeting for the 18 December. He opened the proceedings with an address in which he emphasized the value of the work done by the sub-committee on land purchase, their report constituting 'a monument of industry and of historic value'. He praised the 'exemplary conduct' of the labour men on the electoral systems committee who had recognized that there was no hope of an agreed settlement 'without some very undemocratic arrangements'. Coming to Midleton's scheme, he was careful not to give any opinion as to its merits, but he did point out that, if it was accepted that the control of customs should not be reserved to the imperial parliament, the convention 'should leave the Irish question just where it had been, with all the nationalists for home rule and all the unionists against'. He ended by explaining that his task was child's play compared to Washington's at the Philadelphia convention of 1787 – Washington had half a dozen Ulsters to deal with.

Midleton then gave notice of a motion he intended to propose

[81] Midleton to Plunkett, 6 and 8 Dec. 1917, Plunkett to Midleton, 7 Dec. 1917 (Plunkett papers).
[82] Plunkett, Diary, 4 Dec. 1917.

at the next meeting to the effect that, if an Irish parliament were set up, the control of imperial services, including customs, should be reserved to the imperial parliament, the Irish parliament controlling all purely Irish services, including taxation. Lord MacDonnell and Stephen Gwynn both welcomed Midleton's proposal as providing the basis for a settlement. Murphy tried to get the Ulstermen to express an opinion on it. Writing in confidence, he explained: 'I want them to reject it first . . . As I am opposed to half measures being accepted, such an attitude would greatly strengthen my hand.' But the Ulstermen avoided the trap. Barrie, having paid a tribute to Midleton's eloquent and impressive speech, explained that the northern unionists would have to refer his proposal to their advisory committee. Having regretted that the proposal made an advance on the fiscal provisions of the 1914 act, he hoped that the convention would disperse in a hopeful spirit – the spirit of Christmas and a larger charity.[83]

On the same day, 18 December, immediately after the convention adjourned, the Ulster delegation met to consider Midleton's scheme. They decided to move two amendments, one stating specifically that the imperial parliament had the right to impose conscription, the other reserving to the imperial parliament the control of excise as well as customs. A fortnight later, on new year's day 1918, the delegation, meeting in Belfast, not only reaffirmed its decision to present these two amendments but decided that a scheme for exclusion should be 'put in' – it being left to the chairman of the group to decide the point at which this should be done.[84]

After the convention adjourned, the nationalist group (with Redmond snowed up in Wicklow) discussed the Midleton proposals amongst themselves. Devlin seems (for the moment) to have been favourable; McCarron (the labour representative from Derry) remarked: 'if we do not accept Midleton we would get nothing'; two county councillors, McDonagh from Galway and Brodrick from Youghal, were concerned about how the amount of the Irish revenue was to be ascertained but seem to have been implicitly in favour of the proposals. Dr O'Donnell was 'very strong against agreeing with Midleton', arguing that

[83] *Confidential report*, pp. 57–8.
[84] Minutes of the Ulster delegation, 1, 2, 3, Jan. 1918.

if the nationalists stood firm the government would split the difference between them and Midleton. Stephen Gwynn retorted that, in his opinion, 'no agreement, no legislation'.[85]

Gwynn, who was soon to come to the fore as leader of the section of the nationalists who were eager for an alliance with the southern unionists, had already expressed his views in a memorandum addressed to Redmond, which he said could be shown to O'Donnell and Devlin. He admitted that, if the nationalist leaders recommended a dominion home-rule scheme with large representation for Ulster, both the southern and the Ulster unionists would vote against it. On the other hand, if they drew up a report which the southern unionists would agree to, Murphy would break away and the *Independent* come out against them. He realized too that O'Donnell was bound to be influenced by his friendship with Devlin, and that 'Devlin's instincts will be to seek to rally and hold together nationalist forces by increasing the movement in the direction of Sinn Fein. Devlin's lifelong opposition to the Orangemen will push him in the same way. Russell will be driven and help to drive in the same direction by his economic theories. He is theory-ridden and is largely responsible for the present concentration on the taxing power as the sole instrument for national development.' What then did Gwynn suggest should be done? He argued that the 'line of real advance' was to bring Irishmen together 'in practicable association and unity will develop'. Was it, Gwynn asked, intolerable that Ulstermen with great localized business interests should distrust the business capacity of a new parliament mainly representing agriculture? Given an Irish parliament, it would demand and get increased financial freedom. Gwynn was therefore ready, for the sake of getting a parliament by agreement, that all Ireland should accept for a term of years a scheme of 'contract finance' (that is to say a scheme which provided that taxation in Ireland should be imposed by the imperial parliament and a sum of money handed over annually to the Irish government). The alternative, he pointed out, might be 'permanent partition'. Gwynn was convinced that the policy he advocated was the best in the circumstances. But he was afraid that it would not be adopted by his party. The party, he wrote, was being led by Redmond,

[85] Gwynn to Redmond, 29 Dec. 1917 (Redmond papers).

Devlin and O'Donnell. And the two last named were probably in touch with Dillon, whose policy was certainly not Redmond's. Writing, 'with brutal frankness', to Redmond, he said: 'I fear, as too often happens, Dillon and not you will shape the line. Dillon has more tenacity and more persistence and by these qualities he has again and again, as I am convinced (and God knows I am not single in that opinion), prevailed against your larger and wiser judgement.'[86]

About the time he was pressing his leader to work with the southern unionists, Gwynn was trying to persuade the government to take some that action would encourage southern unionist-nationalist co-operation. He suggested to Adams that the government should give a written guarantee to Midleton and Redmond that if a report was agreed to by all sections in the convention except the Ulster unionists, the government would introduce legislation based on it. Adams replied that it was impossible for the government to give such a guarantee. Before taking action it would have to see the report and know what measure of agreement it represented.[86A]

During December 1917 there was some justification for believing that the convention was moving towards a settlement. There was a faint indication that the Ulster unionists might not prove immovable. Londonderry seems to have told Plunkett and Southborough 'that if a good scheme was produced under the auspices of the southern unionists' it would justify him in pressing for a reconsideration of the position by the northern unionists.[86B] There was a possibility too that the bulk of the nationalists might accept the Midleton proposals. Shortly after Midleton circulated his memorandum, Powell had a talk with the bishop of Ross, 'the brain-carrier of the sane nationalists'. The bishop, Powell reported to Midleton, 'told me your statement contained the basis of a settlement and I think he can carry the Murphy – AE – Lysaght section'. The bishop attempted to discuss customs in 'a fair minded way', arguing that

[86] Memorandum by Gwynn, 17 Nov. 1917; Gwynn to Redmond, 17 Nov. 1917 (Redmond papers).

[86A] Gwynn to Adams, 22 Dec. 1917, Adams to Gwynn – (Lloyd George papers, F 66/1/57).

[86B] Southborough to Adams, 17 Dec. 1917, Plunkett to Londonderry, 21 Dec. 1917 (Lloyd George papers, F 65/1/29, F 64/5/8),

even tariff reformers realized that duties could not be imposed on food imported into England, and that England might impose duties on raw materials in a form which would hit Belfast; but he did not press the matter when Powell told him that Midleton was 'inexorable' on that point and that the southern unionists would adhere to his leadership. 'One supreme consideration', in Powell's opinion, that nationalists had to keep in mind was that any scheme which handed over the control of customs to an Irish parliament was bound to be fiercely opposed in both the house of commons and the house of lords. Though he thought the future 'clouded and overcast', Powell was sure the Ulstermen would accept the inevitable if the rest of the convention were in agreement, and he had heard the cheering news that, if the convention agreed on a constitution, seventy or eighty per cent of the Sinn Feiners would accept it.[87] Moreover Murphy, who was determined not to cede the control of customs to the imperial parliament, had an uneasy feeling that 'Devlin, Clancy and Co. would be glad if they could get agreement on the southern unionist basis if they could safely give their adherence to it without their lost popularity being continued'. Murphy was not sure even of the bishop of Raphoe. He seemed 'a whole hogger' on the fiscal issue. 'But if Redmond bolts', Murphy wrote, 'he will probably follow as well as the bulk of the county council chairmen'.[88]

The bishop of Raphoe at this time was being subjected to considerable pressure. A moderate fiscal autonomist, his position in the nationalist group might be described as being left of centre. Obviously, therefore, his reaction to the Midleton proposals would have considerable influence on the group as a whole. Midleton at the beginning of January 1918 appealed to O'Donnell to support his amendment, arguing that the government would be greatly influenced by the size of the majority behind any scheme produced by the convention. And he stressed that the southern unionists had gone as far as they could. 'If we went further', he wrote, 'we should not only lose the support of our own people but turn the attitude of Ulster from that of non-acceptance to militant opposition'. He added a possibly somewhat tactless *argumentum ad hominem*: if the

[87] Powell to Midleton, 1 Dec. 1917 (Midleton papers).
[88] Murphy to W. L. Murphy, 22 Dec. 1917 (Murphy papers).

catholic bishops in the convention played a prominent part in the defeat of southern unionist compromise, it would strengthen the theory that the hierarchy did not really want home rule and would help those who were against all concessions to Ireland.[89]

On the other hand, George Russell about the same time, tried to impress on the bishop of Raphoe that, if the nationalists accepted the Midleton compromise, the Ulstermen would seize on that acceptance as a starting point for further negotiations. Russell was convinced that the 'bold attitude, the demand for full fiscal autonomy, is the best and only one that will result in us winning anything'. The government, he prophesied, would desert Ulster if Ireland remained firm and the empire was in danger.[90] Murphy fired a salvo of letters at the bishop in which he bluntly stated his views. He saw no hope of the Ulstermen agreeing to anything and he 'would not approve of an incomplete scheme to bring them into an agreement in the hope that in years to come they would be more amenable'. He thought the nationalists should 'press without faltering their demand for full fiscal powers for the Irish parliament' and that the best procedure for the convention to follow would be to arrange for each section to produce its own report and leave the responsibility for further action to the government.[91] About the same time MacLysaght was pressing the bishop to agree to positive and drastic action on the part of the nationalist group. He thought the group should draft and get accepted by the convention as quickly as possible a majority report, stating in the most unreserved terms the Irish claim for full dominion powers – which would of course imply fiscal autonomy and no representation at Westminster. The report, having outlined the southern unionist proposals, would declare that the nationalists would have accepted them in spite of their defects if the Ulster unionists (who, MacLysaght thought were throwing dust in Plunkett's eyes) had done so.[92]

The bishop of Raphoe himself was trying to make up his mind what was the best course to follow. Towards the end of December, writing to Redmond, he agreed that the southern unionists

[89] Midleton to O'Donnell, 7 Jan. 1918 (Logue 19).
[90] Russell to O'Donnell, n.d. (Logue 20).
[91] Murphy to O'Donnell, 29 Dec. 1917, 1, 2 Jan. 1918 (Logue 19).
[92] MacLysaght to O'Donnell, 1, 5 Jan. 1918 (Logue 19, 20).

had 'made a remarkable advance'. But they had not advanced on the fiscal question and the northern unionists had not made their attitude clear. In these circumstances for the nationalists 'to water down . . . with the danger of getting left, would seem to me to be a crazy proceeding. The southern unionists are our helpers in this matter, but any compromise that is not with the north is no good, for an agreed settlement at least.[93] A week later writing to Murphy, the bishop stated the same point of view but with a different emphasis. He told Murphy that he thought they could have the support of a solid majority in the convention for their policy of fiscal autonomy. And, he added, he was against 'watering down' their programme for the sake of an agreement with the southern unionists, because such an agreement would be still further watered down before it reached the statute book. But, O'Donnell emphasized, he saw a great difference in an agreement with the southern unionists and an agreement with Ulster. He reminded Murphy that at one stage in the committee of nine 'our Ulster friends said "let us begin with limited powers such as our people may be got to agree to and let us then later reunitedly demand larger powers when we feel we need them".' He concluded by stating that he 'inclined to think that Ireland as a whole would be strong against rejecting a settlement with Ulster that set up an Irish parliament with British taxing power at the start'.[94]

Plunkett, on the other hand, was afraid the bishop was determined not to come to terms with Midleton, because, as he had explained to Plunkett, he was convinced that if the nationalists were firm the government in the end would sweep away unionist resistance. Nevertheless, in a conversation with Plunkett the bishop made an admission which would have confirmed Murphy's fears. He granted that the situation would have been entirely different if the Ulstermen had joined Lord Midleton.[95]

At the close of December, Plunkett made an attempt to secure Devlin's support for the Midleton scheme. He explained to him that the reason why the southern unionists favoured imperial control of customs was because their main objective was the

[93] D. Gwynn, *Life of John Redmond*, pp. 575–6.
[94] O'Donnell to Murphy, 30 Dec. 1917 (Logue 18).
[95] Plunkett to Redmond, 18 Dec. 1917 (Plunkett papers).

maintenance of Irish representation at Westminster. 'The Irish landlords', he wrote, 'have a big family connection with imperial service. To them the large freedom of separate tariffs even if (as they do not believe) it were of material advantage to Ireland, does not give to the dominion status a tenth part of the national pride and influence which Ireland's participation in imperial affairs under their plan would secure.' But having given Devlin this insight into the southern unionist mentality, Plunkett went on to assure him that, once a united Ireland had 'a home parliament', any powers which 'the material welfare of Ireland might demand', would ultimately be granted to it. Should Midleton's scheme secure unanimous nationalist support, Plunkett argued, the Ulster delegation might see what it could do with friends in the north. 'That to me', Plunkett declared, 'would be an ideal evolution towards an ultimate settlement'.

Devlin was not convinced that Plunkett's optimism was justified. He thought it would be a mistake for the nationalists to assent to a settlement 'which would not satisfy the unionist Orangemen and which would let loose again with fresh intensity all those violent forces condemned in the past by everyone anxious for a peaceful settlement'. The Irish party, in Devlin's opinion, had been almost destroyed by the intense desire it had shown over the past ten years for a reconciliation with England and the Ulster protestants, and he himself during the last five years had been often unwillingly drawn into supporting proposals for a settlement, 'which had turned out unsatisfactory to the people of Ireland and even then did not materialize'. What he wanted to know was, would the British government regard an agreement between the nationalists, the southern unionists and the labour representatives as a substantial agreement. And he also wanted Midleton, when the convention met, to press the Ulster unionists to state what their position was. 'If the Ulster unionists stand out and continue to adopt a policy of veiled, implacable hostility to every effort made to bring about peace on home-rule lines, then I do not think it is for Irish nationalists to keep on sacrificing things they regard as vital.' Plunkett replied immediately that he believed that, if the nationalists, the southern unionists and labour agreed on a plan, the government would tell the Ulster unionists that if they did not come into it coercion would be applied. The situation, Plunkett considered, was very different from what it had been in 1914 or even 1916. There was now a larger measure of agreement in Ireland, the house of lords would be persuaded by Midleton's friends to accept a plan approved by the southern unionists, and 'after a splutter by Sinn Fein' the whole world would be behind the settlement.[96]

[96] Plunkett to Devlin, 22, 28 Dec. 1917; Devlin to Plunkett, 26 Dec. 1917 (Plunkett papers).

IV

THE CONVENTION, 1918

THE CONVENTION'S FIRST MEETING in 1918 was held on 2 January, and 'after much waste of time about procedure' (apparently caused by the necessity of getting an amendment of Murphy's transferring customs to the Irish parliament post-poned),[1] Midleton began a three days debate by moving the motion of which he had given notice in December. His motion was to the effect that if an Irish parliament was established it would have control over all purely Irish services, including excise duties, the levying of customs duties being reserved to the imperial parliament. Midleton 'took Raphoe's paper (on fiscal autonomy) to pieces with much ability', arguing that it was calculated to confirm the fears of Ulstermen, who considered the closest possible relations with Great Britain essential to their industry and commerce. Dunraven, seconding Midleton, showed how many concessions both the nationalists and the southern unionists had made. He himself had decided not to press for a federal plan (though he thought the new Irish constitution could be fitted into a federal scheme). He defended his change of front on fiscal autonomy by explaining that he had advocated it because he had 'misgivings about hostile action from England'. Now he had come to the conclusion Ireland could defend herself. Two other peers, Desart and Oranmore, both supported Midleton. Desart pointed out to the nationalists how many concessions the southern unionists had made,

[1] Mahaffy notes.

appealed to the north to help, and declared that a proposal to give the control of customs to an Irish parliament could never be carried in England. Gwynn thought Desart's speech 'an able argument',[2] Mahaffy's comment on it was, 'not very audible, nothing new'. Oranmore pointed out that in all federal systems taxation was in the hands of the federal government, not 'the small parliament', and that the position of the unionists in the new Irish parliament would be so much better than it would have been under the 1914 act that 'Belfast should allow it larger powers'. Indeed, he thought that, if the Midleton proposal was accepted, the only possible Irish government would be 'unionist in its complexion'. Another peer, Londonderry, retorted, according to Mahaffy's notes: 'Oranmore's conversion too recent . . . won't take his advice'.

A number of other members supported the Midleton compromise. Kavanagh, a country gentleman and the chairman of a county council, made, in what Mahaffy described as 'a really good speech', 'a most moving appeal for agreement'. He said 'we must all give in something. We must make concessions.' Indeed he was prepared to give the unionists forty per cent representation on the county councils as well as in parliament. Speaking as an imperialist and a protestant, he called on the north to accept the compromise. Another protestant nationalist, Gwynn, repudiated the notion that by accepting the compromise nationalists were 'hauling down the flag'. And, alluding to a remark of Bernard's to the effect that the customs duties would be collected by Irishmen, he said that this would greatly weaken the nationalists' opposition to Midleton's scheme, since 'Ireland will know all about it' (the working of the tariff system). He was interrupted by Midleton who said the archbishop had only made a suggestion. Gwynn prophesied that labour would not allow indirect taxation to rise, 'hence Ireland should be safe in its hands'. And he appealed to the Ulster members 'to put the thing boldly to their people'. 'Ulster trade', he declared, 'is as dear to us as to them'.

MacDonnell reiterated that he still favoured full fiscal autonomy – subject to the qualification that there should be free trade between Great Britain and Ireland. But appreciating that 'the southern unionists were for appeasement', he supported the

[2] S. Gwynn, *John Redmond's last years* (1919), p. 318.

Midleton compromise, emphasizing however that the collection of customs duties should be under the control of the Irish government. Andrews said that the Dublin and Cork chambers of commerce would accept imperial control of customs at least for the duration of the war. Windle, from Cork, stressing 'the good feeling which had radiated from the room, declared that though a fiscal autonomist he accepted the compromise. Dempsey, a catholic from Belfast, agreed to the Midleton scheme, though he hoped that the duties on tea and sugar, 'the food of the poor', would be controlled by the Irish parliament. Whitley, a labour man, who declared himself to be an imperialist, agreed with Midleton, emphasizing that it was better for the present that customs should be under imperial control. And he made what Plunkett termed 'the significant remark', that if Ulster working men could hear the debates in the convention they would see that the danger to their interests from an Irish parliament was wholly imaginary'.[2A] Plunkett reported that another labour man, McCarron, also supported Midleton. But according to Mahaffy, McCarron said that 'they must have full fiscal autonomy and so far differed from Lord Midleton'.

On the first day of the debate Murphy, who felt they had 'been evading (I might say dodging)' the fiscal issue, made a frank, forcible speech. Control of customs, was, he argued, 'the most essential right that a country with any pretence to self-government should possess and without which no country can have any real control over its most important interests'. If a country was denied control over customs it could not develop its trade and industry. On the other hand, he argued, it was unreasonable to suppose that customs were 'an imperial right'. The Channel islands, Trinidad and Jamaica all had control of customs duties. The convention, he emphasized, which did not represent half the country, had 'to make a bold bid to capture the imagination of the people'. 'I did not come here', he said, 'to find a way to make the loyalists more loyal – some of them are more loyal than the king already . . . The purpose I came for was to find a means for converting a disloyal into a loyal people, to make friends of the unfriendly and to put my country on the way to prosperity and contentment by endowing it with a free constitution.' Sinn Fein, he thought, was only 'a name which

[2A] *Confidential Report*, p. 61.

represented an ideal. If you satisfy the sentiment behind it, it would cease to exist as a militant body, and some of the men who compose it would probably be amongst the best elements of the new Ireland.'[3]

Murphy was supported by the bishop of Raphoe, who wanted Ireland to have the power to impose tariffs to prevent unfair competition and dumping. He expressed the hope that Midleton would agree to limit the period during which the imperial parliament would control customs (which implied that the bishop seems to have been at this point prepared to consider the reservation of customs to the imperial parliament for a term of years). Mahaffy thought his speech 'rambling'. It seems to have impressed Plunkett, who was especially struck by the bishop's emphasis on the importance of customs duties to a country such as Ireland, since indirect taxation was bound to press more heavily on the poor than on the rich.

Barrie summed up the northern unionist standpoint in a phrase – 'we came here to find some compromise between the act of 1914 and what has since been suggested' – the latter alternative being partition. But, he complained, the nationalists, 'entirely owing to outside influences', had enlarged their demands since 1914, which was 'not fair to Ulster'. Barrie hoped that the convention would agree on some modest scheme. Once an Irish parliament was established, he believed that the Ulster unionists would, if they were satisfied that it was wise and for the good of the empire that further powers should be given to the new parliament, join in securing 'a larger amount of elbow room for a parliament that had proved itself worthy of trust and confidence'.

On the last day of the debate Redmond spoke. On the evening of 2 January, at a meeting of the nationalists, 'with the art of which he was a master', Redmond had 'indicated support for the Midleton proposal without forcing a conclusion'. An immediate agreement, he pointed out, would enable them to obtain facilities for land purchase and protect Ireland against the burden of war taxation. Clancy, 'in his downright manner said he would not yet press his view publicly', but in the privacy of the meeting he admitted that he would not reject the Midleton offer for the sake of taxes on tea and sugar. It was also

[3] Murphy papers.

pointed out that the nationalists should not run the risk of driving the southern unionists and Ulstermen together against them. On the other side it was argued that, by accepting the proposal, Ireland was giving up the management of the taxes which pressed on the poor, and there was no guarantee that the proposal would be embodied in legislation. But, in Gwynn's opinion, the general sense of the meeting was in favour of accepting.[4]

When two days later Redmond addressed the convention it was in 'his best vein'.[5] He emphasized the sacrifices for the sake of agreement made by the nationalists, the southern unionists, and labour. Then he attacked the Ulster delegates as being pledge-bound to consult an outside body and for refusing 'to give an inch'. Surely this attitude, so unworthy of Ulster, did not represent its last word? For himself, his only remaining ambition was, having brought the convention to a successful conclusion, to serve under the first unionist prime minister of Ireland. It seemed to Mahaffy 'a very telling speech', and that afternoon Redmond tabled an amendment to Midleton's motion asking the convention to agree to Midleton's proposals provided that they were adopted by the government as a settlement of the Irish question and legislative effect given to them forthwith. This amendment, drafted by an old parliamentary hand, was obviously designed to attract the hesitant nationalists by throwing the responsibility for making a success of the convention back on the government.

At the beginning of January it seemed as if a large majority of the convention might agree on a settlement along the lines laid down by Midleton and Redmond. Goodwill was in the air, and it looked as if the fervent fiscal autonomists and the Ulstermen might find themselves isolated and that the convention might succeed in producing a scheme that would command widespread support in the country. In the middle of the debate, on the night of 3 January, a great party, attended by the whole convention, was given by Lord and Lady Granard. It was, in Gwynn's opinion, 'the most festive moment of our comradeship'; and according to Midleton, Barrie, on leaving the house, turned to him and said, 'I think you can count on us. We shall

[4] S. Gwynn, *John Redmond's last years*, pp. 318–19.
[5] *Confidential report*, p 63.

certainly not be against you.' Admittedly, just after being the recipient of this outburst of cautious friendliness, Midleton was walked round the Green until two in the morning by a catholic bishop (probably MacRory of Down) who kept asking at intervals, 'what would prevent the English parliament ruining Irish trade as in the eighteenth century?'[6]

But for ten days the convention dropped the discussion of the constitutional question, during its meetings in the second week of January debating a scheme of land purchase. In his contemporary report Plunkett explains that the reason for adjourning the constitutional debate was to enable Midleton and other members of parliament to attend at Westminster. And in fact Midleton did take part in a lords' debate on 8 January. Midleton himself, writing nearly twenty years later, complained sharply that at this critical moment Plunkett 'found reason for postponing the discussion from the first week in January until certain committees had reported', thus giving the extremists on both wings an opportunity to press their views on members of the convention.[6A] But though Midleton's memory was at fault, his complaint reflects his feelings of twenty years earlier when he had been extremely critical of Plunkett as chairman of the convention. It seems obvious now that, by the beginning of 1918, speed, which would take full advantage of generous emotional impulses, was essential if a settlement was to be achieved. A more autocratic chairman would probably at this point have driven the convention hard. But Plunkett, though he had great determination, had too much respect and liking for his fellow men to act the autocrat. Also, it is not unfair to say that he had a strong predilection for a debate on land purchase. Not only was rural improvement his main interest in life, but land purchase was a subject on which Irishmen of very different opinions had in the past co-operated in hammering out a settlement. The land conference of 1902 had been a magnificent example of what could be achieved by Irishmen of different schools of thought, working together (and, a cynic might add, ganging up for some purposes against the treasury). Plunkett also was convinced that 'in Ireland the political and the agrarian questions

---

[6] Lord Midleton, *Records and reactions*, pp. 241–3; S. Gwynn, *John Redmond's last years*, p. 321.

[6A] Lord Midleton, *Records and reactions*, p. 242.

had been so intertwined' that no settlement of the former would be satisfactory unless accompanied by a settlement of the latter. And one of the sub-committees which he persuaded the grand committee to set up early in November 1917 was appointed to inquire into land purchase. Under the chairmanship of Mac-Donnell, this committee produced an able report, detailing a scheme for the rapid completion of land purchase, a report which was thoroughly debated during three days (8, 9 and 10 January). As Plunkett observed, many members of the convention 'were deeply interested in the land question and far more familiar with its details than they were with constitutional theory'.[7] After a vigorous discussion the report was accepted.

Redmond, after attending the meeting on 4 January had gone down to the country; and as he was not at all well and had a heavy cold he cut himself off from politics for ten days. Returning to Dublin on the 14th he had a talk with Gwynn, whom he asked to find a leading county councillor to act as the seconder of his motion.[8] He also sent a conciliatory letter to his old political associate, the bishop of Raphoe. 'You will notice', Redmond wrote, 'this amendment of mine does not commit anyone to giving up customs unless the government accepts the scheme and gives it legislative effect *forthwith*. If they did this I am quite convinced we should be guilty of a grave dereliction of duty if we do not accept the compromise regardless of what Sinn Feiners might say outside. I dare say my amendment will receive a certain amount of opposition – certainly from Murphy, Lysaght and Russell. But I am moving it entirely on my own responsibility and everybody will be quite free to vote as he likes, and I will say so.' Redmond's letter crossed one from the bishop of Raphoe, written on the day on which O'Donnell declared that he would oppose Redmond's amendment. If Ulster had come in, the nationalists, the bishop argued, could have given something away. But with Ulster out, the cabinet could not carry a settlement excluding customs because 'there would be no Irish opinion at the back of the measure'. There was nevertheless, the bishop thought, the possibility of the Midleton proposals becoming the basis for a settlement. If the majority of the convention were in favour of fiscal autonomy

[7] *Confidential report*, p. 66.
[8] S. Gwynn, *John Redmond's last years*, pp. 322–3.

and the Ulster unionists and the southern unionists presented minority reports, the southern unionist report might be accepted as a compromise solution. But, in O'Donnell's opinion, 'the very worst service that can be done to the chances of legislation on the Midleton lines would be by our concurrence in the absence of a promise from Ulster to come'.[9]

On the following morning, the 15th, Redmond, on arriving at Trinity shortly before the convention met, discovered that there was very strong support for fiscal autonomy amongst his followers, Garahan and Gubbins (the chairmen of the Longford and Limerick county councils)[9A] informing him that a number of county councillors intended to vote against his amendment. Many county councillors were 'furious at being rushed' and the bishops of Raphoe and Down, it was said, had 'got at' Devlin, who informed Redmond that the bishops and Devlin himself would not support the compromise.[9B] But when Redmond took his seat in the Regent House, Gwynn told him that he had secured a seconder for the amendment, Martin McDonogh, the chairman of the Galway urban district council, 'the kind of man', Gwynn later wrote, 'who in America would certainly have been a millionaire and who even in Galway had become a really important manufacturer and merchant'.[10] Redmond, 'with characteristic brusqueness', replied to Gwynn: 'he need not trouble. I am not going to move it, Devlin and the bishops are against me.'[11] And shortly afterwards, when the proceedings started, rising to his feet, in a few short sentences Redmond told the convention that the amendment embodied 'his deliberate advice', that he had just learned that some very important nationalist representatives were against it, that he believed that if it went to a division he would probably carry it, but that 'such a division could not carry out the objects I have in view'. Therefore he was not going to move his amendment

It was a moment of profound and humiliating defeat for Redmond, and his abdication of authority brought home what

[9] D. Gwynn, *Life of John Redmond*, pp. 584–5.
[9A] MacLysaght, diary, Feb. 1918.
[9B] Southborough to Adams, 15 Jan. 1918, Plunkett to Adams, 15 Jan. 1918 (Lloyd George papers, F 65/1/35, F 64/6/10).
[10] S. Gwynn, *Experiences of a literary man*, p. 294.
[11] S. Gwynn, *Last years of John Remond*, pp. 322–3.

had been steadily becoming apparent that constitutional nationalism was ceasing to be a decisive force in Irish politics. It is not surprising then that when Redmond sat down there was 'a pause of consternation'.[12] But speechlessness was not a characteristic of Irish public men. Plunkett, who had just received 'the worst shock of my public life',[13] rose and explained that 'he had only heard the thing a few minutes ago. [He] did not know what to do.' After some talk it was agreed that the general discussion should continue, and McRory, the bishop of Down, revived the debate by a very vigorous restatement of the case for fiscal autonomy. He agreed with Midleton that no single nation could make as good a bargain as the empire, but the question was not what the empire could do but what it would do. If England adopted protection she would manipulate tariffs in her own favour, protecting manufactures but not agriculture, so that Ireland would be compelled to buy in a closed and sell in an open market. Midleton's scheme, he said, would produce rebellion in a fortnight. 'If there is to be a settlement', McRory declared, 'then in God's name let it be a settlement that will bury the hatchet and enable us to sit down in harmony and good will'. Plunkett in his report, commenting on the speech, could not help remarking that the bishop had made rather free use of the hatchet he proposed to bury, but he reflected: 'a Roman Catholic prelate with Belfast in his diocese may be somewhat sorely tried'.[14] To counterbalance the bishop of Down's speech Plunkett read a letter from Dr Kelly, the bishop of Ross, who was too ill to attend the meeting. In this letter Dr Kelly, while emphasizing that 'the power to impose customs duties by an Irish parliament is part of the full completion of home rule', implored his fellow nationalists to yield on this point to the southern unionists 'for the sake of a settlement'.[15]

Another northern nationalist, Devlin, made a powerful speech which greatly impressed Mahaffy. He did not dwell on fiscal autonomy, over which he had broken with his leader, but attacked the northern unionists, who, he asserted, had 'contributed nothing and conceded nothing' and whom he compared

[12] Ibid., p. 323.
[13] Plunkett, diary, 15 Jan. 1918; Mahaffy, notes.
[14] *Confidential report*, p. 68.
[15] Ibid., p. 69.

to Prussians, 'in their assertion of superiority to the other inhabitants of Ireland'. And in reply to Barrie's suggestion of a compromise between partition and the act of 1914, he emphasized that the act was on the statute book. The speeches of Devlin and the bishop of Down stimulated Anderson, the mayor of Derry, and Pollock into replying for the northern unionists. Anderson, who made 'a very telling speech', asserted: 'Ulster has played a big part in the great war', and, to the charge that the Ulster delegation had continuously to consult their friends in the north, he retorted that Redmond's career had demonstrated the danger of losing touch with one's supporters. Both Anderson and Pollock argued that the nationalist had not made any concessions; indeed Pollock pointed out, they were making fiscal demands which had not occurred to O'Connell, Butt, Biggar or Parnell. 'I stand where Parnell stood', Pollock asserted, a remark which in the middle of a sombre debate produced a burst of laughter.[16]

Though Pollock and Anderson were supported by the moderator of the presbyterian church, who complained about the propaganda directed against Ulster, and the financial autonomists secured the backing of the archbishop of Cashel, a number of speakers dwelt on the supreme importance of a speedy settlement. Two leading businessmen, Goulding and Jameson, supported Midleton's scheme. Jameson pointed out that the Ulster unionists had threatened that, if they were not satisfied, they would fall back on partition. 'Speaking as a manufacturer of one of the main excisable articles', he declared that it was practicable to place customs and excise under the control of different authorities. And he implored the nationalists to yield on the customs question, arguing that Devlin underestimated the influence the convention would have on the country 'when it makes up its mind and puts forth a settlement'. Granard praised the southern unionists and urged the county council representatives to vote with them. In the course of his speech he stated that England would never allow Ireland to make customs treaties with foreign powers. Russell interrupted him to ask what was his authority for this statement, and the bishop of Raphoe asked him how did he know that England would accept Midleton's scheme. Gwynn, who was one of the

[16] Mahaffy, notes.

leading moderate nationalists, asked what were the nationalists to do. He suggested that an effort should be made to secure legislation giving Ireland protection against dumping, and debarring Great Britain from imposing a tariff that might injure an Irish industry. 'All we want', he said, 'is a bridge, perhaps from Lord MacDonnell'.

The next day (17 January) Lord MacDonnell produced an amendment to Midleton's scheme to the effect that the control of customs be reserved to the United Kingdom parliament for the duration of the war and until parliament had considered the report of a royal commission which would be appointed to inquire into the financial relations of Great Britain and Ireland. Midleton at once made it clear that in his opinion his own scheme 'embodied the best offer ever made to Ireland' and that he was not prepared to make further concessions, though he was willing to agree that all questions relating to Ireland's taxable capacity should be referred to a royal commission.[16A]

On the same day, in conversation, Midleton told Granard that even if the cabinet were prepared to concede customs, the southern unionists would insist on their remaining under imperial control, voting with the Ulster unionists on this point. In Granard's opinion, 'people like Lord Iveagh have got at him [Midleton] and say, what is to become of us at the end of 15 years unless the imperial government controls the customs. It is an agricultural country and it is naturally in the interest of the people to get their tea and sugar cheap; surely the first thing they would do would be to increase the income tax out of all knowledge and tax us out of existence.'[17]

But if Midleton was immovable, Granard for a day or two hoped to rally nationalist support behind the Midleton proposals. He had heard that Devlin and the bishops of Down and Raphoe were inclined 'to wobble', and many of the county councillors had told him they were not deeply concerned about customs. They wanted the issue to be settled at Westminster so that they could say to their Sinn Fein friends 'we voted for the customs, but the English government threw the proposal out'.[18]

[16A] On the same day, 17 March, Midleton expressed the same views in a letter to Adams (Lloyd George papers, F 66/2/3).

[17] Granard to Asquith, 19 Jan. 1918 (Asquith papers).

[18] Granard to Asquith, 18 Jan. 1918 (Asquith papers).

The bishop of Ross, Granard discovered in a long talk, was strongly in favour of the Midleton compromise. The bishop was not afraid of Sinn Fein but was 'very nervous of Mr Murphy and his paper', and Granard made inquiries as to what that 'old gentlemen wants'. He came to the conclusion that Murphy was guided purely by self-interest, and that his opposition to the Midleton proposals could be bought off if it was arranged that the townships of Pembroke and Rathmines were incorporated in the city of Dublin, with the result that the conservative elements in the city corporation would be much strengthened – which would be to Murphy's advantage as the head of several public utilities.[19] Granard was probably unaware that Murphy had already been tentatively approached along these lines. Tim Healy after dining with Duke had telephoned Murphy and told him that, if he remained neutral on the customs issue, Duke would get embodied in the new franchise bill a scheme for amalgamating the townships with Dublin – a plan Healy was extremely keen on. Murphy's comment was: 'I don't take much interest in his township scheme while I take a deep interest in the customs'.[20]

'Marking time with desultory debate' (to use Plunkett's phrase) carried the convention through its meetings in the third week of January until it adjourned on the 17th to the following week. And during this adjournment an effort seems to have been made to rally a substantial number of nationalists behind the southern unionist compromise. 'We got Redmond up to the point of convening a meeting of his supporters for the evening of 22 January', Granard wrote. But at the last moment, Redmond, in Granard's bitter phrase, 'funked' – he was a sick man who on the following day was again forced to retire to bed.[21]

Meanwhile Plunkett, who had crossed to England on the 17th, had an interview with the prime minister on the 19th. Lloyd George considered Plunkett to be diffuse and difficult to follow,[21A] but on this occasion Plunkett's task was simple. He had merely to say that the convention was making little or no headway and might break up without achieving an agreement. The prime

[19] Granard to Asquith, 23 Jan. 1918 (Asquith papers).
[20] Murphy to W. L. Murphy, 6 Jan. 1918 (Murphy papers).
[21] Granard to Asquith, 23 Jan. 1918 (Asquith papers).
[21A] Riddell, *War diary* (*1933*), p. 311.

minister told Plunkett that Redmond had written to him pressing him to announce the government's intentions. And he suggested that Plunkett on his return to Ireland should confer with Redmond. The next day Plunkett saw Redmond, obviously a very sick man. The nationalist leader said he would fight for the compromise but had no hope of success without a definite promise of legislation from the government. Plunkett telegrammed the substance of this conversation to Lloyd George and Redmond forwarded the draft of a letter which he thought should be sent to Plunkett.[21B] It suggested that the convention should send a representative delegation to London and Lloyd George at once responded by suggesting that if the point was reached at which the convention found it could make no further progress, representatives of the various groups should confer with the cabinet.[22]

When, on 24 January, Plunkett informed the convention of the prime minister's offer, MacDonnell, Clancy, Gwynn, McCarron and the southern unionist leaders were in favour of accepting the invitation, Midleton complaining that the southern unionist attempt to bring about a settlement had been met by demands for further concessions. The archbishop of Amagh, the bishop of Raphoe, Devlin and Fitzgibbon, all thought they should go on exhausting the possibilities of agreement. The lord mayor of Dublin made a short speech which decided the issue. He rose to speak just before lunch. Plunkett, who felt that he would have something useful to say, at once adjourned the meeting so that the lord mayor 'should speak with all the advantages of an audience which had satiated the cravings of the inner man'. The pith of the lord mayor's speech consisted of asking Midleton, Barrie and the bishop of Raphoe in turn were they prepared to recede from the position they had taken up on the customs issue. Having heard their terse replies, he declared 'it is nonsense to say we are not at a standstill. We are in an absolute quagmire.'[23]

The convention therefore resolved that though it 'did not feel that the possibilities of agreement are exhausted', it con-

---

[21B] Redmond to Lloyd George, 21 Jan. 1918 (Lloyd George papers, F 64/-/15).

[22] *Confidential report*, p. 73.

[23] Ibid., p. 77.

sidered that they would be increased if representatives were nominated to confer with the cabinet. The grand committee selected a carefully balanced delegation of 16 and the convention adjourned. It was understood it could meet again on the 12th February but in fact, as will be seen, circumstances prevented it reassembling until 26 February.

By the time the convention adjourned it had lost two members by resignation. On the last day of 1917 MacLysaght and Russell had come to see Plunkett 'in a very bad temper'.[24] And shortly afterwards MacLysaght wrote to Lloyd George asking for an assurance that the government would implement the decisions of a majority of the convention and requesting a definite statement explaining what the prime minister would regard as 'substantial agreement'. Lloyd George replied that if the convention failed to reach agreement then 'the responsibility will fall upon the government of determining whether the measure of actual agreement is such as to justify them submitting legislation to parliament'. On receiving this letter MacLysaght informed Plunkett that the only course open to him was, by resigning from the convention, 'to make it clear that self-determination lies not with a nominated convention but with the people of Ireland'.[25]

MacLysaght thought 'it would reinforce my action tremendously' if Russell simultaneously sent in his resignation. But Russell hesitated for ten days. Then on 1 February, after 'brooding much on the state of Ireland', he told Plunkett that he was resigning. He thought that Midleton's scheme would not assuage anti-British feeling in Ireland. What was needed, he asserted, was a much bigger measure giving Ireland complete control of Irish affairs. A few days later, in a letter to the prime minister, he complained that, hampered 'by pledges of ministers to the people of Belfast', the convention could not arrive at an agreement, and he warned the government that 'we have for the first time in Ireland a disinterested nationalism not deriving its power from grievances connected with land or even oppressive government but solely from the growing self-consciousness of nationality, and this has with the younger generation all the

[24] Plunkett, diary, 31 Dec. 1917.
[25] MacLysaght to Lloyd George, 12 Jan. 1918; Lloyd George to MacLysaght, 17 Jan. 1918; MacLysaght to Plunkett, 22 Jan. 1918 (MacLysaght diary).

force of a religion, with the carelessness about death, suffering or material loss which we find among the devotees of a religion'. As for himself, Russell admitted that he was 'unfitted for the practical business of bartering bits of my convictions in meetings obviously arranged for compromise'.[26] Plunkett, having failed to get Russell to withdraw his resignation, thanked him for the brilliant part he had played in the convention and for refraining from stating publicly his reasons for resignation. Writing to Bullock, who had worked with Russell, he remarked: 'I am not sure that he is not guilty of intellectual vanity, though I feel rather that his fault is a want of balance. His aloofness from party politics has misled him.'[27]

At this time Lloyd George was 'beset by difficulties any one of which would have amounted to a first class crisis in normal times' – failure on the western front, the impending German onslaught, the submarine campaign, food shortages, air raids, immense difficulties with labour.[28] Nevertheless, at intervals snatched from his other preoccupations, he threw himself with his accustomed energy, enthusiasm and eloquence into trying to persuade and force the Irish leaders to agree on a settlement which would get the Irish question out of the way at least for the immediate future.

The discussions may be said to have begun when at the end of January Adams, acting for the prime minister had a talk with Barrie, who put forward the idea – to which he did not commit himself – of an Ulster committee in an Irish parliament which could both veto and initiate legislation affecting Ulster.[28A] Immediately afterwards Adams had two interviews with a more important Ulster leader, Carson. Carson had just resigned from the war cabinet, having become extremely critical of Lloyd George's handling of naval and military matters. Nevertheless he professed to be anxious 'to meet the *non possumus* attitude in Ulster'. He and Adams discussed possibilities. Carson spoke of a Dublin and an Ulster house of commons. Adams replied that he did not think the nationalists would accept two parliaments and

[26] A. Denison, *Letters of A.E.*, pp. 135–41.
[27] Plunkett to Bullock, 11 Feb. 1918 (Plunkett letters).
[28] Lord Hankey, *The supreme command*, pp. 11–780.
[28A] Memorandum by Adams of interview with Barrie, 28 Jan. 1918 (Lloyd George papers, F 63/2/5).

referred to the suggested Ulster committee. He also touched on the possibility that sessions of the Irish parliament might be held alternately in Dublin and Belfast. Carson agreed that these were 'useful points', but he made it quite clear at the close of the conversation that the fundamental question was would the Ulster unionists accept the idea of an Irish parliament.[28B]

On 6 February, Lloyd George, with Curzon and Bonar Law, met Midleton, Bernard and Desart. Midleton told the prime minister that the possibility of agreement being reached on the basis of the southern unionist proposals had diminished since January. The split in the nationalist party had affected Redmond's 'nerves'; telegrams from the United States published in *The Times* had encouraged the extreme nationalists to hope that Great Britain would concede everything they demanded; and Ulster refused to accept anything. Lloyd George was sympathetic. 'The difficulty was', he explained, 'that Belfast was impervious to any public opinion other than that of Ulster . . .; they were a very narrow, self-centred community and difficult of persuasion'. To illustrate the Ulster attitude the prime minister read a letter from the archbishop of Armagh to Walter Long in which the archbishop described Midleton's proposals as 'mad', and declared that if they were accepted the Ulster artisans would 'down tools'. Midleton somewhat acidly remarked that the archbishop had given the impression of not knowing his own mind. Desart said that the Ulstermen, after their protestations of loyalty, would never dare to down tools, and Midleton suggested that the government 'might have to face placing Ulster in this quandary'. Bernard asked a blunt question. Had the Ulster delegates, before entering the convention, been fortified by a promise from the government that no legislation would be passed which they disapproved of. 'If this were the case and were discovered', Bernard pointed out, 'the temper of the convention would be severely tried'. Lloyd George emphatically repudiated this suggestion, explaining that what had been promised was immediate legislation if there was a substantial majority in favour of a scheme. But of course, he added, 'if Ulster stood out, it would be difficult to describe the residual majority as substantial'.

[28B] Memorandum by Adams of interviews with Carson, 29, 31 Jan (Lloyd George papers, F 63/2/15).

Lloyd George mentioned three subjects which Ulster was apprehensive about, the liquor trade, education and industrial legislation, but he thought that Ulster's fears might be set at rest by empowering an Ulster committee in the Irish parliament to deal with these subjects in so far as they affected the area. Midleton and Bernard were prepared to agree to this but stressed that the grand committee should not have 'such powers as would for example disturb the budget'. Bernard also doubted if the catholic bishops would agree to educational questions in Ulster being decided by the grand committee. A tentative suggestion of Curzon's that there should be four educational authorities in Ireland, a catholic and a protestant in each area, received short shift. Above all, the southern unionists insisted that 'the one thing all Ireland (outside Belfast) would *not* allow was partition'. Lloyd George warmly agreed with them that partition was impossible.[29]

The next day Lloyd George had a twenty minutes talk with Murphy, Duke being the only other person in the room. Murphy stated 'that the only way Ireland could be made a source of strength instead of weakness to the empire was by a full measure of fiscal and legislative autonomy such as had been granted to the dominion of Canada'. In reply Duke argued that, if the control of customs was granted to an Irish parliament, there would be no means of recovering the contribution which it was generally agreed Ireland should pay towards defence and imperial services. Murphy retorted 'that England was lending money to all the governments of the world, trusting to the fact that repudiation would be the ruin of any wilfully defaulting country' and that there was a variety of means by which Great Britain could make Ireland, in its own interests, honour its obligations. The prime minister concluded by saying that 'he should feel his way to find out what kind of measure it would be possible to pass through parliament'.[30]

On 13 February Lloyd George, who on the previous day had been seedy with a temperature, and who was engaged in the Herculean task of getting rid of Robertson as C.I.G.S., met the

[29] Memorandum of interview with the war cabinet, 6 Feb. 1918 (Add. MS 52781).
[30] Memorandum in Murphy papers.

delegation from the convention.[31] Seated and in a conversational
tone, he made a long and eloquent statement, aimed at forcing
the parties towards an agreement along the only lines that
seemed to him possible. At the outset he frankly admitted that,
having with all the advantages of a Celtic imagination taken
part in many cabinet discussions on the Irish question, he had
come to the conclusion it could only be solved by Irishmen.
Now, when he heard that the convention was likely to recommend 'two or three almost irreconcilable proposals which
would leave the problem in a more insoluble condition than it
had ever been in', 'he was filled with despair. And he implored
them to make another real effort to arrive at a substantial
agreement', emphasizing that the government guaranteed (as
far as it could pledge parliament) that any solution 'which
represented a substantial acceptance of Irish opinion' would be
given legislative form.

He then laid down three 'governing considerations' which the
delegates should bear in mind. It was impossible to legislate as
freely in wartime as in peace, so for the duration of the war the
control of the police and Anglo-Irish fiscal relations should
remain as they were. And it was impossible during the war to
break up the fiscal unity of the United Kingdom 'to the extent
of giving Ireland the powers the colonies possessed a thousand
miles from our shores'. Secondly, a settlement was only possible
if partition was ruled out. He regretted the failure of the partition proposals of 1916, because he believed that if they had been
accepted the unity of Ireland would soon have been achieved.
'The unionist majority in the north would', he was sure, 'have
been helpful to the unionist minority in the south'. However he
was now convinced that nothing but the unity of Ireland as a
whole could be successful and that 'it would be idle to propose
partition again'. Lastly, safeguards had to be provided for the
Ulster unionists. The industrial and commercial interests of the
province, he considered, should not be left at the mercy of a
legislature dominated by agriculture. 'Labour must be protected
against the peasant.' In educational matters the Ulster protestants must be protected against a catholic majority. Again, on

[31] There are accounts of this interview in *Confidential report*, pp. 84–5.
Convention papers, T.C.D. box 2, Murphy papers, and in Lloyd George
papers 50F/66/6.

the liquor question local feeling in Ulster must be considered. And there must be guarantees against administrative unfairness. Lloyd George suggested some possible safeguards. The Irish parliament might sit alternately in Dublin and Belfast. There might be additional M.P.s from Ulster in the Irish parliament; or there might be an 'Ulster committee' in the Irish parliament with powers to protect Ulster. The prime minister, according to Murphy, was 'vague as to the powers of this committee but I understood it would be administrative as well as legislative for Ulster'. Lloyd George also suggested that, as labour in the north of Ireland did not like the prospect of being 'cut off' from future British legislation favourable to their class, 'any such legislation passed in England should be adopted for Ulster'. McCarron, the labour nationalist from Londonderry, at this point interrupted the prime minister to say that the labour members of the convention had made no such claim and he wanted to know who had raised the question. The prime minister could not recollect.

After the prince minister made his statement there was 'a long and desultory discussion'. The bishop of Raphoe asked, would the control of customs and excise 'be given to Ireland *now*?' The prime minister answered 'no, you cannot break up existing fiscal unity at this moment'. Gubbins, the chairman of the Limerick County Council, said that Ireland must have at least a promise of customs after the war. Pollock declared that Ulster would object to the control of customs or excise being entrusted to an Irish parliament. Murphy said that, 'unless full powers of taxation were given *in the bill* to the Irish parliament after the war, nationalists would not be satisfied'. Then Midleton bluntly mentioned a delicate if fundamental point. He asked the prime minister what was the attitude of the Ulster delegates? Barrie, Midleton explained, had during the convention said that 'Ulster was willing to listen to any proposal, and if they found it reasonable to accept it. For more than six months now we have gone on their system and at the end of each discussion they have indicated they have been unable to accept or entertain our proposals.' The government, Midleton declared, must give an undertaking that 'other matters agreed what they the government put forward as to Ulster will with the agreement of the convention, be put to parliament'. The prime minister did not give any definite answers to these queries and comments, and he concluded the interview by saying that during the next few days he hoped to have further meetings with groups and individuals belonging to the delegation.

On the 14th the delegates met at the Colonial Institute to decide when the convention should next meet. The lord mayor of Dublin complained about being detained in 'the murkey atmosphere' of London, and Plunkett, who, Desart thought, was more 'wandering' than ever, allowed the delegates to drift into a general discussion. Raphoe repeated his case, Devlin attacked the Ulster unionists, Barrie replied to him, and Midleton stated that 'he would never give way'. Plunkett later wrote 'it was noticeable that no two speakers seemed ever to be agreed upon the actual words, or even the meaning, of the prime minister's utterances upon the vital differences it had been hoped he might compose'.[32]

On the evening of the 14th Lloyd George saw the bishop of Raphoe, the lord mayor of Dublin, Devlin, Gubbins and Murphy. He said he had just seen the Ulster deputation, who were still unable to make any proposals. They were going the next day to see Carson, who had been laid up, and 'after that they would have to consult their committee in Belfast'. Murphy remarked: 'we have frequently heard that story from them'. The discussion then turned mainly on customs and why it was desirable that they should be under Irish control. The bishop of Raphoe again expounded his case. The prime minister, Murphy wrote, 'said the state of the American union did not possess such powers and he thought that if Ireland got the status of an American state that American would accept that as a settlement of the Irish question . . . I said that the settlement America would accept would be what nationalist Ireland would accept.' According to Murphy, the prime minister said at the end of the discussion that if a majority of the convention agreed on a scheme, the government would endeavour to give legislative effect to it. The bishop seems to have enjoyed the meeting since later he wrote to Plunkett; 'I wish you had been present at our last meeting with the prime minister and the chancellor. It was a real pleasure to discuss the principles involved and the

[32] *Confidential report*, p. 85; Desart to Bernard, 16 Feb. 1918 (Add. MS 52781).

analogies offered by the colonies and other countries with the chancellor. He knew the ground and he was quite fair.'[33]

When the Ulster delegation saw Carson, who was at Littlehampton, he almost certainly told it that if the south and west of Ireland were given home rule Ulster should stand out. After all, the exclusion of the six counties at least 'preserved the union for the vast majority of those who desired it'. The only other solution for the Irish question which seemed to Carson possible was the creation of a federal system for the whole United Kingdom. In such a system Ulster could be a unit or part of another unit. He quickly added that in such a federal system the United Kingdom parliament must possess 'an actual and active supremacy', and he admitted that the Irish question was probably too pressing to wait for the creation of a federation. But putting forward the suggestion, he thought, would show 'how untrue it is that Ulster presents a *non possumus* attitude'.[33A]

Lloyd George does not seem to have secured any explicit concessions from the representatives of the main groups in the convention, but he gained an impression of the balance of forces and the development of ideas in the assembly. After the delegates left London, he addressed a long letter to Plunkett, dated 25 February, suggesting the basis of a compromise and indicating what the government was prepared to do. Having summed up in a few competent lines the arguments pro and con on fiscal autonomy, he emphasized that it was not a matter which could be settled during the war. So he suggested that, for the duration of the war and two years afterwards, customs and excise should be reserved to the imperial parliament. At the end of the war a royal commission should conduct a thorough inquiry into the financial relations of Great Britain and Ireland and submit proposals on the best means of adjusting them. During the war all revenue raised in Ireland should, after the deduction of an agreed imperial contribution, be paid to the Irish government. The government also thought, he wrote, that the unionists should be given additional representation in the Irish legislature and that an Ulster committee in the Irish parliament should

---

[33] Memorandum in Murphy papers; O'Donnell to Plunkett, 3 May 1918 (Plunkett letters).
[33A] Carson to ——, 14 Feb. 1918 (Carson papers).

have power to modify or veto legislative or administrative action 'not consonant with the interests of Ulster'. Finally, the prime minister promised that the government would as part of the settlement introduce a bill giving effect to the recommendations of the convention on land purchase and make 'a substantial provision' for dealing with the Irish housing problem.[34] This letter was 'concocted' for the prime minister by Plunkett, Adams and Shaw. But on Monday 25th Plunkett was dismayed to discover that the draft had been completely destroyed by Lloyd George, Milner and Philip Kerr, 'who had been weekending together'. However, after a forcible telephone call from Adams to Kerr, the original draft was sanctioned.[35]

A few days earlier, Lloyd George had written a powerful and conciliatory letter to Barrie in which he both set out the government's proposals for a settlement and endeavoured to impress on the Ulster unionists how important it was 'not only for the peace of Ireland, but both for the union and strength of the empire and for our relations with the United States in the prosecution of the war', that the convention should not fail. Also he pointed out that it would seriously impair Britain's influence in 'that council of nations', the peace conference, if 'we have to go there with Ireland unsettled and possibly in a state of coercion'. 'The Irish question', he declared, 'is within reach of settlement. There is to-day one of those opportunities, which, if lost, may never return', and he implored the Ulster unionists to return to the convention with authority to accept a single legislature for a united Ireland.[36]

The Ulster response was not encouraging. Montgomery, a vigorous member of the advisory committee, dismissed Lloyd George's reasons for an immediate settlement as 'bunkum'. Would, he asked, handing Ireland over to the friends of the enemy help us to win the war? 'I was never', he added, 'able to see the force of the argument that once the war began we should join the Redmondites. It appears to me [they] had better join us.'[37] When the Ulster delegation and its advisory committee met on 25 February, it was made clear to Barrie and Londonderry that

[34] *Confidential report*, pp. 85–7.
[35] Plunkett, diary, 25 Feb. 1918.
[36] Lloyd George to Barrie, 21 Feb. 1918 (Montgomery papers).
[37] Montgomery to Londonderry, 26 Feb. 1918 (Montgomery papers).

they were not authorized 'even tentatively to accept Lloyd George's dodgy proposal in its present shape', but they were given 'a free hand to play with it in the hopes of getting it rejected by one or all the home rule factions in the convention'. Barrie himself, writing to Montgomery, remarked, 'the more I think over the position the less I am inclined to give anything away and I think this view is generally shared by our friends. The state of a large portion of the country is in itself a sufficient justification for standing firm.' And he decided to send the prime minister 'a short, explicit statement which in effect turns down his proposals'.[38]

While the prime minister was appealing to the imperial loyalties of the Ulster unionists, Erskine Childers had thought of another method of reducing their resistance. He suggested to Plunkett that English labour opinion might be brought to bear on labour in the north of Ireland, and in a letter he blocked out the arguments which he thought English labour might use. It would bluntly tell Ulster labour men: 'your reactionary unionism is a drag on the wheel'. Since Ulster labour, incapable of asserting itself, could not win a parliamentary seat even in Belfast, Ulster was bound to be represented by capitalists or reactionaries of some sort, so keeping Ulster in the union meant ten conservative M.P.s at Westminster. As long as Ulster was unionist it would be, so far as English labour was concerned, outside the pale. Labour legislation would not apply to Ireland, affiliation to English trade unions would cease. 'Until you learn the A.B.C. of democracy we wash our hands of you.' But once Ulster labour threw off its shameful bondage to privilege and bigotry, all the friendship and help of English labour would be at its disposal. Irish nationalists and English labour men were fighting the same battle, and the latter would ask Ulster labour men, 'Do you expect us to turn into Prussians and shoot down Sinn Feiners for you'. 'This', Childers remarked, at the close of his letter, 'is rough and over-coloured but gives the idea'.[39]

At this point it should be said that while the Ulster unionists formed a solid, unbudgeable bloc, the southern unionists were

[38] Montgomery to Fisher, 27 Feb. 1918; Barrie to Montgomery, 2 Mar. 1918 (Montgomery papers).
[39] Childers to Plunkett, 19 Feb. 1918 (Plunkett letters).

beginning to split. Within the convention Midleton held his group together. Outside it, schism was developing fast. When, at the beginning of January 1918, Bernard explained the situation to the standing committee of the general synod of the Church of Ireland, he was strongly attacked by Richard Bagwell, a country gentleman who had written solid works on Irish history and who had been for years an ardent and active unionist. Bagwell said he was too old to turn his coat and that Bernard was now a home ruler. The scheme he supported was not a compromise but a surrender. The archbishop protested that he was still a unionist, since he would prefer to maintain the union if it were possible to do so. He was supported by Coote, Maconchy and Cole Bowen who, in the opinion of a northern unionist, made 'drivelling speeches'. The Ulster unionist point of view was expressed by D'Arcy, then bishop of Down, Stronge, and John Leech. D'Arcy pointed out that the Ulster unionists had saved the empire from the danger of an Irish parliament sitting during the war. Leech remarked that the southern unionists had sold the pass. This aroused loud protests, and Montgomery intervened to explain that he agreed with Leech in so far as he meant so-called unionists but that he himself respected real unionists. However, Montgomery privately criticized even one of the real unionists. Bagwell, he wrote to Barrie, in an otherwise admirable speech had shown himself bitterly opposed to partition. Montgomery had tried to weaken his opposition by pointing out 'that most of us believed that no home rule could be set up with Ulster excluded'.[40]

In February hostility towards Midleton amongst the southern unionists became organized. Early in the month it was rumoured that Charles Guinness was on the warpath trying to get up a demonstration against Midleton. But Guinness and Henry Macnamara of Ennistymon and MacKay Wilson of Curryrane (a brother of the field marshal) were regarded as 'wild men' who did not carry much weight, and Bagwell, though furious at 'the betrayal of the cause by Midleton and Bernard', was suffering from gout and old age.[41] However on 20 February a group of fervent and unyielding southern unionists

---

[40] Montgomery to Barrie, 21 Jan. 1918 (Montgomery papers).
[41] Montgomery to A. Maude, 9 Feb. 1918; Montgomery to Stronge, 9 Feb. 1918; Montgomery to Fisher, 4 Feb. 1918 (Montgomery papers).

met at the Shelbourne. Bagwell was put in the chair and it was decided to issue a manifesto.[42] Entitled 'A call to unionists', it appeared at the beginning of March. It began by asserting that the only hope for Ireland lay in the maintenance of the union and the impartial administration of the law. The revolutionary movement derived support only from the young and irresponsible, and the demand for home rule found 'no echo in the hearts of those who had a real stake on the country'. At the end of the manifesto a four-point programme was ennunciated – the enforcement of the law, the development of Ireland's natural resources, the completion of land purchase, and an effort to ensure that Ireland should share the burdens and obligations imposed by the war on the rest of the United Kingdom. The signatories included two peers, a baronet, a general, two historians (Bagwell and Elrington Ball, the editor of Swift's correspondence), five country gentlemen, three K.C.s, three other barristers, a Cork businessman, an English M.P., Newman, who was a member of a Cork landed family.[43] The *Irish Times* deplored the publication of the manifesto as unnecessary and unwise: unnecessary because all unionists were convinced that the union was the best system of government for Ireland; unwise, because, with three-quarters of the population opposed to the union, unionists had to be prepared to accept a compromise. But the Dublin *Daily Express*, the other leading unionist paper, gave 'the call' plenty of publicity and the supporters of 'the call' set to work to try to remove Midleton and his associates from the party leadership. However this took time and Midleton was not deposed while the convention was in being.

When the convention met on 26 February Plunkett opened the session by reading the prime minister's letter, recapitulating its contents, stressing its main points and driving home the view that the limitations of the powers of the Irish parliament were, in his opinion, temporary and that, on the points of principle in dispute, the government had abstained from giving a decision. Though, as he said himself, not often guilty of inflicting cruelty on dumb animals, he spoke for over an hour.[44] When he sat

[42] Stronge to Montgomery, 22 Feb. 1918; Jellett to Montgomery, 21 Feb. 1918 (Montgomery papers).
[43] *Irish Times*, 4 Mar. 1918.
[44] *Confidential report*, p. 88.

down he was conscious of an atmosphere favourable to agreement. If in fact it existed it was dissipated by a sudden intervention of Mahaffy's. The southern unionists had been growing steadily more alarmed about the maintenance of law and order in Ireland, a subject with which they were always profoundly concerned. A law-abiding group, led by men of property, with resentful memories of the extra-legal methods employed by their opponents, they always emphasized the need to enforce the law – partly because it protected their own interests and upheld a system to which they were attached, and partly because they had a genuine respect for law and order. At the end of November Mahaffy had written an angry letter to *The Times* complaining that the 'atmosphere' created by the government with the aim of facilitating the convention was alarming to the loyal and a cause of 'jubilation and insolence' amongst the rebellious. 'Between confident ignorance, over-scrupulous indecision, weary indolence and placid acquiescence we are going down the slope of a precipice'.[45] Now at the end of February he rose to propose that the convention should refrain from discussing the prime minister's letter until it was assured that the government was going to take prompt and effective steps to restore law and order throughout Ireland. A heated debate began over whether the provost's motion was in order. The chairman ruled the 'old pantaloon' out of order. But Mahaffy kept jumping up every time anyone else sat down and finally got himself into order by moving the adjournment. He was defeated by 50 votes to 33 – the majority being composed of nationalists, the minority of unionists.[46] The minority seem to have transmitted a memorial on the state of Ireland to the prime minister who replied by assuring Mahaffy that the government 'were determined to take all the necessary steps with a view to dealing with disorder in Ireland', adding that in his opinion 'neither the task of the government nor that of the convention would be made easier by the publication of the memorial at the present time'.[46A]

---

[45] *The Times*, 26 Nov. 1917.

[46] Barrie to Carson, 26 Feb. 1918 (Carson papers), Plunkett to Adams, 27 Feb. 1918 (Lloyd George papers, F 64/7/1).

[46A] Lloyd George to Mahaffy, 28 Feb. 1918 (Mahaffy autograph letters).

The next couple of days (27 and 28 February) were spent in discussing the situation created by the prime minister's letter. MacDonnell and Dunraven supported his plan, Dunraven cheered by the prospect that it offered for a federation of the United Kingdom. Murphy and the bishop of Raphoe were against accepting the prime minister's proposals, the bishop suggesting that each section of the convention should present its own report and leave it to the government to take whatever action it pleased. Several nationalists pressed the Ulster unionists to state their attitude to the proposals. Barrie promptly rose and explained that the convention had reached a deadlock not because of Ulster but because the other parties could not agree. When the convention made up its mind on the fiscal issue, the Ulster delegation might declare its views. When the convention adjourned for lunch after Barrie had spoken, the nationalists held a meeting, and, according to Plunkett, in view of Barrie's speech 'decided to take an extreme course'. And Bernard, possibly sensing the effect of the speech, when the convention reassembled pointed out in measured words that the prime minister had definitely stated that there should be a single Irish parliament. Would Ulster, he asked, accept such a parliament if customs and excise were excluded from its control? There was no response from the Ulster delegation. Some time later Londonderry, however, hinted that a solution might be found in federalism, if of course, the demand for Irish fiscal autonomy was dropped.

At this stage Lord MacDonnell enumerated a compromise solution in the form of six resolutions. These were to the effect that the convention accepted the plan suggested in the prime minister's letter, subject to the following conditions – that though customs and excise were to be left under the control of the imperial parliament for the duration of the war, the question was to be finally settled within seven years of the conclusion of peace, and from the creation of the Irish parliament these duties were to be administered by a board of members nominated in equal numbers by the British and Irish governments, with a chairman appointed by the crown; the Irish police and postal services were to be administered by the imperial government during the war and on its termination were automatically to come under control of the Irish government; and a royal commission was to be set up to determine the amount of Ireland's imperial contribution and the practicality of establishing a free trade agreement between the two islands. Gwynn attempted a compromise on a compromise by drafting an amendment to MacDonnell's motion to the effect that the convention would accept the prime minister's financial proposals for the period of the war, provided that it was recognized that the Irish parliament, when constituted, would be the taxing authority for Ireland. In addition, the amendment laid down that the act constituting the Irish parliament would establish a free trade agreement between Great Britain and Ireland and bind the Irish parliament for ten years after the war to enact the same customs duties on similar articles as were imposed by the imperial parliament and to impose no other customs duties. Gwynn hoped that the nationalists and the southern unionists would be able to unite in supporting this amendment, 'for the sake of agreement even if it should be barren'. However, at the end of February, when he had a long talk with Lloyd George, Gwynn received political tuition from an old hand. An agreement between the southern unionists and the nationalists, Lloyd George pointed out, might drive the Ulster unionists out of the convention. But he did not think the prospect of legislation would be seriously endangered if the nationalists reported in favour of Irish control of the customs. Then Lloyd George could say to the Ulster unionists, 'well, I have to refuse things to the nationalists as well as to you'. However what really made Gwynn reluctant to insist on southern unionist support for his amendment was, he explained to Midleton, that he did not want 'any support from you that cannot be *ex animo*'. His hope was that while his amendment was being debated, Midleton, while refusing to accept it, would 'contrive to give the discussion on it a friendly tone', so that they would extract from the convention 'the reality of an agreement'. Gwynn's aims were to drive home to the rank and file that the prime minister's offer was extraordinarily advantageous from the nationalist standpoint and to 'shape the report which the bishop of Raphoe proposes to draw up that you [Midleton] will be able and willing to sign most of it'. In return he hoped Midleton would join the nationalists in demanding the automatic transfer at the end of the war of the post office and the police to Irish control. 'We cannot' Gwynn thought, 'get an agreed report on all details. But we can lay the foundations of a convention party – a constitutional self-government party'. He did not think they could arrive at an agreement with the Ulster unionists but they could avoid giving the Ulster unionists all the cards required to wreck home rule.[47] Gwynn's ideal was 'an Ireland morally more in sympathy with Great Britain than ever in the past and having close commercial relations'.[48]

And talking to county councillors who were pleased with the Lloyd George proposals but intended to vote for their rejection in the expectation they would be implemented by parliament, Gwynn pointed out that 'the Irish party would scarcely go against the convention's line and if it did it would be overwhelmed by clamour in the country. So they must decide on the merits'.[48A]

As soon as he heard that the government would not accept Gwynn's amendment, Plunkett set to work to put every ounce of pressure he could upon the bishop of Raphoe, 'the nationalist dictator', with the aim of getting him to accept the government's proposals. Simultaneously Plunkett pressed the government, through Adams (of the cabinet secretariat), to concede something. He told Adams: 'I still think the government would be extremely unwise and would be acting unfairly not only to Ireland but to all the great interests which have become – illogically no doubt – entangled in this important question if they did not go to even greater lengths than the prime minister has gone in making it possible for those who are co-operating with the government to bring about a settlement'. And he warned Adams that if Dillon succeeded Redmond as leader of the parliamentary party, the moderate section of the nationalists were only too likely to enter into tacit agreement with the revolutionary forces. Adams replied that it was extremely important to get from the convention a scheme which could be carried through the house of commons. Gwynn's fiscal proposals would be strongly and successfully opposed by Ulster and the unionists. MacDonnell's scheme might prove acceptable to the house of commons. It was simple and compatible with a federal settle-

[47] Gwynn to Midleton, 1 Mar. 1918 (Add. MS 52781).
[48] *Confidential report*, p 92.
[48A] Gwynn to Adams, 31 Mar. 1918 (Lloyd George papers, F 66/2/29).

ment, and federalism, Adams noticed, was 'making some headway in the house of commons'.[49]

Just before the convention assembled on 5 March, the southern unionists held a meeting and decided not to support the Gwynn amendment even though, as Plunkett pointed out, it included the proviso that the taxing powers of the Irish parliament should cease on a federation of the United Kingdom coming into existence (possibly they thought this an unlikely contingency). When the convention itself met later in the morning, the proceedings opened with 'a rather bitter fight' between Murphy and the chair. Murphy was anxious to move his fiscal autonomy amendment to Midleton's motion, and he suspected the chairman who thought it a 'wrecking amendment', of trying to block it. Midleton resolved the issue by withdrawing his motion. Then MacDonnell introduced his resolutions. Next Gwynn moved his amendment and Midleton made his position clear. He could not, he said accept the Gwynn amendment but he supported MacDonnell's scheme though he asked for one change, the omission of the requirement that Irish representation at Westminster should be in proportion to population. And, speaking with 'a good deal of feeling and eloquence' he appealed to the convention 'not to lose the opportunity of registering a measure of agreement far beyond anything that was expected at the outset'. The new fiscal autononomy demand, he asserted, had been encouraged by members of the convention and he doubted if it was supported by outside public opinion. He was followed by P. J. O'Neill, the chairman of the Dublin county council and director of national service, 'whose platitudes', Plunkett wrote, 'are only interesting as indicating the probable attitude of the dominant party which he anticipates will have the distribution of jobs'. O'Neill denounced the idea of accepting a scheme from the government. After his speech the convention adjourned for lunch.

During the luncheon interval the bishop of Raphoe summoned a meeting of the nationalists and Plunkett gloomily reflected that 'now the nationalist party . . . have taken a leaf out of the Ulster delegates' book and all speak as one man, the hope of any reasonable agreement, which always rested on

[49] Plunkett to Adams, 4 March 1918; Adams to Plunkett, 7 March 1918 (Plunkett letters).

independent thought and action, has become somewhat remote'. He had the consolation of hearing that the meeting was rather irritated by O'Donnell's domineering tone. When the convention reassembled after lunch, Murphy and the bishop of Raphoe took up 'a very intransigent attitude', their speeches showing that the Gwynn amendment would not lessen their opposition to the MacDonnell scheme. McCarron, who rambled a bit, spoke strongly in favour of a settlement, for the sake of which, he said, he would 'gulp down a lot'. And Fitzgibbon remarked that Lloyd George's letter offering, on behalf of the government, fifteen shillings in the pound they owed Ireland, should appeal to everyone's business sense. Gwynn withdrew his amendment, and Plunkett, after vigorous prodding from Midleton, agreed to get on with the MacDonnell motion. The bishop of Raphoe at once put down amendments and MacDonnell wanted to amend his own motion, so, as Plunkett wrote, 'We soon got into a tangle'.[50]

When the convention assembled the next morning, Wednesday, 6 March, it learned that John Redmond had died some hours before, and it was decided to adjourn until after the funeral, which meant for a week. Bernard and Midleton, stressing parliamentary precedent, were for a much shorter adjournment, but the nationalists and the Ulster members ('the latter', Plunkett wrote, 'I am afraid for business reasons') agreed in postponing the next meeting until 12 March. Both Midleton and Plunkett thought this long adjournment unfortunate. Plunkett was convinced that on the morning of the 6th the tide was running strongly in favour of agreement; 'an extraordinary change', he felt, had come in the night, and if the discussion on MacDonnell's scheme had continued during the day he was sure that Murphy and the bishop of Raphoe would have secured the support of only a minority of the nationalists.

Immediately after the adjournment, the nationalist members again met, with the bishop of Raphoe in the chair. O'Donnell stated that 'nothing would induce him to change his attitude'. According to Plunkett 'the strong feeling of the majority was they must not tolerate the dictation of the bishop any more'. 'I think', Plunkett added, 'there is a thoroughly healthy split

[50] Plunkett to Adams, 5 Mar. 1918 (Plunkett letters); *Confidential report*, pp 92–3.

between the bishops and Murphy on the one hand and the majority of the nationalists on the other. The latter mean to accept the MacDonnell amendment as a basis for an immediate settlement, appending a note stating their views upon the ultimate settlement of reserved questions. Before the meeting the bishop of Raphoe begged me to induce MacDonnell to withdraw his motion as he said: "We shall have to oppose it in every clause". He meant to infer that "we" implied an overwhelming majority, whereas he knew, I believe, that it now means a small minority of extremists.'[51]

During the adjournment Plunkett made a desperate and indiscreet effort to obtain support for the Lloyd George proposals. He composed a long letter or short essay (it ran to about 2000 words), which on 9 March he circulated among the members of the convention. 'Without wishing to influence anybody's opinion in controversial matters', he argued that acceptance of the prime minister's proposals was the only way of securing practical results from the convention. He indicated what Ireland could obtain from the government by accepting them – a parliament, complete control of all sources of revenue except customs and excise, the completion of land purchase, assistance towards the solution of the urban housing problem. As for the question of principle involved in the control of customs and excise, Plunkett pointed out that the prime minister was postponing the fiscal issue *'without prejudice'*.[52] When the convention met on 12 March, Plunkett was severely criticized for distributing this piece of propaganda, and he had to agree that it would not appear among the official publications of the convention. This awkward matter disposed of, the convention continued the discussion on the MacDonnell resolutions, and after a debate in which well worn arguments were reiterated MacDonnell's first resolution was carried by 38 votes to 34. And the next day his third resolution was taken. By the combined efforts of Bernard, Midleton, the bishop of Raphoe, and Windle, it was reshaped into a form which took account of the immense disparity between the British and Irish yields from customs and excise. The amended resolution provided that there should be at least one person nominated by the Irish treasury on the

[51] Plunkett to Adams, 6 Mar. 1918 (Plunkett letters).
[52] *Confidential report*, pp 95–8.

United Kingdom board of customs and excise and that there should be an exchequer board, consisting of two members nominated by the Irish treasury and two members nominated by the crown, to decide the revenue of Ireland. The amended third resolution was carried by 39 to 33.

In the critical division of 12 March the majority of 38 (in Murphy's opinion a combination of southern unionists and weak-kneed nationalists)[53] was composed of an independent (Provost Mahaffy) two liberals (Granard and MacDonnell), four labour men, ten southern unionists and twenty-one nationalists, including eighteen representatives of local bodies, the chairman of the Cork chamber of commerce, Gwynn, and Windle. Windle by the close of the convention had come to the conclusion that the southern unionists were ' "the men who really appeal to me", and of course by birth and associations I belong to them, and understand them. They are gentlemen, and you know that their word is their bond. I liked all of them, though I began with the greatest prejudice against Midleton, Jameson, and several others, e.g. Stewart. Yet I was wrong. These men acted in a most patriotic spirit, and if all the rest had been like them the convention would have been a great success.' The Ulster delegation did not make such a favourable impression on him. 'If to make money and the best of this world', Windle wrote, 'is all, Ulster is right, but if not, *not*. They have not "vision" beyond money, so it seems to me, and are not really Irish. Can they ever amalgamate with the rest of the country? It is difficult to imagine it.'[53A]

The minority, in Plunkett's eyes, 'an alliance between the Ulster Dervishes and the Bolshevik bishops'[53B] consisted of seventeen Ulster unionists (including eight representatives of local authorities), the archbishop of Armagh and the moderator of the presbyterian church, fifteen nationalists (including Devlin, Murphy, the archbishop of Cashel, the bishops of Down and Raphoe and eleven representatives of local authorities) and two labour men (Hanna and Lundon). In the division of 13 March on the third resolution the majority was reinforced by Patrick Dempsey (a government nominee and a

[53] Murphy to W. L. Murphy, 16 Mar. 1918 (Murphy papers).
[53A] M. Taylor, *Sir Bertram Windle: a memoir* (1932), pp 268–9.
[53B] Plunkett to Bernard, 13 Mar. 1918 (Plunkett letters).

nationalist), the minority gained four new voters (two Ulster unionists and two nationalists), and lost five (one Ulster unionist and four nationalists). So taking the two divisions together, the moderates who favoured the MacDonnell or Lloyd George compromise had the narrowest possible majority of one.

On the 13 March MacDonnell's fourth resolution, that a royal commission should be appointed to determine the amount of Ireland's imperial contribution and the practicality of establishing free trade between Great Britain and Ireland in the event of customs and excise coming under Irish control, was defeated by 44 to 27. Eleven of the nationalists who favoured the compromise resolutions, thinking a royal commission an unsuitable instrument, voting with the Ulster unionists and the fiscal autonomists in the majority. The minority which supported MacDonnell consisted of southern unionists (10), nationalists (12), labour representatives (3) and liberals (2). On the 14 March the convention began work by taking Mac-Donnell's second motion, which provided that the Irish police and postal service should be reserved during the war and thereafter automatically become subject to Irish control. The bishop of Raphoe wanted to substitute 'joint' for 'imperial control' for the duration of the war and an amendment embodying his views was carried by 36 to 33. The majority consisted of 33 nationalists, two labour men and a liberal (Lord Granard). The minority consisted of 18 northern and nine southern unionists, two labour men, two nationalists (Kavanagh and Quin), Lord MacDonnell and the provost.

Then, with the fiscal issue at last out of the way, the convention was able to start dealing with all the remaining aspects of the future Irish constitution. Exhaustion and a sense of urgency combined to shorten discussion. Moreover, Mac-Donnell persuaded the convention to agree to organize its debates by discussing in turn the points on which provisional agreement had been reached by the grand committee. The result was that by 22 March, twenty-one resolutions, embodying a scheme for the government of Ireland, had been passed.[54]

[54] In its main outline it resembles the home rule act of 1914 with of course the changes which have been mentioned. Its clauses are summarized in *Report of the proceedings of the Irish convention*, pp 24–9.

Light relief was provided by an attempt of Lord Oranmore and Browne to have the senate renamed the Irish house of lords. The Ulster and southern unionists and a few nationalists voted for his motion, the bulk of the nationalists voted against, and it was defeated by a majority of one. The labour men tried to secure a more democratically chosen senate, but receiving no support they were unsuccessful. Then two of them supported by the Ulster unionists, voted against the resolution constituting a second chamber, but it was carried by 48 votes to 19.

Before the scheme for the government of Ireland was discussed the Ulster unionists had decided that, 'to prevent any misdescription of the alleged agreements' in the report of the convention, 'the group should divide against everything that could have been alleged to have been agreed on'.[54A] Their positive policy was expressed by Barrie when, on 14 March, he proposed that the authority of the Irish parliament should not extend to the province of Ulster. Two days earlier he had circulated a memorandum, which Plunkett characterized as 'a crude proposal'.[55] It laid down that the home rule act of 1914 should not apply to Ulster, termed 'the excluded area'. The executive in the excluded area was to be under the direction of a secretary of state and was to be administered through such officers and departments as might be instituted by order in council. The cost of government in the area was to be defrayed by the imperial exchequer, to which all taxes in the excluded area were to be paid. Judicial power in the area was to be exercised by a supreme court and county courts. In short, the union was to be preserved in respect of nine counties. Lastly in a somewhat incongruous final clause the Ulster unionists chivalrously declared that their representatives in the convention would support such safeguards as the southern unionists thought necessary.[56]

Barrie, when moving his exclusion resolution, was seconded by the moderator and supported by Hanna, Londonderry and the archbishop of Armagh. Hanna said that only by the union 'could the social position of labour be safeguarded and further

[54A] Minutes of the Ulster delegation, 13 Mar. 1918; Barrie to Plunkett, 30 Mar. 1918 (Plunkett letters).
[55] *Confidential report*, p. 11.
[56] *Report of the proceedings of the convention*, p. 116.

economic victories won'. Londonderry regretted that the convention 'had not been able to offer to Ulster some compromise between the two extremes of partition and the act of 1914'. The nationalists, he complained, had advanced their demands beyond his expectations. The primate, stressing his own 'absolute independence', declared that the convention could not force the scheme which was being devised by the majority on Ulster. A determined, united, democratic party in the north whose 'strong antagonism to home rule in any form has been drunk in from their mothers' breasts', would not accept it. And Crozier himself was not prepared to 'use the loyalty and self-sacrifice of the people I have known so well to force on them a measure which would strain their loyalty to the breaking point'. As for one of the suggested guarantees for Ulster which had been suggested, artificially created over-representation, it was so distinctly opposed to modern principles of government that it would never appeal to a great democratic community like Belfast. But Crozier regarded the prospect of partition with horror, and while voting for Barrie's amendment he would not support his scheme. Instead he suggested that the convention should consider the provost's scheme, a central parliament for Ireland, with 'absolute provincial autonomy' as 'not an expedient but an experience'.[57]

Mahaffy himself early in his speech explained that any scheme for Irish self-government which did not include Ulster would be acceptable only to the Sinn Fein section of the population as being a prelude to separation from England and the ruin of protestant Ireland. Having dwelt on 'the contempt' which had been shown 'for an old and respectable member of the convention who knows the history of this and other constitutions as well as any of you and has no personal ambitions', he congratulated the Ulstermen for extending their views beyond the six counties. This 'enlargement' brought the protestant farmers of Monaghan and Donegal into the area which would be controlled by the northern unionists, while the large catholic minority in the area would be able to check religious intolerance. But Mahaffy, though voting for Barrie's amendment, did not accept his scheme. He did not approve of Ulster being

[57] Speech by the primate, 14 Mar. 1918 (Irish convention papers, T.C.D.).

governed from England 'by Birrells and Dukes'. Let Ulster, he urged, govern itself and let the other provinces do likewise. Later the fragments would come together 'in some sort of design and make up some kind of reasonable unity'. If any member of the convention thought this 'an idle vision thrown out in his study by an antiquated pedant', Mahaffy reminded him of Switzerland and Canada.[58]

In the discussion over the adoption of the report of the sub-committee on defence and police the Ulster unionists fought hard and even won a few votes. The report recommended that for naval defence Ireland should be considered as integrally connected with Great Britain. It assumed that the historic Irish regiments would continue to form part of the regular army and that Ireland would remain a valuable recruiting ground. It also laid down that it was desirable Ireland should raise a local force for service in Ireland in peacetime and in any part of the United Kingdom in war, and that, assuming a scheme of self-government for Ireland was adopted, 'it would in practice be impossible to impose a system of compulsory service in Ireland without the assent and co-operation of the Irish parliament.' The police, the report recommended, should be controlled by the Irish government. The section on naval defence was unanimously adopted. But Colonel Wallace moved that the section on military defence should be deleted and replaced by a declaration that military defence was a question exclusively for the imperial government. He was defeated by 49 votes to 22, the northern unionists being reinforced by three southern unionists (Goulding, Jameson and Midleton) and the provost, while two southern unionists (Desart and Powell) and the two liberals voted in the majority. The resolution on compulsory service dealt with a subject which might at any moment become a burning issue, and, though it was cautiously worded and contained a hypothesis, it could be used to support the contention that the imperial parliament had not the moral right to impose conscription in Ireland. Goulding moved that it should be omitted but was defeated by 48 votes to 29, the minority being composed of Ulster unionists (18), southern unionists (7), two labour men (McCarron and Whitley), the archbishop of Armagh and the provost.

[58] Speech by the provost, 15 Mar. 1918 (Irish convention papers).

178

The majority included two southern unionists (Mayo and Powell) and three labour men (Lundon, McKay and Murphy) and the two liberals. Finally when Barrie moved that the Royal Irish constabulary and the Dublin Metropolitan police should for at least six years be reserved services under the imperial government, he was beaten by 57 to 18, the southern unionists voting with the nationalists in the majority.

As the convention speeded up its work it became obvious that a report would soon have to be produced. Plunkett discovered that Southborough and Vernon were anxious to have 'a colourless, non-committal report' and that Vernon, 'who understands officialese literature and reduces it with great skill almost to algebraic formula', had prepared a draft which Plunkett dismissed as inadequate.[59] Vernon himself was sure his draft would not appeal to the chairman from its 'elimination of adjectives, of literary allusions and of the journalistic touch'.[59A] Plunkett's attitude as to what sort of a report was required was clearly discernable. And when on 21 March the convention began to try to give the chairman instructions on how the report was to be drafted, Midleton, stung by what Plunkett termed, 'some casual remarks' of Plunkett's indicating his intention of putting into the report an outline of the views of each section along with a commentary of his own, declared firmly that what was wanted was a simple narrative. Midleton was supported by a number of members including Barrie, Gwynn and the bishop of Raphoe, all asking for a report (in Plunkett's words) 'so colourless that everybody can sign it'; Powell added that if Plunkett attempted to expound the views of the different sections they would 'have to sit until Christmas.'[60] Plunkett was exasperated. He understood why Barrie did not want the public to know what the convention was prevented from achieving. But he regretted that the southern unionists and the moderate nationalists had failed to grasp what the advanced nationalists were aiming at. What the bishop of Raphoe wanted was 'a bald and forbidding' report, 'unreadable as the pages of Bradshaw which the public would gallop through until they came to a minority report in which the bishop would make a powerful case for

---

[59] Plunkett to Adams, 19, 27 Mar. 1918 (Plunkett letters).
[59A] Vernon to Adams, 19 Mar. 1918 (Lloyd George papers, F 65/3/14).
[60] Plunkett to Adams, 23 Mar. 1918 (Plunkett letters).

dominion status and fiscal autonomy'.[61] Naturally Plunkett's political and literary instincts reacted vigorously against permitting this to happen. But a few days after the convention adjourned, Midleton warned him that if he tried in the report to interpret the opinions of the various sections of the convention he would not carry a word of that portion of the report. 'You have in mind', Midleton went on, 'a brilliant exposition of all that has taken place . . . but the sort of report we want should be written by the secretariat'. Irritated by Plunkett's confidence in his own tactical skill, Midleton went on to drive his case home by dwelling on the mistakes Plunkett had already made. His questionnaire ('the examination paper') which he had addressed to the members of the committee of nine 'and the consequent replies had caused infinitely bad feeling'. The letter of 9 March, though admirably expressed, 'had produced so much contention that you publicly withdrew it'. Plunkett defended himself with some vigour. He had been a silent spectator of the committee of nine, intervening only 'when it was practically agreed to throw up the sponge'. As for his letter of 9 March, if it had not been written, 'the most critical of all our divisions . . . would have been lost'; and 'having saved the situation I could be happy in a white sheet'. He also felt that Midleton had made a mistake by insisting that the customs issue must be settled before the convention dealt with other questions which did not involve serious differences. 'I should not think it necessary to justify my own views', Plunkett told Midleton, 'upon these points only that you are so frequently reminding me and telling others that I prevented you carrying your motion at the psychological moment – I think if I remember right after a booze at Granard's on 3 January.' However, he promised that when he told the whole story he would credit Midleton with having played the biggest part in the convention. And Midleton in return emphasized that he did not underestimate 'the generosity and patience' with which Plunkett had treated 'the various discordant elements and situations which have arisen'.[62]

After the convention adjourned on the 22nd, Plunkett set to

[61] Plunkett to Adams, 23 Mar. 1918; Plunkett to Midleton, 25 Mar. 1918 (Plunkett letters).
[62] Midleton to Plunkett, 27, 30 Mar. 1918; Plunkett to Midleton, 28 Mar. 1918 (Plunkett letters).

work to draft a report, 'which did the convention as much justice as it would allow to be done to itself'. It was a lively and objective narrative, ending in a 'statement of conclusions' – in fact the resolutions passed during the second half of March. This draft report was ready when the convention assembled for its final sittings on 4 April. Plunkett had intended to ask the convention to dinner on the night of the 4th, but a few days before the convention met he received a telegram from Barrie saying that his group had a previous engagement for that night.[63] And since it would not have been advisable to hold a convention dinner with the Ulster unionists absent, he dropped the idea.

When on 4 April the convention began to consider the draft report, Murphy moved a group of amendments with the object of emphasizing how his efforts to carry a resolution in favour of fiscal autonomy had been blocked and the extent to which the prime minister's position had altered between May 1917 and February 1918. Though on one amendment, the aim of which was to remove a phrase emphasizing that on 12 March the opinion of the majority of the convention on 'the main financial question' had been expressed, he was backed up by the Ulster unionists, all his amendments were defeated. On 5 April the report of the committee on urban housing was received. Then after some discussion a formula was found for authenticating the convention's report. Plunkett suggested a resolution to the effect that it was an accurate narrative of the procedings and 'as such the members would sign it'. But instead it was decided to use the phrase, 'the chairman and the secretary have the honour by the direction of the convention to submit the foregoing report of its proceedings to his majesty's government'. The report was then approved by 44 votes to 29 (the majority being composed of 26 nationalists, 9 southern unionists, 5 labour representatives, Granard and the provost; the minority being made up of 18 Ulster unionists and 11 nationalists). The proceedings, which had more than filled the morning, terminated with hasty votes of thanks. The luncheon to which the chairman had invited the members was getting cold and members were thinking about their trains when the convention adjourned *sine die*.

[63] Plunkett to Barrie, 30 Mar. 1918 (Plunkett letters).

In addition to the report of the convention members handed in two reports and five 'notes'. The longest of these was the report produced by the fiscal autonomists, who, emphasizing that Ireland was a nation, laid down that it was essential 'to abide by the principle that Irish affairs, including all branches of taxation, should be under the Irish parliament'. The taxing power so deeply affected the welfare of the people, the dignity of parliament and the wise and economical administration of the government, that no part of it could be placed under external control. Ireland, the report urged, should have the form of constitution enjoyed by the self-governing dominions. Nevertheless the report ended by listing the concessions the signatories were prepared to make to meet the doubts and objections of the unionists – generous additional representation in the Irish parliament, a guarantee for a reasonable period of free trade between Great Britain and Ireland, a joint advisory commission to secure co-operation in commercial and postal matters, continued Irish representation in the imperial parliament (the Irish M.P.s in Westminster being elected by the Irish parliament), a statutory Irish imperial contribution, suspension for a term of years of the power to raise local defence forces, and suspension until the end of the war of powers over customs and excise.[64]

The Ulster unionists also produced a fairly long report in which they explained that they had expected that the real work of the convention 'would have been directed to a sincere and patriotic endeavour to find common ground somewhere between the 1914 act on the one hand and the views of Ulster on the other'. Though they realized that fiscal autonomy was valued by the nationalists 'not only on the ground of supposed economic advantage but as an essential symbol of national independence', the Ulster unionists declared 'Ulster takes a firm stand on the people's common prosperity, and maintains that the fiscal unity of the United Kingdom must be preserved intact'.

The majority of the nationalists, the southern unionists and the labour men produced short notes. The nationalists stated that since they held it to be of paramount importance that an Irish parliament should be established, in order to reach agree-

[64] Plunkett thought it was written by Childers (Diary, 5 Apr. 1918).

ment with the unionists they would not 'at this moment' press their objections to the prime minister's fiscal proposals, though they put on record their conviction that an Irish parliament was entitled to be and ought to become the sole taxing authority for Ireland. The southern unionists enunciated six points they thought vital to any satisfactory settlement, viz, that all imperial services, including customs, should be left in the hands of the United Kingdom parliament; that Ireland should send representatives to Westminster; that the whole of Ireland should participate in any Irish parliament; that Ireland should make an imperial contribution; that the safeguards agreed to by the convention should be established, and that in any scheme for the federation of the empire or the United Kingdom, Ireland should occupy the same position as other parts of the United Kingdom. The labour men stressed that, because they believed that self-government was in the best interests of the country, they had agreed to certain temporary concessions, in regard to the constitution of the Irish parliament, which 'we as democrats and representatives of labour regard with strong dislike'.

Lord Dunraven in a short note reiterated his belief that a plan based on the federal principle would give Ireland the fullest measure of self-government while providing an Irish constitution which would 'fit into the complete federation of the United Kingdom' and 'form a consistent link in the chain that may lead to constitutional synthesis within the empire'. Finally the archbishop of Armagh and the provost of Trinity, in a very short report almost certainly from its style drafted by Mahaffy, declared they could not accept the policy supported by the majority of the convention because it involved either 'the coercion of Ulster, which is unthinkable' or 'the partition of Ireland which would be disastrous'. They suggested a federal scheme based on Canadian or Swiss precedent, which 'would be capable of being adapted to some larger scheme of imperial federation for the whole British empire'.

Plunkett had a final opportunity which he seized of officially expressing his views on the convention's work. When he transmitted the convention's report, the minority reports and the notes to the prime minister, he prefaced the whole collection by a letter in which he tried to give a clear idea of the real significance of the convention's achievement. 'We had', he wrote, 'to find a way out of the most complex and anomalous political situation to be found in history – I might almost say in fiction'. The difficulties facing the convention he summed up in two words – Ulster and customs. But the nationalists and the southern unionists by mutually making concessions and by agreeing to postpone a decision upon the ultimate control of customs and excise had managed to agree on a complete scheme of self-government for Ireland. 'Is it too much to hope', Plunkett asked, 'that the scheme embodying this agreement will forthwith be brought to fruition by those to whose call the Irish convention has now responded'?

V

AFTERMATH

∿∿∿∿∿∿∿∿∿∿∿∿∿∿∿∿∿∿∿∿∿∿∿∿∿∿∿∿∿∿

ON 21 MARCH, the day on which the convention began
to consider the problem of preparing a report, the great
German attack on the west opened on the stretch held by
Gough's fifth army. By the 24th, the day on which the convention adjourned, leaving Plunkett to prepare a draft report,
Gough's first two lines had been pierced, and his shattered army
was struggling to re-form. By 9 April, when the convention
finally approved its report, the British army was engaged in a
desperate effort to save Amiens, and it seemed likely that, if
Amiens fell, the whole British defence system in France might
crumble. It was not the best time for the government or parliament to consider constitutional change in Ireland, and at the
end of March the Irish situation was further complicated by the
emergence of a new issue – the extension of conscription to
Ireland. Between 21 March and the end of April the British
army lost over 300,000 men. It was urgently necessary to find
drafts to fill the ranks in France, and in spite of other important
demands on British man-power the cabinet on 24 March
decided to raise the age limit for liability to military service
from 42 to 50 (in some specialist categories to 55). At once the
question came up, was Ireland still to be exempted from compulsory military service?

In February 1917 Lloyd George, with characteristic force,
had summarized the probable results of trying to apply conscription to Ireland: 'scenes in the house of commons, a possible

185

rupture with America, which is hanging in the balance, serious disaffection in Canada, Australia and South Africa. They would say, "You are fighting for the freedom of nationalities. What right have you to take this little nation by the ears and drag it into a war against its will?" If you passed the act you would get only 160,000 men. You would get them at the point of the bayonet and a conscientious objection clause would exempt by far the greater number. As it is, these men are producing food which we badly need.'[1] By 1918 America was in the war and the British people, after four years of endurance, were definitely feeling the strain. A sense of duty and a determination to persevere kept the country going, but there was a growing consciousness of the burdens which had to be carried and a critical awareness of exemptions from the obligations imposed by the military service acts. How then, when men of fifty were being called up, would the British public opinion react to the exemption of a part of the United Kingdom, a part too which was prospering as a result of war prices and escaping comparatively lightly from war-time deprivations?

On the 28 March the war cabinet considered both whether conscription should be extended to Ireland and the related question, on what date was the new military service bill to be introduced into parliament. Curzon, Balfour, Smuts and the prime minister were all in favour of extending conscription to Ireland and simultaneously introducing a scheme of home rule based on the convention's report. This policy of course implied waiting until the convention's report arrived, which meant a delay of about a week. Milner energetically protested. From the military point of view, he said, there should not be a moment's delay, and 'if time were allowed to slip by, the public would become accustomed to the critical state of affairs'. Bonar Law despondently doubted if the convention's report would make the government's position easier. It was bound, he thought, to arouse antagonism amongst the Ulster unionist M.P.s. The final decision was not to summon parliament, which had adjourned for the Easter recess to 9 April, to meet a week earlier, a decision which implied postponing the introduction of the military service bill until the arrival of the convention's

[1] Lord Riddell, *War diary*, p. 239.

report[2] – a decision which led Henry Wilson, the C.I.G.S., to remark to Duke: 'that when the convention heard that the moment they had signed the government would put on conscription, it would be found they would all get measles and the whole convention would fall down'. Duke (probably disliking both the substance and style of his comment) disagreed with him.[3]

When five days later the war cabinet, with the viceroy, the chief secretary and Sir Henry Robinson, the vice-chairman of the local government board in Ireland, in attendance, discussed Ireland, it seems to have been assumed that conscription was to be extended to Ireland and a home rule bill introduced. Robinson, a highly efficient civil servant, with thirty-five years official experience of Irish public life, whose absurdities he good-naturedly enjoyed, was, on the whole, reassuring. If conscription was applied to Ireland, he thought, the shopmen in the towns might give trouble and the farmers' sons would probably try to avoid being called up, but if the government was firm Ireland would accept conscription. And if conscription was successfully enforced Sinn Fein would die. What he was afraid of was trouble in the north over home rule. He did not anticipate a strike in the shipyards – the men were making too much money – but he expected unrest, especially among the women linen workers employed on aircraft work, and a fall in output. Duke also was unexpectedly cheerful. He believed in 'the practicability of government for Ireland under the convention scheme', and he thought that the Irish administration which would be installed once the convention scheme was implemented could be trusted to enforce conscription.

The lord lieutenant, Wimborne, was less optimistic. He pointed out that to apply conscription in Ireland before implementing the settlement proposed by the convention would cause an explosion. His general appreciation of the situation was that if the nationalists were promised home rule followed by conscription they would not accept it; if the unionists were asked to accept conscription followed by home rule they would be equally hostile. If conscription and home rule were brought in simultaneously, opposition would be general. But on the whole

---

[2] War cabinet minutes, 28 Mar. 1918 (Cab. 23/14).
[3] C. E. Caldwell, *Field Marshall Sir Henry Wilson* (1927), ii, 88.

187

he favoured introducing the two measures at the same time. Bonar Law agreed with him but was afraid of trouble in Ulster. Milner argued that, 'however strange it might appear, an attack from both sides would not be a bad thing. The government would undoubtedly receive great support in this country, a great deal in Ireland and the support of the world if it were seen to be dealing with the whole Irish question firmly and impartially'. And he and Smuts both expressed the opinion that an Irish settlement would never be attained unless imposed. Towards the close of the discussion Balfour dwelt on what he thought was 'the fundamental point' – whether they should be stronger if they got a few men from Ireland and ran the risk of disturbances or if they did nothing. If they adopted the latter policy, it would be difficult to persuade England to accept the decision. 'We should have to state the naked truth', he remarked, 'that Ireland is a sheer weakness, but it would be a greater weakness if we did something than it was if we did nothing'.[4]

The government at the beginning of April 1918 was certainly not happy about its Irish policy. Conscription would not be popular in nationalist Ireland. And the Ulster unionists had already flatly rejected the scheme of home rule sponsored by a majority in the convention. Moreover there was an awkward if minor technical problem to be faced. The military service bill could not be delayed but a home-rule bill based on the recommendations contained in the convention's report, which was bound to be a lengthy and complicated measure, had still to be drafted. The existence of this difficulty was demonstrated by the wording of the Irish clause in the military-service bill. It was provided that the bill would not necessarily come into operation in Ireland immediately it was enacted, but might be applied to Ireland by order in council.

The government's Irish policy was expounded by the prime minister on 9 April, when in a powerful, energetic speech he surveyed the war situation and introduced the military-service bill. Immediately he sat down Devlin tried to move the adjournment, and during the next few days the Irish nationalist M.P.s in a series of impassioned speeches denounced the proposal to impose compulsory military service on a country without obtaining the consent of its people, Dillon going so far

[4] War cabinet minutes, 3 Apr. 1918 (Cab. 23/14).

as to declare that the bill would open up another front in Ireland. And Ireland loomed so large in the debates on the bill that J. H. Thomas was driven to complain that anyone listening would think they were discussing an Irish bill.[5] In Ireland all sections of nationalist opinion were united in a crusade against conscription. Demonstrations took place all over the south and west, and a one day's general strike was organized.

However during the spring of 1918 the government seemed set on its policy of home rule and conscription. The prime minister impressed on Austen Chamberlain, a member of the war cabinet who had suggested that the proposed Irish parliament should not operate until a federal scheme for the British Isles was implemented or Ulster accepted home rule, that these stipulations would make it impossible to carry a home-rule bill in the immediate future, and that 'the Irish would say we were trifling with them and they would have the sympathy of a very large number of people in this country who would think we were not holding the balance fairly between protestant and catholic Ireland'.[6] About the same time, Amery, who was working in the cabinet secretariat, sent Chamberlain some suggestions for dealing with passive resistance to conscription in Ireland. 'The great thing', he wrote, 'is to do it as good humouredly as we can'. Males between 18 and 55 violating the law should forfeit any exemption from military service they might possess; and general resistance in any area could be weakened by the government suspending their public services such as railways and banks.[7]

At the beginning of May a new Irish executive was installed, French, an Irishman and in earlier days a dashing cavalry commander, replacing Wimborne as viceroy, and Shortt, an expert on national-service problems, succeeding Duke as chief secretary. The new executive was obviously expected to administer Ireland firmly, but French and Shortt began by insisting that in Ireland, as in Great Britain, the introduction of compulsory service must be preceded by a recruiting campaign on the lines of the Derby scheme. The war cabinet agreed, and discussed a proclamation to be issued by the viceroy calling for

[5] *Hansard* **5** (*commons*), civ, 1338–70, 1715.
[6] Lloyd George to Chamberlain 13 Apr. 1918 (Chamberlain papers).
[7] Amery to Chamberlain, 1 May 1918 (Chamberlain papers).

recruits. Balfour and Curzon wanted it to be expressly stated that conscription had not been given up. Shortt retorted that his draft though 'by no means tantamount to the abandonment of conscription would have the effect of convincing many people that it was not the intention of the government to deluge Ireland in blood'.[8] The proclamation, which called on Ireland 'to play her part fully and freely in the world struggle for liberty' by supplying 50,000 recruits by 1 October, was issued at the beginning of June, and the unprofitable and almost impossible task of obtaining by compulsion reluctant recruits from an embittered community was indefinitely postponed.

About this time it was suggested that the convention might be revived. Sir Henry Robinson at the beginning of May suggested to Stephen Gwynn that a provisional Irish executive, responsible to the imperial parliament, might be installed. Gwynn at once sketched out a bold plan for an Irish coalition government, which would, broadly speaking, take over the functions of the chief secretary until the end of the war. The work of this government would be subject to review by an Irish assembly, which could perhaps prepare the heads of bills though legislative and financial power would remain with the imperial parliament. The Irish assembly, Gwynn thought, could be the convention. It was, he pointed out, already known in Ireland, the members knew each other and it was 'essentially coalition in atmosphere and tradition'. Moreover Ulster had accepted it. The aims of the new government should be to tranquillize the country, to bring about united action between sections of Irishmen and to bring back Ireland into the war. Gwynn suggested that the new Irish administration should be composed of Plunkett ('chief'), Healy (chancellor), Powell (attorney general), Barrie (agriculture), Pollock (finance and works), Waugh (labour), Boland (education), Clancy (lands), Devlin or Gwynn (local government). All the men he suggested had been members of the convention, with the exception of Healy and Boland. The latter, one of the whips of the Irish parliamentary party, had been educated at the universities of Oxford and Bonn.[9]

French and Shortt were not only confronted by the great anti-

[8] War cabinet minutes, 10 May 1918 (Cab. 23/14).
[9] Gwynn to Hayden, 4 May 1918 and enclosed memorandum (N.L.I.MS 8380).

conscription agitation. They were also painfully impressed by the disturbed condition of much of the country. Defiance of authority was loudly expressed, drilling was continuously going on; toward the end of May the Irish executive, having asserted that there was evidence that the Sinn Fein leaders were attempting to co-operate with Germany, made numerous arrests. The war cabinet scrutinized with some scepticism the evidence for what was melodramatically termed 'the German plot' – Curzon remarking that much of it was a year old and that the material supplied by Admiral Hall provided proof of German designs but not of Sinn Fein complicity.[10] Nevertheless it was obvious that there was widespread disaffection. To proceed with a home-rule bill with hostility in the south and strong opposition to home rule in the north, seemed to Lloyd George 'folly'. And on the 25 June he announced that the government was not going to introduce the home-rule measure in the immediate future. With conscription and home rule indefinitely postponed, the government's Irish policy, as enunciated in April, was in disarray, though Curzon tried to put a good face on it. 'It was necessary', he explained at the end of July in the lords, 'I will not say to abandon the policy – that would be a most unfair description of our position – I will not say to change the front, but it was our duty to recognize the facts of the case as they were before us and adjust our policy to them'.[11]

By the summer of 1918 the tide was beginning to flow rapidly in favour of the allies and by mid-November all the central powers had sued for peace. The all-absorbing, exhausting struggle was over, but immediately the allied leaders were confronted by a distracting multiplicity of urgent problems. Over much of Europe and Asia political authority and economic organization had collapsed, and the peace conference which began at Versailles in January 1919 had both to adjust a large number of claims in three continents and endeavour to reconstruct ordered existence over wide areas in Europe and Asia. At home, the British government had to handle demobilization, dismantle much of the elaborate machinery which had been built up during the war and cope with outbreaks of bitter industrial strife. Thus for months after the war ended,

[10] War cabinet minutes, 22 May 1918 (Cab. 23/14).
[11] *Hansard 5,* xxx, 330.

circumstances made it difficult for the government to get down to dealing with the Irish problem, and yet all the time the situation in Ireland was growing more critical.

The general election of 1918 had swept most of the constitutional nationalists out of parliamentary life. At the dissolution they held 76 seats. But in December 1918 only six constitutional nationalists were returned for Irish constituencies. Of these, two, Devlin and Captain Redmond (the son of John Redmond) defeated Sinn Fein candidates. The other four were returned as a result of an agreement with Sinn Fein. At the end of November 1918, Cardinal Logue of Armagh and seven catholic bishops, whose dioceses included parts of Ulster, in a published manifesto pointed out the danger of Ulster seats being captured by the unionist minorities because of contests between 'men on the popular side', and on the matter being referred by both parties to the cardinal he assigned four Ulster seats to the constitutional nationalists and four to Sinn Fein.[12] Sinn Fein won 73 seats in all and the unionists 26. Of the unionists 23 came from Ulster. Carson, who was returned for the Belfast division of Duncairn, emphasized that the war had brought home to him the need for social reform. 'I wanted', he declared, 'a better condition of affairs for my fellow men whatever their rank or class, as they call it, may be'. And two of the Ulster unionist M.P.s from Belfast were returned as labour unionists, Carson explaining that, as he understood it, 'they are true to the union and on questions affecting the union will follow me but on questions relating to labour and the working classes they will vote just as freely as any member of the labour party in England'.[13]

The southern unionists won three seats. Dockrell, chairman of an important Dublin firm of builders' suppliers, won Rathmines, a constituency which included sections of highly respectable Dublin suburbia, and of course the unionists held the two Trinity seats. There were four candidates for the university constituency, Samuels, the attorney general, a pillar of southern unionism who had been returned in 1917, Jellett, a K.C. (and son of a nineteenth-century provost), Woods an eminent Dublin surgeon, and Stephen Gwynn, the nationalist M.P., himself an Oxford man but, as he reminded the constituency, the son of a

[12] *Irish Times*, 28 Nov., 2, 3, 4 Dec. 1918.
[13] *Belfast Newsletter*, 29 Nov. 1918.

Trinity professor, three of whose sons had been elected to fellowship. Carson, who was one of the sitting members, withdrew just before nomination day, stating in a letter to the provost that it was desirable for him to do so since the convention had brought out differences of opinion between the northern and southern unionists. A week later Carson enlarged on this. 'Never', he told a Belfast audience, 'was Ulster in a more dangerous position than it was when the convention was drawing to a close because the southern unionists lost their courage' and under Lord Midleton's leadership 'they were prepared to say "if we go down Ulster must go down too".'[14]

Mahaffy publicly expressed his surprise at Carson's action in 'bartering his university seat for a very new constituency in the slums of Belfast'. A week or so before Carson announced his intention, Samuels wrote in confidence that if Carson went to Belfast it implied that 'the game was up'. The Belfast businessmen, Samuels went on to say, 'are a poor lot in politics. They cannot find a decent candidate, I hear, for even one of their many new seats. Their local manufacturers are too busy with money making to even make a rota among themselves to attend parliament.' They were also afraid, Samuels gathered, that if Carson did not stand three seats might be lost to labour. When Carson and Craig explained to Samuels that they had tried unsuccessfully to get the big merchants and manufacturers of Belfast to come forward, Samuels retorted that he thought the 'patriotism, so-called, of these Belfast men is absolutely contemptible'.[15]

Jellett was more sympathetic to Ulster. He explained publicly that, while opposed to home rule for any part of Ireland, at the same time he quite recognized that should home rule become inevitable, Ulster had an absolute right to insist that 'she should not be dragged into the waste and ruin entailed by any such scheme'. Woods took up a position which allowed him a little more manœuvreability – the union, he declared, was the only alternative to a settlement by consent. Gwynn explained that he was driven by the logic of facts to accept the policy put forward in the convention by two of its most distinguished members, the

[14] *Irish Times*, 23 Nov.; *Belfast Newsletter*, 4 Dec. 1918.
[15] *Irish Times*, 23 Dec. 1918; Samuels to Bernard, 12, 19 Nov. 1918 (Add. MS 52783).

provost and the primate – federalism. And he advocated the summoning of a fresh convention limited by its terms of reference to drafting a federal constitution for Ireland.[16] Samuels and Woods were returned, Jellett did satisfactorily, and Gwynn secured a small number of votes. When Samuels was put on the bench Jellett was returned unopposed for Trinity in July 1919.

Shortly after the election the southern unionists finally broke into two distinct sections. A month after the convention finished its work a determined attempt was made at a meeting of the Irish Unionist Alliance to censure the southern unionist delegation. Jellett moved a resolution to the effect that the meeting disagreed in toto with the findings of the convention and affirmed its undeviating support of the union. An attempt was made to get the Ulster members (whom Jellett had urged to attend) to withdraw. This was unsuccessful, but Desart made what Montgomery grudgingly described as a clever speech, deprecating an uncompromising declaration against home rule at the very time that a home-rule bill might be destroyed by the nationalists and in the end the adjournment was carried by 80 to 51.[17] The unionists who had signed 'the call' then set to work to capture control of the Alliance, or, as Montgomery put it, to show that, with 'the exception of a few scheming peers and whiskey and manure sellers', they were opposed to home rule.[18] Their efforts were rewarded when the delegates assembled in Dublin in the summer to choose a new executive committee. Of the 20 members elected, the first 16 were 'call' supporters.[19] At the beginning of 1919, Midleton's group tried to reassert their leadership. At a meeting on 24 January a resolution was brought forward providing that the Ulster members should be excluded from the deliberations of the Alliance if a scheme involving partition came up for consideration. Jellett opposed this motion, it was defeated, and a number of leading southern unionists, including Midleton, Jameson, Stewart and Iveagh,

[16] *Irish Times*, 27 Nov., 5 Dec. 1918.
[17] *Dublin Evening Mail*, 3 May 1918, *Irish Times*, 4 May 1918; Montgomery to Dawson Bates, 4 May 1918 (Montgomery papers).
[18] Montgomery to Willis, 20 May 1918 (Montgomery papers).
[19] *Dublin Evening Mail*, 8 June 1918; Printed paper, signed J. E. Walsh, 31 Aug. 1918 (Montgomery papers).

194

withdrew from the Alliance and immediately formed the Unionist Anti-partition League. The league in its programme emphasized that it stood for the maintenance of the union and was against partition. In the event of opposition to home rule proving futile, it would strive for safeguards for the unionists of the south and west. The Alliance emphasized its complete hostility to home rule and tried to bring home to the British public the dangers of surrender.[20]

Towards the end of 1919 the cabinet began to consider the preparation of a major measure to meet the Irish problem, which since the end of 1918 had become more difficult and urgent. In January 1919 those of the Sinn Fein M.P.s, returned at the 1918 general election who were not in gaol had met at the Mansion House in Dublin, declared themselves Dail Eireann, and adopted a declaration of independence. Soon afterwards, efforts were made to establish under the authority of Dail Eireann rudimentary administrative services which attempted to take over as far as possible the government of the country. Simultaneously, the more militant republicans tried to prevent the existing governmental machinery from functioning. The government struck back, guerrilla warfare developed and spread. By the beginning of 1921 large areas were under martial law and over much of the south and west of Ireland the king's writ was ceasing to run.

Finding a solution for the Irish question was a daunting task, especially for a coalition cabinet. It was only five years since the unionist and liberal members of the administration had been fighting fiercely over the Irish question. And the attempts which had been made to solve the Irish problem between 1914 and 1919 had merely demonstrated its apparent intractibility. It was scarcely surprising then that the first general cabinet discussion on Ireland ran on pessimistic lines. It was pointed out that any home-rule bill which was practicable would inevitably put the northern unionists under a different régime from that of the rest of the United Kingdom, inflict hardship on the southern unionists, 'who had made as great sacrifices in the war as any part of the empire', and give the southern provinces rather less than they had secured under the 1914 act. But it was also clear, when relations with the United States and the dominions were

[20] *Dublin Evening Mail*, 24 Jan. 1919, *Irish Times*, 25 Jan. 1918.

taken into account, that a home-rule bill could not be postponed. And a momentary gust of irritation seems to have swept through the cabinet room: for it was suggested that since Ireland gained more from the union than Great Britain, it should be enacted that the three southern provinces would be cut off from Great Britain, unless, before a certain date, their inhabitants by a plebiscite declared themselves in favour of the union. But it was apparently realized that a majority in the southern provinces might be misguided enough to vote against their own interests and the union, because the principal reason urged against the proposed plebiscite was 'that an Ireland which in time of war could remain neutral might, owing to its geographical position, prove a great danger to the British empire'.[21]

About a month later the cabinet again discussed what should be the government's ultimate objectives when formulating its Irish policy. It was agreed that these should be a united Ireland with a parliament of its own, bound by the closest ties with Great Britain. It was pointed out that lifelong unionists naturally preferred having a single parliament in the United Kingdom. But the cabinet was reminded that it was important to make a good impression on the self-governing dominions, the United States and other foreign countries; and that this could only be achieved by a bill which at least paved the way for an Irish parliament when both north and south were willing to accept it.[22]

According to Lloyd George, in framing a home rule bill three basic facts had to be taken into account – that Irishmen claimed the right to control their own domestic concerns; that there was a section of the people of Ireland just as opposed to Irish rule as the majority of Irishmen were to British rule; and that any arrangement by which Ireland was severed from the United Kingdom would be fatal to the interests of both. England was Ireland's best customer and Ireland was of the greatest strategic importance to England. And Lloyd George emphasized that if Great Britain during the war had not had control over the Irish coast, 'the area of submarine activity would have been greatly extended' and the allies cut off from the United States and the dominions.[23]

[21] Cabinet minutes, 11 Nov. 1919 (Cab. 23/18).
[22] Cabinet minutes, 3 Dec. 1919 (Cab. 23/18).
[23] *Hansard 5 (commons)*, cxxiii, 1170–4.

These general considerations largely determined the pattern of the measure 'to provide for the better government of Ireland' which the government laid before parliament early in 1920. In its general outline the bill closely resembled the scheme which Lloyd George had put forward in May 1917 as an alternative to summoning a convention. Ireland was to be politically divided into two areas, Southern Ireland and Northern Ireland, the latter comprising the six north-east counties. Each area was to have a parliament consisting of a house of commons with an executive responsible to it, appointed by the lord lieutenant. 'With a view to the eventual establishment of a parliament for the whole of Ireland, and to bring about harmonious action between the parliaments and governments of Southern Ireland and Northern Ireland', a council of Ireland was to be constituted, consisting of a president, nominated by the crown on the advice of the United Kingdom government, and of forty persons, twenty nominated by each of the Irish parliaments. The parliaments were empowered to establish by identical acts a parliament for the whole of Ireland, to which parliament the powers possessed by the council of Ireland and any other powers which the parliaments of Southern and Northern Ireland agreed to surrender, were to be transferred.

The parliaments of Southern and Northern Ireland were each empowered to legislate for its own area in all matters except the crown, defence, foreign affairs, external trade, light-houses, cables, currency and aerial navigation. And certain services – police, postal services, the registry of deeds and the public record office – were provisionally reserved for imperial control, the police for three years, the other services until the date of Irish union, unless the two parliaments by identical acts provided for the transfer of the services to the council of Ireland or for their joint administration by the two Irish governments. Land purchase was to be reserved until the parliament of the United Kingdom should otherwise determine. The council of Ireland was entrusted with certain functions in relation to private bills and with legislative and administrative powers in respect of railways and the contagious diseases of animals; and the parliaments of Southern and Northern Ireland might by identical acts delegate to the council any of their powers.

Each area was to have its own supreme court and there was

to be a high court of appeal for Ireland. Each parliament was empowered to impose within its respective jurisdiction any tax except a customs or excise duty. The imperial parliament retained control over customs, excise and income tax but the Irish parliaments were empowered to raise the rate of income tax in their areas. Any time after the date of Irish union the control of customs and excise might be transferred to the Irish parliament. Ireland was to make an imperial contribution (for two years at £18,000,000); and a joint exchequer board, on which the imperial government and both Irish governments were to be represented, was to allot the proceeds of reserved taxes between the areas and fix the imperial contribution. Ireland was to be represented at Westminster by 42 M.P.s.

The Irish sub-committee of the cabinet was largely responsible for the preparation of the bill but while it was being put into shape several important points were raised by individual ministers or discussed by the cabinet itself. The terms Northern and Southern Ireland were, it was explained, adopted 'in order to escape if possible from the terms associated with the old and long protracted controversaries'.[24] But one of those controversaries could not be avoided – what area was to be comprised in Northern Ireland. Though county option was mentioned, the government seems to have felt that the choice lay between the whole province of Ulster and the six counties. It was strongly urged in the cabinet that if their ultimate aim was the unity of Ireland it would be desirable to place the whole province, which contained large numbers of both catholics and protestants and a good balance of rural and urban areas, under the jurisdiction of the Northern Ireland parliament.[25] But Balfour was strongly opposed to the creation of a *Hibernia irredenta*,[26] and the cabinet was informed that the Ulster unionist leaders preferred the six county area, being very doubtful if they could effectually govern the whole province. James Craig, the future prime minister of Northern Ireland, suggested a boundary commission to examine the denominational distribution of the population on the borders of the six counties and to take a vote

[24] Cabinet minutes, 10 Dec. 1919 (Cab. 23/18).
[25] Cabinet minutes, 19 Dec. 1919 (Cab. 23/18).
[26] Balfour to prime minister, 10 Feb. 1920 (Cab. 24/98).

by districts.[27] And when, near the end of December 1919, Lloyd George outlined in the house of commons the government's plan for the future government of Ireland, he seems to have inclined towards this proposal, since he implied that Northern Ireland would be constituted by 'taking the six counties as a basis, eliminating where practicable the catholic communities, while including the protestant communities from the coterminous catholic counties of Ireland, in order to produce an area as homogeneous as it is possible to achieve under these circumstances'. But during the drafting of the bill no attempts appear to have been made to insert provision for plebiscites on the borders of Northern Ireland; and Macphearson, the chief secretary, referring to the area problem in introducing the bill, said that the 'soundest and most practicable' plan was the one discussed if not decided on in 1914 and decided upon in 1916, that is to say treating the six counties as a unit. Dealing with the same problem in the lords, Birkenhead pointed out that 'the main trend of the business activities' in Tyrone and Fermanagh was towards Belfast, and he asserted that the presence of a powerful minority in the Ulster parliament might 'prove to be corrective of undue haste or partiality if such tendencies should unfortunately disclose themselves'.[28]

The cabinet discussions on home-rule finance followed familiar lines. H. A. L. Fisher, the historian, who was minister for education, was strongly in favour of transferring the control of customs and excise to the Irish parliaments. He admitted that this would be a bold step, but, he argued, it would ultimately promote the principal object of the bill, the reconciliation of the English and Irish races. Taking into account the great power of retaliation possessed by the wealthier country, Fisher did not think the concession he urged would damage British trade. In reply to the question, would not his policy lead to the emergence of a customs barrier between Northern and Southern Ireland, he remarked that the two areas would probably remain separated from one another for a long time.[29] The cabinet sub-committee, however, argued that to give the Irish parliaments control over even excise duties might have unfortunate

[27] Cabinet minutes, 10, 15 Dec. 1919 (Cab. 23/18).
[28] *Hansard 5 (commons)*, cxxvii, 927, *Hansard 5 (lords)*, xlii, 846.
[29] H. A. L. Fisher, cabinet paper, 31 Jan. 1920 (Cab. 24/97).

o   199

consequences. If the Irish duty on an article was lower than the British, the Irish producer would be protected against the British in the Irish market. If the article was one which was exported from Ireland to Britain, 'the lowering of the Irish excise duty would be particularly objectionable. British producers could migrate to Ireland more easily than to foreign countries and they might do so on a large scale in order to produce for the British market at a lower rate of duty. This would not only be an artificial displacement of industry but it would also occasion a serious loss of revenue to the imperial exchequer'. Moreover if Ireland was given control of excise duties, with variations between the excise rates in the two islands counteracted by customs duties, it would be impossible, the sub-committee thought, to refuse Ireland control over customs. And 'control of customs is likely', the sub-committee emphasized, 'to lead to control of tariff policy'.[30]

Customs and excise were as has been seen, reserved in the bill, but Ireland's imperial contribution was fixed on a basis very favourable to Ireland and the government promised to introduce a scheme of land purchase based on the convention's report. There was some opposition in the cabinet to giving what was regarded as a financial bonus to the south and west of Ireland, which 'had deserted Great Britain in her hour of need'. And Balfour hoped that when settling the financial provisions of the bill they would not be absurdly lavish, 'I would', he wrote, 'treat the rebels over money matters as one gentleman treats another in a matter of pure business'. He would not 'over-pay Ireland either on the false ground that Ireland had been treated ungenerously in the past', nor on 'the principle which induces a man to give a large sum to an organ grinder'. Balfour 'would pay neither conscience money nor blackmail'.[31]

Other points raised while the bill was being drafted related to defence, unemployment insurance and the representation of Ireland at Westminster. Attention was drawn to the danger that an Irish parliament might recruit an abnormally large police force which could be employed in war time to capture imperial naval bases in Ireland. And it was suggested that the parliamentary draftsman in charge of the bill might look to the clause

---

[30] Irish sub-committee, cabinet paper, 31 Jan. 1920 (Cab. 24/97).
[31] Balfour to prime minister, 10 Feb. 1920 (Cab. 24/98).

in the peace treaty limiting the size of police forces in Germany.[32] It was also suggested that unemployment insurance and labour exchanges should be reserved services, since otherwise trade unionists would be exasperated by variations in benefits and rates. But, it was retorted, the existing rates fixed on British standards were regarded in Ireland as grossly extravagant and it was therefore decided that the services should be transferred.[33]

In the first draft of the bill there was an 'in and out' clause whereby the Irish members at Westminster were to be excluded from voting on purely British issues. But this provision was dropped on the ground that its retention would offend the Ulster unionists, who claimed that their area was an integral part of the United Kingdom and might lead to a government having a most unstable parliamentary majority. It was also pointed out that the Ulster unionists would object to the representation of their province at Westminster being reduced, and it was suggested as a means of meeting this grievance that each Irish area should be given the same number of M.P.s at Westminster. But it was quickly pointed out that this plan would 'furnish an undesirable precedent against England in the event of a federal parliament' and in the end members were assigned to the Irish constituencies roughly in accordance with population.[34]

The debate in the commons on the second reading of the bill, which was part of a heavy legislative programme, began at the end of March, and the bill was still in committee when the house adjourned for the summer recess. It did not receive its third reading until 11 November and only reached the committee stage in the lords on 1 December. The debates on the bill, both in the lords and commons, are interesting as reflecting complex varieties of opinion, but a growing sense of futility generated boredom in the commons, and as early as April *Punch* summarizing the second reading debate, said that ' "the yawning chasm" which according to its opponents the bill is going to insert between the north and south of Ireland' was to be seen on the countenances of many members while the chief secretary

---

[32] Cabinet minute, 3 Dec. 1919 (Cab. 23/18).
[33] R. S. Horne, cabinet paper, 9 Dec. 1919 (Cab. 24/94), cabinet minutes, 10 Dec. 1919 (Cab. 23/18).
[34] Cabinet minutes, 3, 10, 19 Dec. 1919 (Cab. 23/18).

was outlining its provisions.[35] When however the bill reached the lords, the vigorously voiced apprehensions of the peers from the south of Ireland, the determination of the house to assert itself and the antagonism aroused by the arrogant ability of the lord chancellor, Birkenhead, infused some spirit into the discussions.

On its second reading in the house of commons the bill was attacked by the Irish nationalists, the labour party, the Asquithian liberals and by a section of the unionists. Devlin denounced it as a proposal to divide a nation permanently, and he emphasized that, in the convention, the southern unionists, the labour men and the nationalists had all agreed that 'national unity was sacrosanct', the nationalists being prepared for this reason to make considerable concessions to obtain a parliament for the whole of Ireland. Clynes, for the labour party, denounced partition and urged that an Irish constituent assembly should be summoned; Asquith, describing the bill as embodying 'a large, cumbersome, costly and unworkable scheme', also suggested an Irish constituent assembly and argued that the Ulster problem could be met by county option. Lord Robert Cecil considered that the government should rigidly enforce law and order in Ireland before embarking on a constitutional experiment.[36] The minority of 98 which opposed the second reading was composed of nationalist (7), labour (44), liberals (19), southern unionists (3) and British unionists (23). The Ulster unionists abstained from voting on both the second and third readings of the bill.

Early in March the Ulster unionist council had agreed to accept the bill without accepting responsibility for it. And a resolution moved by Lord Farnham and seconded by Knight, substituting the province of Ulster for the six counties, was defeated.[37] Shortly afterwards Charles Craig, M.P. for South Antrim and brother of James Craig, the first prime minister of Northern Ireland, pointed out that in a nine-county parliament the unionist majority would be so slender that 'no sane man would undertake to carry on a parliament with it'. And Carson, having referred to his 'passionate longing to get in with

[35] *Punch*, 7 Apr. 1920.
[36] *Hansard 5 (commons)*, cxxvii, 944–66, 1107–20, 1133–52.
[37] *Belfast Newsletter*, 11 Mar. 1920.

us the unionists who are in Cavan, Donegal and Monaghan', explained that 'after anxious hours of discussion and anxious days of going into the whole matter, almost parish by parish and townland by townland' they had come to the conclusion that there would be no chance of successfully starting a parliament in Belfast if it was to be responsible for all nine counties.[38]

The attitude of the northern unionists to the bill as a whole was frankly expressed by Craig and Carson. The bill, in Craig's words, confronted Ulster 'with a most extraordinary paradox'. While the Ulster unionists loathed and detested home rule and the break up of the United Kingdom, nevertheless they saw in the bill the realization of what they had aimed at when in 1913–14 they took steps which, Craig admitted, were illegal, to prevent the imposition of home rule 'on practically a million of the kingdom's most loyal and patriotic citizens'. Accepting that home rule was inevitable, the Ulster unionists stated that they simply wished to remain part and parcel of the United Kingdom. And when Lord Robert Cecil in committee proposed that a parliament should not be established for Northern Ireland, the area remaining in all respects part of the United Kingdom, the northern unionists supported him. But it is probably true to say that, though they voted with logical consistency, they did not expect the amendment to be carried. Clearly a local parliament had its advantages. Even on the second reading Craig admitted that the Ulster unionists saw that a parliament of their own would put them 'in a position of absolute security'. Carson, believing that there should and would soon be 'a great devolution of the business of the United Kingdom', said that he did not 'look upon a parliament in Ulster as altogether without a ray of sunshine' and in a letter to Birkenhead, read during the debates on the bill in the lords, he stated that Ulster wanted peace and to be removed from the arena of British party politics, and that the Ulster unionists had decided that in the interests of Ireland, Great Britain and the empire, they should accept the bill and work it loyally.[39]

There were some points of detail in which the northern

---

[38] *Hansard 5 (commons)*, cxxvii, 990–1, 1299, ccxxix, 1315–16.

[39] *Hansard 5 (commons)*, ccxxix, 1996–8, ccxxx, 941, 1186–93; cxxxiv, 926. *Hansard (lords)*, xlii, 433–4.

unionists unsuccessfully tried to have the bill amended. The bill provided that the Irish parliaments should be chosen by proportional representation and prohibited them from altering the method of election for three years. The northern unionists, who considered P.R. to be an unpopular and expensive system, wanted this prohibition removed. They also tried to get rid of the court of appeal for Ireland, arguing that the legal system constituted by the bill was too elaborate and that it would be better if appeals went directly from the northern and southern supreme courts to the house of lords. They wanted to transfer the administration of railways from the council of Ireland to the two parliaments. Craig indeed referred to the council as that 'very miserable council', which instead of bringing the two parliaments together was going to 'act as a sort of lever for keeping them apart'. Carson spoke of the council (an invention of his own) with more respect as 'the liaison between north and south', and said he considered 'the conception of this council . . . the biggest advance towards unity in Ireland'. However he was in favour of depriving it of its functions in respect to railways. Another minor amendment advocated by the northern unionists was to the effect that the lord lieutenant should spend at least three months every year in Belfast, Whitla, the member for Queen's University, Belfast, asserting that 'a great deal of the misgovernment of Ireland could be traced to the fact that the lord lieutenant goes over to Dublin and knows less about Belfast than he knows about Moscow'.

The southern unionists took a far more active part in the debates on the bill, which they wanted to reshape in a number of important respects. A week after the bill was introduced two leading southern unionists, Midleton and Desart, approached Carson to see what were the possibilities for common action. They wanted him to oppose the bill vigorously, attacking especially the absurdities of partition, the absence of second chambers in the Irish parliaments, the proposal that those parliaments should have unlimited power over income tax and the handing over control of the police to the people who were shooting at them. Carson was sympathetic but what he said implicitly emphasized the gap between northern and southern unionism. He explained that the Ulster unionists preferred the *status quo* but would accept the bill rather than the 1914 act.

However he agreed that if Jellett and Dockrell pressed for the postponement of the bill until peace was restored in Ireland the Ulster M.P.s might support them. When Midleton and Desart emphasized there must be second chambers 'or everything that landlords and capitalists valued would be taken away from them in a week', Carson pointed out that if a protestant second chamber was set up in the south a catholic second chamber would be asked for in the north, and this would mean that in a joint assembly (i.e. the council of Ireland) the unionists would be in a minority. Desart tried to reassure him by saying 'sane men should be nominated to the council or belong to it ex-officio'. Carson then went on to explain to Midleton and Desart that Belfast was largely socialist and that when the fear of the pope disappeared constituencies like his own, which was ninety per cent working class, would be of little use to the southern unionists. Indeed he mentioned as an argument for including all the nine counties of Ulster the possibility that 'the outside counties might counteract the socialism of Belfast'.[40]

When the bill was in committee the southern unionists tried to obtain safeguards for themselves, to maintain as far as possible Irish unity and to make the bill more acceptable to moderate nationalist opinion. In the commons Walter Guinness strove strenuously and with some success to secure constitutional safeguards and in the lords the southern unionist peers obtained two safeguards – both financial. They deleted the words which empowered the Irish parliaments to raise the income tax and they added a phrase prohibiting them from taking property 'without just compensation'. The government considered that this latter amendment implied a vital constitutional change since it meant that a supreme court could sit in judgement on an act of parliament.[41] But the amendment was defended in the commons and the government yielded to the extent of accepting it with the omission of the word 'just'.

When the bill was in committee in the commons Guinness proposed that there should be an Irish senate. Composed of members nominated by both Irish houses of commons and by the lord lieutenant and of representatives of the churches, the

---

[40] Midleton to Bernard, 3 Mar. 1920, enclosing memorandum of conversation with Carson (Add. MS 52781).
[41] Conference of ministers, minutes, 15 Dec. 1920 (Cab. 23/23).

Irish peers and privy councillors, this senate was to provide a second house for both Irish parliaments. Guinness pointed out that it would provide a safeguard for minorities and 'be a great encouragement to Irish unity'. And Pennefather, M.P. for the Kirkdale division of Liverpool but a member of a great Tipperary family, speaking on behalf of 'the unhappy minority in Southern Ireland who are in danger because they are loyalists and friends of Britain and friends of Ulster', appealed to the northern unionists to 'come and help us; place your wisdom and sagacity into the common pool'. But the Ulster unionists, arguing that it was ridiculous to suggest that the decisions of their own democratic parliament should be submitted to such an artificial body as the proposed senate, spoke and voted against Guinness's proposal which was decisively defeated. Sir Samuel Hoare did however manage to carry an amendment providing that each Irish Parliament should be bi-cameral. The government agreed to produce schemes for a northern and a southern senate by the report stage of the bill, but when that stage was reached, six months later, the government announced that, baffled by the problem of devising senates, it had decided to entrust the council of Ireland with the duty – a decision which, Guinness bitterly remarked, meant postponing the matter to the Greek Kalends. In the lords the government was overborne, and on the initiative of Lord Oranmore and Browne each parliament was provided with a senate – the northern senate to be composed of the lord mayor of Belfast, the mayor of Londonderry and twenty-four members elected by the northern house of commons; the southern house of representatives of the churches, of the Irish peers and privy councillors, and of the county councils, and of persons nominated to represent commerce, labour and learned bodies. When this decision was being discussed in the house of commons Devlin complained that, while a most conservative senate was going to be constituted in the south, the minority in the north were given only the same weight in the northern senate as they possessed in the northern house of commons.

Guinness also tried to make an important change in the constitution of the council of Ireland. He wanted its members to be elected by the Irish houses of commons, using proportional representation. Under the bill, he pointed out, there was nothing to prevent the majority in each parliament nominating a solid block of extremists. But if P.R. was instituted they should get 'a certain mixture of moderating influences. There would be a few nationalists in addition to the Sinn Feiners from the south, and possibly a few nationalists side by side with unionists from the north'. Robert O'Neill replied that this would mean that the unionists would be in a permanent minority in the council, and the house rejected Guinness's proposal. But in the lords the southern unionist peers carried an amendment providing that seven members of the council should be chosen by each senate and thirteen by each house of commons, voting, in the event of a contest, to be by P.R. The government, when it considered this amendment, concluded that it might lead to a catholic majority in the council of Ireland. And since 'the whole basis of the constitution of the council of Ireland was that it should consist of equal numbers of representatives from the northern and southern parliaments', when the lords' amendments were being considered by the commons the government secured the rejection of the Southern Unionists' plan for the selection of the council of Ireland. The government argued that, as it was hoped the council would become 'a larger and larger spending body', the Irish houses of commons, which had control over finance, should elect its members.[42]

Guinness in the commons and Desart in the lords tried to maintain a single judiciary for the whole of Ireland. They argued that, if two supreme courts were set up, vested interests would be created which would develop into 'a very strong influence in favour of partition'. And Desart pointed out they had in Ireland a united bar and a united body of solicitors. They were defeated but Guinness managed to carry two fairly important amendments. One of them slightly increased the powers of the council of Ireland by providing that it should be entrusted with the control of fisheries. The other increased the Irish representation in the imperial parliament from 42 to 46 by providing that the Irish universities should continue to be represented at Westminster, it being emphasized that the southern unionists, who otherwise would not be represented, could hope to have their views expressed by the Trinity members.

[42] Ibid.

In an effort to make the bill more acceptable to nationalist opinion, the southern unionists pressed vigorously for drastic changes in its financial provisions. Guinness proposed that control of the reserved taxes should be given to the Irish parliaments. A fortnight before he moved his amendment, the question of granting financial autonomy to the Irish parliaments was considered by the cabinet, and Lloyd George argued the case against it with tremendous verve and dialectical virtuosity. For the United Kingdom to give up the control of income tax would be, he declared, 'to let off Ireland financially', and though 'he was all for justice for Ireland . . . it must be remembered that justice was due to England, Scotland and Wales who had made greater sacrifices in the war than Ireland'. Customs he considered a symbol of unity, and, he said, 'he was still a Gladstonian home ruler and he wished to keep Ireland an integral part of the United Kingdom and that was why he hoped the present bill would be proceeded with. Under the bill it would be possible to keep the United Kingdom, which was a small country, together in some sort of unity.' To these general considerations he added a more immediate and cruder argument. The reserved taxes, he contended, could be used to reduce Ireland to submission. Ulster would work the bill, and Great Britain by merely holding the ports would control three-quarters of Ireland's revenue and have Sinn Fein at its mercy. Such a policy, the prime minister added, was not unprecedented; 'the Roman empire had constantly to do this kind of thing in Sicily'. Finally he implied that the reserved taxes should be retained as a bargaining counter when negotiating with Sinn Fein. 'If', Lloyd George argued, 'we gave up customs, excise and income tax without getting anything in return it would be the worst piece of business which this government has ever done. . . . Such taxes ought to be imperial taxes and it was unsound in principle to part with these things.'[43]

The government opposed Guinness's amendment and he was overwhelmingly defeated, but amongst those who voted with him were four of the six young conservative backbenchers who Bonar Law thought were destined to be cabinet ministers.[43A] A fifth member of this group, Edward Wood, said at this time that

[43] Cabinet minutes, 13 Oct. 1920 (Cab. 23/23).
[43A] N. Waterhouse, *Private and official* (1942), p 214.

he was in favour of offering dominion status to Ireland. The sixth was Guinness himself. Clearly by the summer of 1920 a small but influential section of the conservative party had come to the conclusion that, if granting dominion status to Ireland was a risk, it was a risk well worth taking.

When the bill reached the committee stage in the lords, Mac-Donnell proposed that the Irish parliaments should have complete control over the finances of their areas. He too was defeated but the minority of 37 which supported his amendment included 23 peers resident in Southern Ireland. And Midleton in the debate produced a political apologia, explaining why he had 'very slightly altered his position on the financial issue'. He and his supporters in the convention, he said, had fought hard for the maintenance of imperial control over customs duties but he had been greatly impressed by 'the passionate earnestness' with which large sections in Ireland regarded the question. He himself, while the convention was sitting, had spent some days at the treasury and the custom house trying 'to find out what the case was against a customs barrier between Great Britain and Ireland'. To his surprise he had found that both departments believed that such a barrier could be easily and economically administered, and 'though he was the last man in the house who would wish to see the power of this empire either in finance or anything else cut up or curtailed', now, for the sake of a settlement which would 'carry the bulk of the Irish people', he was prepared to concede control of customs and excise.

The government of Ireland act received the royal assent shortly before midnight on 23 December 1920. The next day a leader in *The Times* declared that 'few indeed believed or believe that this bill will prove in itself a final settlement of the Irish question'. In fact the act only came into operation fully in the six county area. In May 1921 elections were held for the parliaments of Northern and Southern Ireland. In Northern Ireland the unionists secured a large majority and at the beginning of June the lord lieutenant constituted seven government departments in Northern Ireland, defined their functions and powers, and appointed ministers to head them. In the south, Sinn Fein captured all the constituencies with one exception, and when at the end of June the parliament of Southern Ireland met in the council room of the Department of Agriculture, only fifteen senators and four members of the house of commons (the M.P.s for Trinity) attended. When it held another meeting, a fortnight later, a few additional senators signed the roll and the two M.P.s who attended thanked his majesty the king for his message.

While the government of Ireland act was still in committee in the house of commons, the government's faith in it as a solution of the Irish question must have been severely shaken. Near the end of July 1920 several cabinet ministers, including Lloyd George, Bonar Law and Curzon, held a conference with some senior Irish officials. Major-General Tudor, who was in command of the police, was confident that the campaign of outrage in Ireland could be checked if the crown forces were given proper support. But four of his colleagues, all men of weight and ability, urged other courses. MacMahon, the under-secretary, said that repression would fail and suggested a thirty-two county parliament from which Ulster could opt out. In short, he advocated dominion home rule with exclusion. Cope, an assistant under-secretary, said that Tudor's policy would rebound on the government like a boomerang, and quoted Cardinal Logue as being in favour of dominion home rule. The other assistant secretary, Sir John Anderson, one of the outstanding civil servants of his generation, disagreed strongly with Tudor.[44] He was convinced that if force was to be relied on 'it means in effect a military dictatorship' and he favoured home rule as a solution. Wylie, the law adviser, a man of tremendous vigour with a shrewd awareness of the currents of Irish life, vehemently urged the government to negotiate. He explained that he had begun life as a unionist but had been convinced that the Irish were capable of self-government by seeing the marvellous organization Sinn Fein had built up. If the government made an offer of dominion status, Wylie was sure Sinn Fein would respond. He went on to suggest that the six counties should not be given a parliament of their own but kept under United Kingdom control, since the Sinn Fein view was that the administration of the rest of Ireland would be so successful that the north-east area would soon want to come in. James Craig replied that if Wylie's suggestion were accepted the effect on the north would be 'disastrous'. H. A. L. Fisher suggested that after

[44] Note on the Irish situation by Sir John Anderson (Cab. 24/1/09).

the government of Ireland act was passed the prime minister should propose that a convention should be summoned to draft a constitution for the twenty-six counties. To this Wylie retorted: 'the word convention was obnoxious'.[45]

About the time the government received this douche of cold realism from the senior Irish officials it consulted, groups in the south of Ireland with a conservative bias, deputy lieutenants of counties and justices of the peace, and the unionist anti-partition league, distressed by the growing disorder, began to press for a settlement on the basis of dominion home rule. In August 1920 Midleton, who with Desart had been pressing the cabinet to take strong measures to restore law and order, was dismayed to hear that Jameson, a member of the unionist group in the convention, was with a group which had come over to London to demand a dominion home rule settlement. And from the close of the year efforts were being made to get negotiations started between the republican leaders and the government. On 9 July 1921 a truce between the republicans and the government, in the negotiation of which Midleton played an important part, was agreed to; and discussions began which culminated in the articles of agreement for a treaty, signed on 6 December 1921 – a settlement which gave Southern Ireland – the Irish Free State – dominion status. The old parliamentary party, with its following in Ireland reduced and dispirited, played no part in the negotiations. The Ulster unionists, determined to maintain the autonomy they had won, were intent on holding a watching brief for their zone. The southern unionists, proud of their traditions and mindful of their place in Irish life, must have been painfully conscious of their weakness as their representatives in London during the December negotiations hovered uneasily in the background.

In the middle of November, Midleton, Bernard (now provost of Trinity College, Dublin) and Jameson, 'representing the loyalists of Ireland', saw Lloyd George and some of his colleagues. Lloyd George explained that Sinn Fein had accepted association with the empire for a United Ireland and that he was putting pressure on the northern unionists. Midleton emphasized the importance of limiting the armed forces to be maintained by Ireland and Bernard was anxious to obtain securities

[45] Conference with officers of the Irish government, 23 July 1920 (Cab. 24/109).

for church property. The next day the southern unionist representatives met Griffith, one of the leaders of the Irish delegation, who agreed that land purchase should be completed before the Irish government was set up, that there should be a second chamber and that 'before a taxation agreement was reached' (dealing with double taxation) the southern unionists should be consulted. But Griffith refused to discuss Ulster or any large question, taking up the position that he and his colleagues were in London 'as the Irish government to negotiate with the British government and no one else'.[46]

Three weeks later, on 7 December, the day after the treaty was signed, Midleton and his two colleagues were summoned to a meeting with the prime minister. Midleton expressed surprise that the government had gone so far, and when Lloyd George asked him was he not content with the safeguards in the treaty, he pointed out nothing had been said about taxation. Birkenhead then reminded Midleton that in cases of injustice there would be an appeal to the privy council. Bernard pointed out that nothing was said about the government grant of £30,000 per annum which a commission had recommended in 1920 should be paid to Trinity College. The prime minister 'after reflection admitted he had not appreciated that point'. But he was sure Sinn Fein would deal impartially with all creeds and classes.[47] Later, Midleton, referring to Lloyd George on this occasion, remarked: 'I never knew a man so startled as he appeared to be when we pointed out to him that all the pledges that had been made to us had been ignored and that we were left by the treaty without any remedy except that which we could obtain from those who would rule in Ireland'.[48]

From then on the southern unionists lost effective contact with the government of the United Kingdom. When early in 1922 Bernard supported by a group of M.P.s for the universities secured an interview with Lloyd George with the object of obtaining an annual grant for Trinity, the prime minister refused to burden the British exchequer with this liability.[49] However, a few years later the southern unionist peers achieved

[46] Secret memoranda, 15, 16 Nov. 1921 (Add. MS 52781).
[47] Memorandum [? by Bernard], BM., Add. M.S 52781.
[48] *Hansard 5 (lords)*, lii, 122.
[49] Memorandum, 9 Feb. 1922 (Add. MS 52781).

the remarkable feat of twice defeating a conservative government in the house of lords. Land purchase in Ireland had been
completed by two acts: a Free State act of 1923, and an act of
the imperial parliament applying to Northern Ireland, passed
in 1925. The latter act carried out 'the only unanimous recom-
mendation' made by the convention, being based on its report
on land purchase.[50] The Irish Free State act gave the landlords
less advantageous terms, and in 1926 a group of unionist peers,
including Oranmore and Browne, Midleton, Carson and Mayo,
arguing that the British government was morally bound to meet
the difference between the price paid to the landlord under the
Free State act and that contemplated by the convention, prevailed on the house, in spite of government opposition, to
appoint a select committee to consider the pledges given by
the ministers of the crown regarding Irish land purchase. The
report of this committee proved, in Oranmore's opinion, that
'the ministers were pledged up to the hilt' to complete land
purchase in Southern Ireland on the terms granted in Northern
Ireland. And in May 1927, in the face of resolute government
opposition, the lords resolved by 54 votes to 36 that the government should take steps towards the fulfilment of ministerial
pledges on Irish land purchase.[51] These futile victories of the
southern unionists represent a last despairing effort to implement at least a fragment of the convention's findings.

These hollow victories in the house of lords, victories which
merely showed that the southern unionists retained some social
prestige, even if they had scarcely a vestige of political power,
provide, it might be said, a fitting epilogue to the convention's
history. Because, in spite of the high hopes it had aroused and
the undoubted abilities of many of its members, it had failed to
produce an agreed and acceptable solution to the Irish question.
A critic might argue that this might have been foreseen. Within
the convention, no amount of persuasion and argument could
wear down the obdurate determination of the Ulster unionists
to remain in the United Kingdom and not to come under the
authority of a Dublin parliament. Only sheer, irresistible force

[50] *Hansard 5 (commons)*, clxxix, 372.
[51] *Hansard 5 (lords)*, lxiii, 45–9, lxvii, 173–207.

could have compelled them to accept Irish home rule in any shape or form for themselves. It could also be said that any scheme the convention devised which would have satisfied the constitutional nationalists, a substantial group of unionists and the British government, would have been rejected out of hand by nationalist Ireland. Opinion in Ireland had been moving fast since the spring of 1916. Sinn Fein was gaining support and while moderate nationalists were becoming convinced that home rule must include financial autonomy, more advanced nationalists contemptuously dismissed home rule as a shabby and inadequate substitute for an Irish republic. With the tide of opinion flowing so rapidly, the convention, middle-aged, experienced and moderate, could be regarded as a rhetorical irrelevence on the margin of Irish history.

This view of the convention's place in history has the merit that it more or less corresponds with what happened. But, it might be asked, could not the convention with slightly better fortune have attained its objective, or at least have had a more significant effect on the course of events? After all it need scarcely be said that the convention was fully conscious when it met that it might be taking a place in the great succession of assemblies, beginning with the convention at Philadelphia in 1787, which had endeavoured by drafting a constitution to resolve grave conflicts racial, religious, economic, cultural or geographical, within what was taken to be a political community. There was of course plenty of evidence, for instance the American civil war, and the continuous crises in the Hapsburg lands, demonstrating that there were political situations which could not be resolved by constitutional ingenuity. Still, it was widely believed at the beginning of the twentieth century that, given a combination of rationality and the will to keep a community together, in spite of strong differences, a constitution could be manufactured which would ensure such a degree of protection and fair play to minority interests as would prevent dissatisfaction developing into civil strife. This implied, of course, that all parties concerned would be prepared to accept constitutional limitations on their powers of self-expression. And some groups tended to believe that for them to submit to such limitations would, on moral grounds, be impossible. From Irish nationalist literature a catena of quotations could be collected illustrating the almost absolute claims of an acknowledged nationality.

But one of the features of Irish politics from the union has been the predominance of moderate men. Admittedly this has been obscured by the fact that during certain periods large sections of the Irish people – catholics, tenant farmers, strong nationalists – were vehemently opposed to aspects of the status quo, and expressed their feelings in fervent, even martial, language. And England, with its peaceable evolutionary politics, provided a sober background against which the more heroic and dramatic episodes in Irish history stand out in bold relief. Yet the outstanding Irish leaders, who in turn rallied considerable support in the country, O'Connell, Butt, Parnell and Redmond, were constitutionalists and outstanding members of the house of commons. Now parliamentary habits create an attitude to political problems. In parliament there is theoretically an acceptance of the principle that issues are decided by argument, and in practice it is impossible to shut the mind completely to another man's point of view. Understanding permeates, and committee work, in which so much time is spent, encourages, the tendency to seek compromise, at least on points of detail. Of course keen party men do not dwell on these aspects of political life. Politics for many would lose their savour if it was continuously stressed that moderate men in all parties tend to share a considerable amount of common ground. Moreover, as there are often significant differences between the parties over important issues, it is usually inadvisable for a politician, anxious to make an impact on policy, to start by declaring his readiness to make concessions.

Home rule was a striking example of a parliamentary solution to an acute problem. By giving Ireland a substantial measure of autonomy it offered a compromise between Irish independence and a unitary British Isles. To advanced nationalists it was a shameful surrender of Ireland's claims. To many nationalists it was a step towards a greater degree of autonomy. But to some liberals and federalists it was a bold experiment – an attempt both to afford an opportunity to diverse nationalities to express themselves within a larger community and to increase administrative efficiency by providing machinery which would permit policies to be adjusted to local circumstances while leaving major issues to a central authority. And since home rule was a compromise, produced by men who accepted that political arrangements are subject to change and who believed that a modicum of concession may induce opponents to lump what they do not like, it was almost certain that, during the progress of the third home rule bill, modifications calculated to conciliate unionist opinion would be considered. And in fact, while the bill was being debated, negotiations began, negotiations which culminated in the convention.

Each of the main groups represented in the convention stressed that it had an irreducible minimum of conviction, and a quick survey of their respective positions suggests that an agreed solution was logically impossible. But when the convention was at work, it more than once seemed possible that by a process of discussion, examination of relatively uncontroversial issues, tentative concession, compromise and formulae finding, understandings might emerge which would entangle the groups in agreements which would in the event form the basis of a settlement. Meanwhile, an optimist might believe, esprit de corps, reinforced by the trained committee men's natural pleasure in seeing the results of a day's work, would carry the convention forward and impel it to unite behind an agreed scheme for the government of Ireland. Could the convention then, have won a decisive degree of public support for its scheme? Admittedly 1918 was not a year in which moderate men loomed large. All over Europe familiar political landmarks were being swept away, great empires were collapsing and passionate nationalism seemed to be the most potent force in the new era. But Ireland, a member of the convention remarked, was 'a place where the inevitable never happens and the unexpected always occurs'. Violence and bitterness marked the immediate post-war years in Ireland, but during the greater part of the twentieth century Ireland has been politically and socially a remarkably stable community. Change has come slowly and Irish leaders of any weight have been distinguished for their caution and moderation (though on occasion they have employed a political vocabulary romantic in tone and packed with historical allusion). Obviously there were powerful sections in Ireland which might have rallied to a constitutional scheme recommended by a representative assembly of responsible and respected men – especially as the convention's answer to the Irish question would have had a strong sentimental appeal as being the product not only of hard bargaining but of good feeling and mutual understanding. However as a result of Ulster obstinacy and then of the split which developed between the fiscal autonomists and the more moderate nationalists, the scheme that at last emerged from the convention's deliberations lacked the support of that substantial majority in the convention which would have inspired the government to take the necessary steps to put it into operation.

But though the convention conspicuously failed it remains worthy of attention. Its discussions, often conducted with eloquence, acuteness and force, marked the close of the passionate controversy over home rule which had for over forty years absorbed so much time and political energy. And if negotiation is believed to be the best method of resolving political differences, the failure of an assembly, comprising many men of ability and good will to arrive at a settlement, deserves at least examination.

Appendix

LIST OF MEMBERS OF THE CONVENTION

	Representative of	*Political affiliations*	*Religion*	*Profession*
Abercorn, duke of	Tyrone County	Unionist	Church of Ireland	Landowner
Anderson, Sir Robert Newton	Londonderry Borough Council	Unionist	Protestant	Hosier
Andrews, Edward Henry	Dublin Chamber of Commerce	Unionist	Church of Ireland	Wine merchant
Armstrong, Henry Bruce Wright	Armagh County	Unionist	Church of Ireland	Barrister
Barrie, Hugh Thom	Ulster Party	Unionist	Protestant	Grain and product merchant
Barry, Michael K.	Cork County Council	Nationalist	Catholic	Farmer and shopkeeper
Bernard, John Henry	Church of Ireland	Unionist	Church of Ireland	Archbishop of Dublin

Name	Southern Unionist	Unionist	Church of Ireland	Civil servant
Blake, Sir Henry	Southern Unionist	Unionist	Church of Ireland	Civil servant
Bolger, John	Wexford County Council	Nationalist	Catholic	Merchant
Broderick, William J.	Munster Urban District Councils	Nationalist	Catholic	Farmer and victualler
Butler, John	Kilkenny County Council	Nationalist	Catholic	Farmer
Butterfield, Thomas C.	Cork Borough Council	Nationalist	Catholic	Dentist
Byrne, John	Queen's County County Council	Independent	Catholic	Shopkeeper
Clancy, John Joseph	Irish Party	Nationalist	Catholic	Barrister and journalist
Clark, Sir George Smith	Ulster Party	Unionist	Protestant	Linen manufacturer
Clark, Col. James Jackson	Londonderry County Council	Unionist	Church of Ireland	Land owner
Coen, James John	Westmeath County Council	Nationalist	Catholic	Agent

	Representative of	Political affiliation	Religion	Profession
Condren, Daniel	Wicklow County Council	Nationalist	Catholic	Publican
Sharman-Crawford, Col. Robert Gordon	Down County Council	Unionist	Church of Ireland	Landowner
Crozier, John Baptist	Church of Ireland		Church of Ireland	Archbishop of Armagh
Dempsey, Patrick	[Government nominee]	Nationalist	Catholic	Wholesale spirit merchant
Desart, earl of	[Government nominee]	Unionist	Church of Ireland	Landowner
Devlin, Joseph	Irish Party	Nationalist	Catholic	Journalist
Dooly, John	King's County Council	Nationalist	Catholic	Shopkeeper
Doran, Capt. William A.	Louth County Council	Nationalist	Presbyterian	Farmer
Duggan, Thomas	Tipperary (North Riding) County Council	Nationalist	Catholic	Auctioneer

Dunlevy, James	Donegal County Council	Nationalist	Catholic	Solicitor
Dunraven, earl of	[Government nominee]	Unionist	Church of Ireland	Landowner
Fallon, Thomas	Leitrim County Council	Nationalist	Catholic	Farmer
Fitzgibbon, John	Roscommon County Council	Nationalist	Catholic	Draper
Flanagan, John	Connaught Urban District Council	Nationalist	Catholic	
Garahan, Hugh	Longford County Council	Nationalist	Catholic	Farmer
Goulding, Sir William	[Government nominee]	Unionist	Church of Ireland	Company director
Governey, Michael	Leinster Urban District Councils	Nationalist	Catholic	Mineral water manufacturer
Granard, Earl of	[Government nominee]	Liberal	Catholic	Landowner
Gubbins, William	Limerick County Council	Nationalist	Catholic	Farmer

	Representative of	*Political affiliation*	*Religion*	*Profession*
Gwynn, Capt. Stephen	Irish Party	Nationalist	Church of Ireland	Author
Halligan, Thomas	Meath County Council	Nationalist	Catholic	Farmer
Hanna, John	Labour (Shipyards)	Unionist	Protestant	Shipyard worker
Harbison, Thomas J.	Irish Party	Nationalist	Catholic	Solicitor
Harty, Dr John	Catholic hierarchy	Nationalist	Catholic	Archbishop of Cashel
Irwin, John	Presbyterian Church	Unionist	Presbyterian	Clergyman
Jameson, Andrew	Southern Unionists	Unionist	Church of Ireland	Company director
Johnston, James	Belfast Borough Council	Unionist	Protestant	Flax merchant
Kavanagh, Walter MacMorrough	Carlow County Council	Nationalist	Church of Ireland	Landowner
Kelly, Denis	Catholic Hierarchy	Nationalist	Catholic	Bishop of Ross
Kett, Joseph K.	Clare County Council	Nationalist	Catholic	Farmer
Knight, Michel E.	Ulster Party	Unionist	Church of Ireland	Solicitor

Londonderry, marquess of	Ulster Party	Unionist	Church of Ireland	Landowner
Lundon, Thomas	Labour (Land and Labour Association)	Nationalist	Catholic	Political organizer
McCance, John Stoupe Finlay	Antrim County Council	Unionist	Church of Ireland	Linen manufacturer
McCarron, James	Labour	Nationalist	Catholic	Tailor
McCullagh, Sir Crawford	[Government nominee]	Unionist	Protestant	Draper
McDonogh, Martin	Connaught Urban District Council	Nationalist	Catholic	
McDonnell, Martin	Galway County Council	Nationalist	Catholic	Grocer
McDonnell, Lord	[Government nominee]	Liberal	Catholic	Civil servant
McDowell, Sir Alexander	[Government nominee]	Unionist	Protestant	Solicitor
McGarry, James	Mayo County Council	Nationalist	Catholic	Farmer

	Representative of	Political affiliation	Religion	Profession
MacGeagh, Henry Grattan	Ulster Urban District Councils	Unionist	Protestant	Company director
McHugh, John	Fermanagh County Council	Nationalist	Catholic	Farmer
McKay, Charles	Labour		Protestant	Official of Shipbuilding and Engineering Trades Federation
MacLysaght, Edward E.	[Government nominee]	Nationalist	Catholic	Farmer and Publisher
McMeekin, John	Ulster Urban District Councils	Unionist	Protestant	Linen merchant
MacMullin, Alfred R.	Cork Chamber of Commerce		Protestant	Flour miller
MacRory Joseph	Catholic hierarchy	Nationalist	Catholic	Bishop of Down and Connor
Mahaffy, John Pentland	[Government nominee]		Church of Ireland	Provost of Trinity College
Mayo, earl of	Irish peers	Unionist	Church of Ireland	Landowner

Name				
Midleton, Viscount	Southern Unionist	Unionist	Church of Ireland	Landowner
Minch, Matthew Joseph	Kildare County Council	Nationalist	Catholic	Merchant
Murphy John	Labour (National Union of Railwaymen)	Nationalist	Catholic	
Murphy, William Martin	[Government nominee]	Nationalist	Catholic	Company director
O'Donnell, Patrick	Catholic hierarchy	Nationalist	Catholic	Bishop of Raphoe
O'Dowd, John	Sligo County Council	Nationalist	Catholic	Merchant and Farmer
O'Neill, Charles	Leinster Urban District Councils	Nationalist	Catholic	Solicitor
O'Neill, Laurence	Dublin Borough Council	Nationalist	Catholic	
O'Neill, Patrick John	Dublin County Council	Nationalist	Catholic	Farmer
Oranmore and Browne, lord	Irish peers	Unionist	Church of Ireland	Landowner

225

	Representative of	Political affiliation	Religion	Profession
O'Sullivan, John James	Waterford Borough Council	Nationalist	Catholic	Medical doctor
Peters, Patrick O'H.	Munster Urban District Councils	Nationalist	Catholic	
Pollock, Hugh McDowell	Belfast Chamber of Commerce	Unionist	Presbyterian	Company director
Powell, John Blake	Southern Unionists	Unionist	Catholic	Barrister
Plunkett, Sir Horace Curzon	[Government nominee]		Church of Ireland	
Power, Thomas	Waterford County Council	Nationalist	Catholic	Farmer
Quin, Sir Stephen Byrne	Limerick Borough Council	Nationalist	Catholic	Merchant
Redmond, John Edward	Irish Party	Nationalist	Catholic	
Reilly, Daniel	Cavan County Council	Nationalist	Catholic	Publican

226

Name	Organization	Party	Religion	Occupation
Russell, George (AE)	[Government nominee]	Nationalist	Theosophist	Journalist and man of letters
Slattery, Michael	Tipperary County Council (South Riding)	Nationalist	Catholic	Farmer
Stewart, George Francis	Southern Unionists	Unionist	Church of Ireland	Land agent
Toal, Thomas	Monaghan County Council	Nationalist	Catholic	Grocer
Wallace, Robert Hugh	Ulster Party	Unionist	Church of Ireland	Solicitor
Waugh, Robert	Labour (Belfast and District Building Trades Federation)		Protestant	Official of the Amalgamated Society of Carpenters and Joiners
Whitla, Sir William	[Government nominee]	Unionist	Methodist	Professor of medicine
Whitely, Henry	Belfast and District Trades Council		Protestant	National Graphical Association
Windle, Sir Bertram Coghill	[Government nominee]	Nationalist	Catholic	President of University College, Cork

227

BIBLIOGRAPHY

'In order to encourage the utmost freedom in the expression of opinion', the convention's debates were not officially reported. But Sir Horace Plunkett in his *The Irish convention: confidential report to his majesty the king by the chairman* – a series of letters written while the convention was sitting – summarized many speeches (often with quotations). The report was printed and there are copies in the library of Trinity College, Dublin, in the Dillon papers and in the Plunkett papers. J. P. Mahaffy's notes taken during the debates and some of the printed speeches are in the convention papers, Trinity College, Dublin. Agenda papers are in the convention papers in the library of Trinity College, Dublin, and in the State Paper Office. *The report of the proceedings of the Irish convention* [Cd 9019], in its appendices includes reports and statements submitted to the convention, and a number of division lists.

MANUSCRIPT SOURCES

LONDON

British Museum
   Balfour papers, Add. MS 49721.
   Bernard papers, Add. MSS 52781–3.
   Shaw papers, Add. MSS 50547.
   Gladstone papers, Add. MSS 44132, 44255, 44632, 44647.

Public Record Office
   Cabinet papers. Cab. 23/2, 4, 18, 23; Cab. 24/89, 97–8, 109; Cab. 37/32,
      33, 108, 116, 117, 148, 150–2.

228

Bibliography

House of Lords Record Office
    Samuel papers.

Beaverbrook Library
    Bonar Law papers.
    Lloyd George papers.

Plunkett House
    Plunkett letters.
    Sir Horace Plunkett's diary.

DUBLIN

State Paper Office
    Convention papers.

National Library
    MacLysaght autobiography.
    Redmond papers.
    Copies of letters . . . to John Hayden (MS. 8380).

Trinity College Library
    Convention papers.
    Powell notes.
    Mahaffy autographs.

BELFAST

Public Record Office
    Carson papers.
    Duffin papers.
    Vesey Knox papers.
    Montgomery papers.
    Minute book of the Ulster unionist delegation to the convention.

OXFORD

Bodleian Library
    Asquith papers.
    MacDonnell papers.
    Nathan papers.

BIRMINGHAM

University Library
    Chamberlain papers.

LIVERPOOL

University Library
    Birrell letters.

Bibliography

IN PRIVATE POSSESSION

MacLysaght diaries.
Midleton papers.
Murphy letters.

CONTEMPORARY NEWSPAPERS AND MAGAZINES

Belfast Newsletter
Blackwood's Magazine
Cork Examiner
Derry Standard
Irish Independent
Irish Times
New Ireland
The Times

PARLIAMENTARY PAPERS

Supplement to the annual report of the chief inspector of factories and workshops for the year 1900 ... [Cd 841], H.C. 1902, xii.
Report of the committee on Irish finance, [Cd 6153], H.C. 1912–13, xxxiv; evidence [Cd 6799], H.C. 1913, xxx.
Headings of a settlement as to the government of Ireland [Cd 8310], H.C. 1916, xxii.
Report of the proceedings of the Irish convention [Cd 9019], H.C. 1918, x.

OTHER PRINTED SOURCES

Bryce, J. (ed.). *Handbook of home rule.* 2nd. ed London 1887.
Childers, E. *The framework of home rule.* London 1911.
Denson, A. (ed.). *Letters from A.E.* London 1961.
Desart, Earl of, and Lubbock, S. *A page from the past: memories of the Earl of Desart.* London 1936.
Dowden, E. *Letters of Edward Dowden and his Correspondents.* London 1914.
Gwynn, S. *Connaught.* London 1912.
Gwynn, S. (ed.). *The anvil of war: letters between F. S. Oliver and his brother, 1914–1918.* London 1936.
Hamilton, E. W. *The soul of Ulster.* London 1917.
Lysaght, E. E. *Sir Horace Plunkett and his place in the Irish nation.* Dublin 1916.
MacKnight, T. *Ulster as it is, or twenty-eight years experience as an Irish editor.* 2 vols. London 1896.
O'Brien, W. *The Irish cause and the Irish 'Convention'.* Dublin 1917.
Oliver, F. S. *The alternatives to civil war.* London 1913.
Oliver, F. S. *What federalism is not.* London 1914.
Oliver, F. S. *Ireland and the imperial conference.* London 1917.

230

Bibliography

Quin, Windham-Thomas Wyndham, earl of Dunraven. *Past times and pastimes*. 2 vols. London 1922.
Redmond, John. *Home rule speeches*. Ed. by R. B. O'Brien. London 1910.
Riddell, Lord. *War diary 1914–1918*. London 1933.
Russell, George William. *Co-operation and nationality*. Dublin 1912.
Russell, George William. *The national being: some thoughts on an Irish policy*. By A.E. Dublin 1916.
Russell, George William. *Thoughts for a convention: memorandum on the state of Ireland*. By A.E. Dublin 1917.
Shaw, G. B. *How to settle the Irish question*. Dublin and London 1917.
Young, R. M. *Belfast and the province of Ulster in the twentieth century*. Brighton 1909.

LATER WORKS

Birrell, A. *Things past redress*. London 1937.
Blake, R. *The unknown prime minister: the life and times of Andrew Bonar Law*. London 1952.
Bonn, M. J. *Wandering scholar*. London 1949.
Chamberlain, A. *Politics from the inside*. London 1936.
Colum, P. *Arthur Griffith*. Dublin 1959.
Cooper, D. *The rainbow comes and goes*. London 1958.
Digby, M. *Horace Plunkett: an Anglo-American Irishman*.
Fisher, H. A. L. *James Bryce*. 2 vols. London 1927.
George, David Lloyd. *War memoirs*. 6 vols. London 1936.
Gwynn, D. *The life of John Redmond*. London 1932.
Gwynn, S. *John Redmond's last years*. London 1919.
Gwynn, S. *Dublin old and new*. Dublin and London 1938.
Hancock, W. K. *Smuts: the sanguine years*. Cambridge 1962.
Hankey, Lord. *The supreme command*. 2 vols. London 1961.
R. J. Laurence, *The goverment of Northern Ireland*. Oxford 1965.
Lowther, J. W. *A speaker's commentaries*. 2 vols. London 1925.
Marjoribanks, E. and Colvin, I. *The life of Lord Carson*. 3 vols. London 1932–6.
Midleton, Lord. *Records and reactions 1856–1939*. London 1939.
Murray, R. H. *Archbishop Bernard*. London 1931.
Pakenham, F. *Peace by ordeal: the negotiations and signature of the Anglo-Irish treaty, 1921*. London 1935. New edition, 1962.
Petrie, C. *The life and letters of the Rt. Hon. Sir Austen Joseph Chamberlain*. 2 vols. London 1939.
Petrie, C. *Walter Long and his times*. London 1936.
Pound, R. and Harmsworth, G. *Northcliffe*. London 1959.
Spender, J. A. and Asquith, C. *Life of Henry Asquith, Lord Oxford and Asquith*. 2 vols. London 1932.
Taylor, M. *Sir Bertram Windle: a memoir*. London 1932.
Vane-Tempest-Stewart, E. H., Marchioness of Londonderry, *Retrospect*. London 1938.
Waterhouse, N. *Private and official*. London 1942.

231

INDEX

~~~~~~

Persons whose names are asterisked are noticed in the
Dictionary of National Biography

Abercorn, duke of, *see* Hamilton, James Albert Edward
Adams, William George Stewart, 79, 130, 136, 156, 163, 170
Addison, Christopher, 74
Agar-Robartes, Thomas Charles Reginald, 29–30
America, United States of, vii, 44, 82, 186, 195–6
Amery, Leopold Stennett, 46, 69, 189
Amiens, 185
Anderson, John, 210
Anderson, Sir Robert Newton, 151
Andrews, Edward Henry, 91, 144
Andrews, John Miller, 81
Armagh, archbishop of, *see* Crozier, John Baptist
* Asquith, Herbert Henry, negotiates on position of Ulster, 32, 41; on Irish situation in 1916, 48, 64–5; on Lloyd George proposals, 58–9; on Government of Ireland Act, 202; 26, 30, 37, 45, 93, 128
Ashley-Cooper, Anthony, 9th earl of Shaftesbury, 35
Australia, Commonwealth of, vii, 186

Bagwell, Richard, 165–6
*Balfour, Arthur James, 56, 60–1, 99, 101, 186, 188, 190, 198, 200
*Ball, Francis Elrington, 166
Balmoral, 32
Barrie, Hugh Thom, character, 89; relations with southern unionists, 114–15, 118; on fiscal question, 125–6, 129; on Midleton's scheme, 145–6; talk with Adams, 156; places northern unionist scheme before the convention, 176–7; 119, 121–2, 134, 151, 161, 163, 168, 179, 190
Barry, Arthur Hugh Smith, Baron Barrymore, 35, 56
Barrymore, Lord, *see* Barry, Arthur Hugh Smith
Barton, Robert Childers, 84
Belfast, growth of, 18–19; unionist demonstration at, 23; liberals, 26; nationalists, and Lloyd George proposals, 52–3; labour in, 85, 113; visit of convention to, 110–11; Lloyd George on, 157; Lord Birkenhead on, 199; 16, 31, 41, 47–8, 50, 72, 81, 89, 91, 93–5, 144, 160, 193, 204, 206

233

F4